Seeing Wales Whole

Meic Stephens (photograph: Ben Hussein)

Seeing Wales Whole

Essays on the Literature of Wales

In Honour of Meic Stephens

Edited by

Sam Adams

UNIVERSITY OF WALES PRESS
CARDIFF
1998

British Library Cataloguing-In-Publication Data.
A catalogue record for this book is available from the British Library.

ISBN 0-7083-1389-2

Published with the financial support of the Arts Council of Wales

Typeset at the University of Wales Press
Printed in Great Britain by Dinefwr Press, Llandybïe

Contents

Preface

As friends and associates of Meic Stephens in a variety of projects, the contributors to this book are glad of the opportunity to offer their work in admiration and gratitude for his comradeship and his remarkable industry in the cause of literature in Wales. The introductory pages that follow convey something of the range of Meic's interests and achievements, but the essays that make up the bulk of this *festschrift* do not reflect that formidable array. How could they? It would require several volumes to present a tribute that would correspond fully to such diversity. Rather, the essayists have pursued their own disparate literary interests, which in virtually every case have, happily, been shared with Meic in discussions they have had with him over the years. Nor is the wholeness of the vision the title implies to be seen in the contents. How could it be? It is Meic Stephens's own concept of an inclusive, progressive Wales that will take its place confidently in the modern world.

Notes on Contributors

Sam Adams, born at Gilfach Goch, Glamorgan in 1934, read English at University of Wales, Aberystwyth, became a teacher and later H. M. Inspector of Schools. He was editor of *Poetry Wales* from 1973 to 1975, and has published two books of poems and monographs on Geraint Goodwin and Roland Mathias in the Writers of Wales series.

Tony Curtis was born at Carmarthen in 1946 and educated at the University of Wales, Swansea and Goddard College, Vermont. He has been a teacher since 1969 and in 1994 was awarded a personal chair as Professor of Poetry at the University of Glamorgan. He has published seventeen books, most recently *War Voices: Poems 1970–1995* and *Welsh Painters Talking*. He won a Gregory Award in 1972 and the Cholmondeley Award for Poetry in 1997.

Don Dale-Jones, born at Ruthin in 1935, retired from full-time teaching some years ago, and is now involved in freelance teaching, editing and critical writing. He is the author of three monographs in the Writers of Wales series and is currently engaged with a friend, P. Bernard Jones, on a critical biography of the poet T. Harri Jones.

James A. Davies is Senior Lecturer in English at the University of Wales Swansea. He has been Visiting Professor at Baylor University in Texas, and Mellon Research Fellow at the Harry Ransom Humanities Research Centre, University of Texas at Austin. He has published extensively on Victorian literature and on Welsh writing in English. His most recent books are *A Swansea Anthology* (1996) and *A Reference Companion to Dylan Thomas* (1998).

John Harris, formerly Principal Lecturer in Bibliographical

Studies, is currently Research Associate at the Department of Information and Library Studies, University of Wales, Aberystwyth. His publications include a database of Welsh writing about art, articles about Anglo-Welsh publishing history, several editions of the work of Caradoc Evans, and *A Bibliographical Guide to Twenty-four Modern Anglo-Welsh Writers* (1994).

Emyr Humphreys is a distinguished novelist and poet, winner of the Somerset Maugham Award (1953) and the Hawthornden Prize (1959). Born at Prestatyn in 1919, he read history at University of Wales, Aberystwyth, where he learned Welsh and became a Nationalist. For ten years he was a drama producer for BBC Wales, radio and television, and subsequently lecturer in drama at University of Wales, Bangor. A full-time writer since 1972, he has published four volumes of poetry, a collection of short stories, plays, twenty-four novels, and a historical 'quest for the Welsh identity', *The Taliesin Tradition* (1983).

R. Gerallt Jones, born in Llŷn in 1934, read English at University of Wales, Bangor, and subsequently gave much of his life to teaching, including the first principalship of a college in Jamaica and the wardenship of Llandovery College and of University of Wales, Gregynog. A prolific writer of poetry, short stories, novels and literary criticism in the Welsh language, he has also written extensively in English, including a sequence of poems, *Jamaican Landscape* (1969). He is the author of the Writers of Wales monograph on T. H. Parry-Williams.

M. Wynn Thomas is Professor of English at the University of Wales Swansea, and Director of its Centre for Research into the English Literature and Language of Wales. Among the dozen and more books on American and Welsh literature he has written or edited are *Internal Difference: Literature in Twentieth-century Wales* and *DiFfinio Dwy Lenyddiaeth Cymru.*

1
Introduction

Meic Stephens stands out in any company. His long legs and substantial frame, which he attributes to the genes of his Radnorshire forebears, ensure that he overtops the crowd at literary events, which hereabouts usually attract folk of medium height at best. But it is not his height alone that distinguishes him on such occasions. Few who attend them are not known to him, while he is recognized by all, and he is the most amiable and stimulating of companions, his mind and conversation well stocked with knowledge of three cultures – English, especially that of his own south Wales, Welsh and French. He delights in the literary gossip of this and earlier ages, and wins, hands down, any exchange of quips and quotes. His bibliophilia is well known and his interests range from minority languages to popular songs, from maps to journalism, from cinema to philately. The circle of his acquaintance in Wales is very large. It embraces all contemporary writers of note, in Welsh and English, and all involved in book production and promotion. His links with academic life, the media and politics in Wales are hardly less extensive. It is no surprise that he has friends in many countries, from Georgia on the eastern edge of Europe to the Pacific coast of north America.

Meic was born in Trefforest, near Pontypridd, in 1938. Now widely recognized as the home of the University of Glamorgan, Trefforest at that time was a village better known for its nearby 'trading estate' (an attempt during the depressed inter-war years to insert a little light industry into an area dominated by coal mining), and Upper Boat Power Station, where Meic's father was a shift worker. He it was who came of Radnorshire stock, his mother's family, the Lloyds, having for generations practised as bone-setters in places like Glascwm and Michaelchurch-on-Arrow, familiar to the diarist Francis Kilvert.

Family history is an adult preoccupation and Meic's interest in that of his father's family, Radnorshire and Kilvert, came later. The most important influence on his boyhood was his mother's father, a jaunty Londoner, who, about 1900, as a young man, had come to Cardiff to work on the electrification of the trams, replacing the horse-drawn vehicles with a public transport system that now seems enviably characterful and pollution-free. There, in the course of his daily labour, he chanced to meet the love of his life, a Monmouthshire girl, and stayed in south Wales. These were the grandparents Meic grew up with, for they shared the family home, a small terraced house in Meadow Street, a stone's throw from the School of Mines which has since evolved into the University of Glamorgan. The grandfather, tin-whistle player, yarn-spinner, with a penchant for word games and the music hall, brought a dimension of otherness and linguistic diversity to the household that opened the mind of the growing boy to the richness of language. Furthermore, the old man not only knew a good deal about the recent industrial history of south Wales – the strikes, the explosions, the characters – but delighted in talking about it to his grandson. In his autobiographical essay, 'In John Jones's Country' (*Planet,* 82), Meic tells how, one summer afternoon, he and his grandfather walked to the tumulus at the summit of the Garth, that hill overlooking the Taff Gorge, where he viewed 'as if by revelation the valleys of Glamorgan winding smokily to the north, the Beacons in the far distance, and below us, Cardiff shimmering in the heat, and beyond, the Channel and the hazy hills of Somerset'. This experience, he says, first brought to his mind 'that sense of belonging to a particular place, which is at the root of patriotism'. From the crystallization of that childhood epiphany emerges a prominent strand of Meic's later life.

In 1949, having passed the 'scholarship' examination, Meic entered Pontypridd Boys' Grammar, then one of the foremost secondary schools in south Wales. From there, in 1956, he gained a place at the University College of Wales, Aberystwyth, where he read French. This was a wise choice. It gave him his second language, a year in France, of which he took full advantage, and, he has said, 'a non-English view of literature and politics, particularly the belief that they are not mutually exclusive'.

Alongside the formal progress through grammar school and university, an informal, self-directed education went on. It was his grandfather who, with a prescience we can only wonder at, gave Meic Idris Davies's *Selected Poems* as a seventeenth birthday gift, and set him reading Anglo-Welsh writers. He found their books on the shelves of the 'Local Authors' section of Pontypridd Public Library and, during a period when schools and colleges shunned them (as indeed they continued to do for another thirty years and more), he read the work of Jack Jones, Dylan Thomas, Caradoc Evans, Glyn Jones, Gwyn Thomas, Rhys Davies, Gwyn Jones and Alun Lewis, who opened his eyes to the existence of writing about places like Trefforest. He used Saturdays and holidays to mount solo expeditions by bus and on foot to the Rhondda, Aberdare, Merthyr, Rhymney, Ebbw Vale, in those days a single, if discontinuous, bustling industrial zone, though the twilight was already falling across it, and beyond the Beacons to Brecon. On the buses, in market halls and Italian corner cafés, the ubiquitous generic Bracchis (as often as not actually Rabaiottis, Bacchettas, Forlinis and Sidolis), he spoke to the people he met. His sociable curiosity, or, given the characteristic reticence of Welsh working-class youth in those days, his curious sociability, ensured that he steadily added to his stock of local knowledge and his sense of rootedness. The Rhondda he thought 'quintessential Wales', and that early perception conditioned his later conviction about the nature of his Welshness:

> I am aware that for those who take language to be the *sine qua non* of Welsh nationality, my Wales may not have been recognisable as Welsh at all . . . Such a view fills me with dismay, for it seems to deny or ignore the reality of how the people of Wales, or the greater part of them, have lived during the twentieth century . . . We come to see ourselves as Welsh, and to make our commitment to Wales, for different reasons

> and in different ways, and there seems to be little point in falling out over it. Perhaps, instead, we should try now to accept the differences and go on to explore what we have in common and what we might make of it.

Already politically aware and active (1956 brought the Hungarian uprising, and an anti-colonial war was raging in Algeria), during his first year in Aberystwyth Meic made an overt commitment to the principle of Welsh nationhood. Notwithstanding his socialist background and conscience, he joined Plaid Cymru. He was, for that time, an unusual member of the party, in that he was not Welsh-speaking, a condition he ascribes (in his 'Elegy for Mr Lewis') to a failure of his schooling. The college library at Aberystwyth afforded him the opportunity to extend his reading of Anglo-Welsh literature. This, for a student of French, was clearly an extra-curricular activity – as, indeed (if it entered their minds at all), it was for those studying English. Again, at Aberystwyth, Meic began to think of himself as a poet. In the college magazine, *The Dragon*, which he edited in 1961, he published poems that, if tinged with Romanticism, were distinctively about his roots in industrial south Wales, rather different from the usual undergraduate effusions of the period.

His literary apprenticeship did not properly begin, however, until his year in France, at the École Normale in Quimper and Rennes University, was over, the honours degree in French safely in the bag, and he was training to be a teacher at the Education Department of the University College of North Wales, Bangor. The change of college was more than usually deliberate: he went to Bangor with the intention of joining the editorial board of a Plaid Cymru youth magazine, *Y Wawr*. In the event, the magazine soon folded, but in Bangor he became a friend of Anthony Conran, who shared his interest in Anglo-Welsh literature, and took his first Welsh lessons with Islwyn Ffowc Elis. He also discovered an interest in the literature and politics of Ireland, a short, if choppy, voyage from Holyhead. By the end of the year, the characteristic furniture of his intellect was in place. Only a catalyst was lacking to set the course of a career in literature. That was provided by a chance meeting of minds.

In the second of his autobiographical essays, 'The Garth Newydd Years' (*Planet*, 83), Meic tells how, in the late summer of 1962, on the threshold of his first term as a teacher of French at Ebbw Vale Grammar School, he met Harri Webb in the bar of the Old Arcade in Cardiff. They found they had a great deal in common, from working-class, English-speaking backgrounds to membership of Plaid Cymru, from a training in Romance languages to a love of modernist literature. Both regarded poetry and politics as complementary rather than mutually exclusive. At that initial encounter Meic was invited to join the unconventional commune that lived, rent-free, in Garth Newydd, a grand, if somewhat neglected, pile of uncertain ownership in Merthyr Tydfil. The house soon became a hybrid of caravanserai, salon and retreat, affording temporary shelter to political activists of the nationalist persuasion, and to writers and artists from all parts of Wales, en route elsewhere, or seeking change, rest, solace or inspiration. At Garth Newydd, Harri Webb toiled as editor of *Welsh Nation*, Plaid Cymru's newspaper, and Radio Free Wales, the pirate radio station, did its best to beat the broadcasting ban on Plaid Cymru by beaming its nationalist message to a few streets of Merthyr Tydfil from Meic's attic room.

By assisting Harri Webb on *Welsh Nation*, Meic learned proof-reading, typographical design and layout, and within a year or so of taking up residence in the house he had established his own publishing imprint, the Triskel Press. Among its earliest publications were Gerald Morgan's book about Welsh, *The Dragon's Tongue*, a collection of poems, entitled *Triad*, by Meic Stephens, Harri Webb and Peter Griffith, which gave expression to that belief in the easy co-existence of poetry and politics, and the first of the Triskel Poets booklets by John Tripp, Herbert Williams and Leslie Norris.

The happiest inspiration born of the long conversation with Harri Webb was the founding of *Poetry Wales* in the spring of 1965. The first editorial (in the third number) set out the fundamental aims of the magazine and explained the enigmatic cover design, which depicted Arianrhod, 'the bitch muse' to symbolize 'our first commitment . . . to the craft'. 'Our second', it continued, 'is to the country.' The magazine's subtitle, motto or mission statement, 'Cylchgrawn Cenedlaethol o Farddoniaeth Newydd', there in the inaugural number and still used today, expressed the editor's determination to build bridges between Welsh-language writers and the English-speaking Welsh:

> We are aware that, with the movement towards nationhood so properly linked with the language campaign, we inherit the controversy that has always fallen upon Welshmen who write in English. But we protest, on our contributors' behalf, that there is more sympathy for the senior literature among us than there was in our first heyday . . .

Thenceforth, under his editorship, and for some time afterwards, the magazine carried new Welsh poems, often with translations. The reference in that editorial to what (in the adaptation of a phrase used in a keynote lecture on the topic by Gwyn Jones) had become known as 'the first flowering' of Anglo-Welsh literature in the 1930s and 1940s was apt. As his title for an article in the seventh number, in which he looked back on the quantity and quality of new Welsh writing in English, Meic chose 'The Second Flowering' – with justification, for in little more than two years the magazine had established itself and the reputations of an array of talented poets – John Ormond, Leslie Norris, Raymond Garlick, Harri Webb, Sally Roberts (Jones), John Tripp and Anthony Conran among them – who were to dominate the Anglo-Welsh scene into the 1970s and beyond. Meic Stephens is modest about the part he and his magazine played in providing a platform for Welsh writing in English during the 1960s and 1970s, but without his devotion to their work, there could not have been that 'small renaissance' in Anglo-Welsh literature. For not only did he edit and publish their work, he also promoted it, on the radio, in the press and at public readings.

Between the first number of *Poetry Wales* and the second, Meic moved from Garth Newydd to Twynyrodyn, another part of Merthyr. There he set up home with his wife, Ruth, whom he had met during the 1964 election campaign, when they worked together on behalf of the Plaid Cymru candidate, Ioan Bowen Rees, Ruth's brother-in-law. Meic himself stood for the same seat in the general election of March 1966. In the summer of that year, he and Ruth moved to Cardiff where, having left teaching, he was beginning a new job, as a reporter with the *Western Mail.*

That same summer, I returned to Wales from Bristol, where I had been teaching. At the College of Education in Caerleon I was soon befriended by Gwilym Rees Hughes, a fellow lecturer, who in the winter of 1967 became the Welsh-language editor of *Poetry Wales*. This was the connection that led to my meeting Meic Stephens (for, though we contributed to the same issue of *The Dragon*, I had not known him in Aberystwyth) and, in due course, joining the editorial team to look after reviews. Our association, which began then, extends to the present and this volume in admiration of and tribute to his unique contribution to letters in Wales. The story of *Poetry Wales* merits a monograph. Suffice it here to say that Meic's distinguished contribution as editor, with slight intermission, over eight years – still the longest editorial stint in the magazine's history – established it among the foremost literary journals in these islands.

Meic's career with the *Western Mail* lasted barely a year, for in July 1967 he was appointed assistant director of the Welsh Committee of the Arts Council of Great Britain with responsibility for literature; in another year, titles had changed and he became literature director of the Welsh Arts Council. This role, for which there was no precedent, he largely invented for himself. The concept of state patronage for the literature of Wales was new and he explored it with gusto, adding many fresh ideas about support for writers and writing to those few he was able to gather elsewhere. He set up and refined essential structures for running a department and servicing the Council's Literature Committee. He added to the large stock of knowledge and acquaintance in the field that he already possessed. By this time a fluent Welsh-speaker, he was as at home on the Eisteddfod *maes* as he was in his base in Cardiff, or in the offices of publishers and regional arts associations, and with the many individuals and organizations, large and small, which sought the Council's support. The clarity of his vision and the strength of his will to achieve the objectives he had set were soon widely recognized. He quickly became known also for his impatience with inferior standards in book production as in writing; his plain speaking and unwillingness to shirk or fudge issues won him many friends, and some enemies.

By virtue of the gradually changing membership of the Literature Committee nearly every writer of note who had an interest in its work was eventually involved. It was led by a succession of able chairmen, several of whom, like T. J. Morgan, Roland Mathias, Glyn Tegai Hughes, Prys Morgan, Walford Davies and M. Wynn Thomas, were themselves eminent writers and critics. As its secretary, Meic was a fecund source of energy, information and ideas. In this role he deserves much of the credit for the transformation in Welsh literary life after 1967. Instead he was often the recipient of brickbats. No matter how scrupulously the committee took decisions on the distribution of grant aid there was never enough money to satisfy all those who merited support, far less the others. Every year swelled the ranks of the disappointed, and it was not at the committee that the disgruntled sometimes levelled their aim, but at its secretary. Meic took it all in his lengthy stride.

With Welsh Arts Council support, and often subsequently the advice of the Literature Director, magazines like *Taliesin, Barn* and *The Anglo-Welsh Review* expanded, achieved higher production standards and began paying contributors. In a modest way, the professionalizing of writing in Wales thus began. A backlog of individual writers who, usually for scant reward, had contributed greatly to the culture we share – Kate Roberts, Waldo Williams, Saunders Lewis, T. H. Parry-Williams, Euros Bowen, David Jones, Jack Jones, Rhys Davies, Glyn Jones and Gwyn Thomas among them – received their due of recognition at an annual prize-giving. An international prize brought writers of the stature of Eugène Ionesco, Friedrich Dürrenmatt, Astrid Lindgren, Derek Walcott and Margaret Atwood to Wales. Prizes were (and still are) awarded to 'books of the year' in English and Welsh. Writers received travel grants to enable them to represent Wales at literature seminars in Europe and America. Bursaries allowed writers of recognized talent, like John Tripp, Eigra Lewis Roberts and Rhydwen Williams, freedom from other commitments to undertake particular projects. Others, including Emyr

Humphreys and R. Gerallt Jones, benefited from temporary fellowships at colleges of the University of Wales. Competitions were held to find new writers or stimulate fresh writing in poetry, prose and translation. The Writers on Tour scheme was launched, and Writers in Residence, for a while there was Dial a Poem, and local writers' workshops were set up in many parts of Wales. So successful were many of these schemes that the Welsh Arts Council's policies for literature were emulated by its counterparts in Scotland, Ireland and England.

One of the most important developments, a key to many others, was the establishment on a proper footing of Yr Academi Gymreig, the national association of writers in Wales. This had been founded in 1959 as a society of Welsh-language writers and it was a triumph of Meic's enthusiasm for building bridges between the two cultures, and of the goodwill of writers on both sides but especially of those representing 'the senior literature', that an English-language section was formed in 1968. Meic worked hard at nurturing the idea of a writers' society, encouraging Yr Academi to develop its scope and administrative arrangements. As a representative body, an information exchange aiming to stimulate activity and interest in Welsh writing in both languages, it has steadily increased in importance. In 1990, Meic was made a life member.

A parallel development in which, later, Meic became officially involved was the evolution of the committee initially set up to ensure the availability of books in Welsh for schools into the Welsh Books Association and, in 1961, the Welsh Books Council. In 1971/2 four specialist departments were set up within the Council, grant-aided from the Literature Committee's budget, as the means of bringing about improvement in standards of book production and promotion throughout Wales. These were concerns close to Meic's bibliophilic heart, as was the revival of the Gregynog Press in 1977, with which he was closely associated. The investment in quality which encouraged greater professionalism in the publication of literary journals continued with the filling of niches. New magazines were launched, *Planet* and *Golwg,* with the aim of appealing to readers who were also interested in politics and social affairs, *Barddas* for enthusiasts of Welsh poetry. The Literature Committee also commissioned books and series, like Dramâu'r Byd, Bro a Bywyd, and the remarkable Writers of Wales, which, under the joint editorship of Meic Stephens and R. Brinley Jones, now extends to eighty-eight volumes and could be close to achieving its century before the millennium. Children's literature was supported with grants and competitions and, in 1979, by the establishment of the Children's Literature Centre (now absorbed into the Books Council's Children's Literature Department). The opening of Oriel, the Welsh Arts Council's own bookshop and gallery, in Charles Street, Cardiff, in 1974 was a great adventure. It gave the Welsh reading public, for the first time, access to a comprehensive collection of writing from Wales, as well as a selection of poetry publications to rival that of any bookshop in these islands, and an incomparable range of spoken-word recordings and small-press productions. When selling books in Wales was still a drab business, Peter Finch, an inspired appointment as bookshop manager, brought flair and a programme of events that made Oriel a popular salon.

Yr Academi Gymreig, at arm's length from its funding body, the Arts Council, commissioned an important series of Welsh classics, reprints of key Anglo-Welsh texts that had long been unavailable and, in 1976, two huge contributions to Welsh culture: the *English-Welsh Dictionary* and the *Oxford Companion to the Literature of Wales* with its parallel Welsh version from the University of Wales Press, *Cydymaith i Lenyddiaeth Cymru*. Meic Stephens's editing of the *Cydymaith/Companion* was a labour of love, but a labour indeed, that he combined with his demanding role as literature director. It occupied all his leisure and much of his life for almost a decade and, viewed now, another ten years further on, can be seen as a major triumph of his patience, scholarship and editorial skill. His satisfaction is that the books have won a place as essential reference works for anyone with an interest in our literature. In 1997 we saw the issue of a complete revision and updating of the *Cydymaith*, and the *Companion* will follow soon after, in the autumn of 1998, the conclusion of yet more years of painstaking effort.

Before he resigned from the Arts Council in July 1990, Meic played a leading role in the establishment of Tŷ Newydd, the residential writers' centre for Wales at Llanystumdwy, near

Cricieth. With that, what public patronage, via the Arts Council, could achieve had virtually all been accomplished. Not every project was successful, and there were always critics, some within the literary community, ready to take the shine off those that were. Nevertheless, the long list of enterprises that were launched under the aegis of the Literature Committee during Meic's twenty-three years at Museum Place are, in large part, testimony to his personal vision and his determination to create for writers in Wales a professional infrastructure with style and standards.

Since leaving the Arts Council, he has worked as a journalist, editor, translator, literary agent, media consultant and, from 1994, as a part-time lecturer at the University of Glamorgan, where he has taught modules in modern fiction, journalism, and Welsh writing in English. He is secretary of the Rhys Davies Trust, set up through the wonderful generosity of the writer's brother Lewis. In this capacity, with the trustees, he is still devising schemes to support Anglo-Welsh writing, while keeping the name of Rhys Davies green. With Nigel Jenkins and Sally Roberts Jones, he was instrumental in establishing the Harri Webb Prize as an annual award for polemical verse. Meic was made an Honorary Fellow of St David's University College, Lampeter in 1986 and in the Fall semester of 1991, he was Visiting Professor in the English Department at Brigham Young University, Utah. But it is in his connections with the University of Glamorgan, in his native village of Trefforest, that he takes greatest pride, working alongside fellow writers Tony Curtis, Chris Meredith and Sheenagh Pugh. It was at the University, in 1990, that he helped to establish the Centre for the Study of Welsh Writing in English.

Meic's capacity for work is extraordinary. When he is not teaching, he is usually to be found in his study, surrounded by reference works, or among his collection of Anglo-Welsh books and magazines, which is rivalled only by that of the National Library. The select bibliography that concludes this book gives an indication of the scale of activity that he has sustained over the years. It includes important anthologies like *The Lilting House* (1969), co-edited with John Stuart Williams, which looks back to the beginnings of Anglo-Welsh poetry in the twentieth century, and *The Bright Field* (1992), which surveys the remarkable diversity of the contemporary scene; essential reference texts and source books for all who are interested in Welsh and other minority languages, or writers and writing in Wales, and further afield, such as the *Artists in Wales* series (1971, 1973, 1977), *The Welsh Language Today* (1973), *Linguistic Minorities in Western Europe* (1976), *A Dictionary of Literary Quotations* (1989), *The Oxford Literary Guide to Great Britain and Ireland* (1992); and, more recently, translations – from the Welsh of Gwynfor Evans (*For the Sake of Wales*, 1996) and Saunders Lewis (*Monica,* 1997), and from French (*The Basques* by Luis Nunez Astrain, 1997), together with scrupulously annotated editions of the collected poems of Harri Webb (1995) and Glyn Jones (1996) and the collected stories of Rhys Davies (in three volumes, 1996-98). There is also the journalism, usually on literary subjects, in Welsh and English for the *Western Mail*, and occasionally for the *Independent.* Pausing to assess the value of this multifarious contribution, tantamount to arresting a stream in spate, is not easy, but it can be confidently asserted that he has added significantly to our stock of knowledge about the literature of Wales and opened our eyes to political and cultural influences on Welsh and other minority languages.

As an undergraduate, Meic saw himself as a poet. He has not been prolific: his published verse has been brought together in two slim collections, *Exiles All* (1973) and *Ponies, Twynyrodyn* (1997). His poetry has, however, been influential – as younger poets, like Robert Minhinnick, have testified. The poems in both books demonstrate his powers of stylistic variation and his concern for poetic form. He is a witty poet, whether in suitably rumbustious rhythm and rhymes he is greeting fellow practitioners assembled in 'The Lilting House', or with a more sedate, traditional metre, and mischievous intent, penning a 'Ballade for Spring'. With the wit there is the uncommon *gravitas* that distinguishes the several elegies – for Llywelyn Humphreys, Seamus O'Halloran, Mrs Mordecai, Mr Lewis (Welsh), and other poems like 'Eels' and 'Hooters'. They are the expression of a unique view and voice, recognizably Welsh, that awaken reverberations of the past and have a message for the present. If, as appears likely, the labours of the years at the Arts Council, and since, have driven out the Muse, it is a matter for regret, for few of our contemporary poets achieve that subtle combination of austere tone and emotional intensity.

Again in Aberystwyth, in 1961, Meic won the Alun Lewis Prize for a short story subsequently published in *The Dragon*. It is to that genre that he has returned recently, drawing upon his experiences as a young man in fictions like 'Election Fever' (*New Welsh Review* 34). The narrative control and sharpness in the delineation of characters and events suggest that, if he chooses, he could become a short-story writer of some distinction. Meic will certainly continue, with industry, style and conviction, to make a major contribution to literature in Wales. It will be a bonus for the reading public if that includes more of his creative work in poetry and prose.

Meic Stephens and Ruth have lived in Whitchurch for many years. Welsh is the language of the home: their four children and now their grandchildren are Welsh-speaking. Meic will be sixty in 1998. In a letter to me he refers to himself as 'a Hoggart boy', a product of south Wales during the post-war era of austerity, the Welfare State, the grammar school, wireless and the cinema, not unlike the Yorkshire background Richard Hoggart describes in *The Uses of Literacy*. He has, he says in the same letter, 'the highest regard for the decencies of respectable working-class life'. His vision, he has told me, is of a society 'in which the English-speaking Welsh play a full part in the life of the nation', and of a concept of nationhood that is 'inclusive, progressive, out-going, forward-looking and liberal, part of the modern world'. The contributors to this book, and the many subscribers, friends and admirers, will join me in saying Amen to that, and wishing Meic many more productive years.

2

Taliesin's Children

EMYR HUMPHREYS

The edges of Wales could have been designed for the specific purpose of converting people into poets. It is true that from one end to the other of the western seaboard of the British Isles there are bays, cliffs, golden sands and rocky shores and islands in abundance: and over all, unrepeatable sunsets infusing the waters with an illumination that beggars description. But poetry feeds off the specific. I do not know the exact spot where Robert Williams Parry stood when the exultant final couplet sprang into his mind: 'Digymar yw fy mro trwy'r cread crwn / Ac ni bu dwthwn fel y dwthwn hwn', which amounts to saying, in loose and unsuccinct translation, that he had discovered, with that force of revelation which is the essence of poetry, that his native heath in all its resplendent poverty, the truth that lies in the heather and the grudging acres, was incomparable through all creation and that the present moment was life's most elusive miracle.

A poet has to take pride in his place and in his people. This is an elementary truth to be taken into account by every generation as it grows up to confront its own hunger for abiding certainties. There are of course other nagging questions to be answered and these are shaped by the prevailing concerns of the society on whose shores the bewildered would-be bard finds himself washed up by the tide of time. An education system provides him with the reading and writing he will eventually need to pursue his calling: also an intimidating mountain of information. At the end of the twentieth century, he will be told that he shares 98.4 per cent of his genetic material with chimpanzees. By courtesy of television film he will see that apes are more capable than human beings of demonstrating the poetry of motion. He will be squeezed into 1.6 per cent of his being in order to demonstrate any qualitative difference. It is true that he has speech and the facility of written language: but this precious gift he is obliged to share with the global manipulators of opinion who operate ever more sophisticated networks for power and profit – two goals that have always been low on a poet's list of priorities. There was a classic confrontation in Wales between these two unequal forces not so very long ago. In 1979 some two dozen poets and concerned writers signed a letter to the press in support of the benefits of devolution. The tabloids snorted their contempt; but it was the editor of the *South Wales Echo* who delivered the *coup de grâce*. He printed the names and then asked his readers in bolder print 'ever heard of them?' These were not film stars or royalty or politicians or famous footballers: not even authors of airport novels. They were a gaggle of obscure poets worrying the tatters of an old song and about as relevant to contemporary issues as a bin full of discarded newsprint.

Was it ever thus? Taliesin's forebears, we know, were obliged to contend with the vituperative disapproval of Gildas. We know this from his *De Excidio Britanniae* and that oft-quoted description of the praise poets of those early centuries, 'a pack of scoundrels bawling out like drunken revellers their lies and foaming phlegm spattering everyone within reach'. We still need to ask ourselves what they thought they were up to, the bards on the one hand and the querulous monk on the other. The monk has the advantage of writing in Latin and his words still lie before us on the printed page. He is quite specific in his motives.

> I gazed on these things and many others in the Old Testament as though in a mirror reflecting our own time: and then I turned to the New Testament also and read there more clearly what had previously been dark to me . . . I read that the Lord had said, 'I have not come except to the lost sheep of the House of Israel.'

Gildas could boast an impeccable intellectual pedigree. He had sat at the feet of Illtud, at Llanilltud Fawr in the most illustrious seat of learning in Britain. This Illtud, 'the most learned of all Britons' had been a disciple of Germanus of Auxerre, whose business we know, along with St Martin of Tours, was to preserve the remnants of Roman civilization in Europe by converting the barbarian hordes rather than killing them. (It is worth noting that these stalwarts of the faith had been high-ranking military and civil officials of the Empire before this basic change of approach took place.) Germanus visited Britain in 429 to combat the Pelagian heresy, and he is also given the credit for leading the embattled Christian Britons to victory by bidding them shout 'Alleluia!'.

These links with his immediate past help us to understand more fully Gildas's attitude to unruly princes and poets. Apostasy and heresy were more offensive than the pristine innocence of pagans, however fierce. They could at least be saved if they could be persuaded to put down their weapons long enough to take in the message and the means of salvation. The praise poets and their Brythonic princes were lapsing into all sorts of reprehensible habits under the relentless pressure put on them by the land-hungry Anglo-Saxon barbarian invaders. Like Jeremiah before him, Gildas is unsparing in his condemnation of the errant Children of Israel. His chosen people and their disreputable bards were putting their trust in what he considered revived heathen practices, glorifying their ancestry instead of glorifying God.

At the inauspicious start of what some scholars call 'The British Heroic Age' – which we can take to be the two or three hundred years which followed the withdrawal of the Roman legions – there appears to have been a propaganda battle in progress between the Church and a revived order of poets for the hearts and minds of the beleagured British. The bards were committed to a revival of praise poetry that would glorify the courage and generosity of a military aristocracy that was all that stood between their people and slaughter, dispossession and serfdom. 'Then Talhaearn Tad Awen gained renown in poetry and Aneirin and Taliesin . . .' Out of a highland zone that stretched from Edinburgh to south-west England there emerged a resurgence of interest in the Celtic past where there was a wealth of myth and legend to console the British as well as tantalizing glimpses of lost religions that held out promise of earthly paradise and immortality. What could have been more alluring to a minority at the mercy of massive demographic swings than the idea of a 'Cauldron of Rebirth'? The use of this miraculous utensil is vividly demonstrated in the second branch of *Pedair Cainc y Mabinogi*: 'Should one of your men be killed, throw his corpse in the cauldron and by tomorrow he shall be as sound as ever he was and fight as well, except for the loss of speech.' This device for the recycling of soldiers must have had a special appeal for a minority suffering from a manpower shortage.

This was not the only cauldron available. There was the Irish 'Cauldron of Plenty', an invaluable asset that both Culwch and Arthur were willing to fight to possess. Furthermore, and perhaps most challenging of all, there was the 'Cauldron of Inspiration and Knowledge' which was of vital importance to poets in particular. In the folk-tale preserved in *Hanes Taliesin* a country boy is put in charge of the cooking process, and by accident as much as by design acquires the three drops of the magic potion that transform him from a yokel into the most knowledgeable man in the world. His knowledge as it were supervises his metamorphosis and in the end Gwion Bach is reborn as that prince of magic and poetry, the second Taliesin.

Between Gildas and the bards we catch glimpses of a culture struggle in progress. Gildas wrote in Latin and he saw himself as the standard bearer of Romano-British culture as well as an anointed prophet. His influence ranged from Clydeside to Brittany. He was an important agent of the monastic movement that was to preserve so much of classical Christian values throughout two centuries of turmoil. During this same period so often described as the Dark Ages certain features of this culture struggle took root in the Cymric psyche. The contrast between the ease of movement to the west and the growing constrictions and barriers across the land frontiers to the east become a graphic physical expression of a 'Welsh Situation' even before 'Cymru' emerges as a recognizable entity. We need only look at the 'Lives of the Saints' to catch an early reflection of this contrast burgeoning in the Welsh character. Westward all is openness, warmth, generosity, an altruistic enthusiasm to embrace the whole world and share with it the joys of revelation. It is fair to say that the spirit of St David was a vital part of the initial impetus of a movement which flourished around the western sea routes, and in due course sent missionaries ever further afield. Even the praise poets begin to share in the enthusiasm and suffuse their myths and legends with Christian significance.

Facing east all is changed. The Cymric face seems to darken with apprehension and suspicion. There is a palpable withdrawal of the spirit. How could divine Providence allow a heathen invader to triumph and cast down the Christian defending his own country? Should he withdraw to the hills to commune with himself and shrink like a snail into what he hopes is the protective covering of his own saintly shell? The general condition of the British Church in the eighth century is nowhere more vividly illustrated than in Bede's *Historia Ecclesiastica Gentis Anglorum.* Bede relies heavily on Gildas for his outline of the history of Britain before and during the Saxon invasions. As a public-relations expert for the Latin-reading public he makes skilful use of the material to demonstrate how the Saxons became the Chosen People, a new Israel advancing to occupy the Promised Land of Britain. His English nation was predestined to merge the British Isles into God's plan for a universal Roman Church. It is Bede's pleasure to push the unworthy Britons out of a nest that was far too good for them in the first place. In his eyes this was more than one ruling class replacing another or a mere demographic shift. A new nation was being born and he outlines the choosing of the English in scriptural terms. In those dark centuries a new agreement had been forged and this new testament took precedence over the old.

The pivotal character in Bede's drama is Augustine, the apostle of England. He tells us how this imperious and high-minded ecclesiastic called a meeting in AD 603 somewhere in the English Midlands in a place which was still known in Bede's day as 'Augustine's Oak' between himself, sponsored by King Ethelbert, and certain Cambro-British bishops. Augustine made three demands. He wished the British to accept his authority as the representative of the pope; he wished them to bring themselves into line with all the customs and practices of the Roman Church; and he demanded their active assistance in the great business of converting the heathen Saxons. None of these proposals was acceptable to the

British. Less than twenty years had gone by since the bloody and fateful battle of Deorham when the Saxon invaders had ruthlessly destroyed churches in the valley of the Severn, cutting off the British of south Wales from the British of the south-west. It is doubtful whether Augustine had any true understanding of the struggle that was going on.

Bede tells us there were two meetings. At the first his hero Augustine – in a ploy that must have been calculated to remind his readers both of Elijah on Mount Carmel and of St Germanus on his celebrated trip to Britain to combat the Pelagian heresy – arranges a test of miraculous prowess: a blind Englishman is prayed over by the British bishops with negative results. Then Augustine, the missionary from Pope Gregory who wants to make angels out of Angles, restores the blind man's sight. Bede gracefully allows the reader to draw the appropriate conclusion. The uneasy Britons decide to return home for consultations. They could not make changes in their ancient customs without the consent and authority of their people. This could have been an exercise in primitive democracy. Certainly the British would claim that they had a strong line of their own in saints and miracle-workers. It was no part of Bede's brief to mention these. It was only necessary for the sake of the elegant symmetry of his story-telling to inform the reader that the delegation went off to consult a hermit before returning to confront the formidable Augustine. This in itself indicates that in the Celtic order of these things, anchorites took a guru-like precedence over bishops and doctors of the Church. How was the delegation to know whether or not this autocratic missionary to the heathen Saxon was truly a man sent from God? In Bede's narrative, the hermit answers by quoting a verse from St Matthew's gospel: 'Take my yoke upon you and learn of me; for I am meek and lowly in heart.' This must have seemed on the face of it sound scriptural advice. But the British bishops pressed the hermit further. It was a critical turning-point in history, and they felt the need for a sign. The hermit gave it them. And Bede makes certain that his readers understand that the advice they get is so misguided as to make the source whence it came suspect for all time.

> Do you contrive that he with his followers be first to arrive at the place of meeting, and if as you approach, he rises up to

> meet you, with the knowledge that he is a servant of Christ, hear him willingly; but if he despise you, and does not choose to rise up before you, since you are greater in number, let him also be despised by you.

Of course Augustine does not rise to greet them, and the conference, as we would say, gets off to a disastrous start. There was no common ground. Augustine, strengthened by the prerogative of Rome, expected submission to authority. The British, among whom bishops seem to have been two-a-penny, looked in vain for signs of what they would consider spiritual fitness. To the venerable Bede, however, the whole occasion represented a great deal more than the inability of two forms of Christianity to understand each other. The Britons were in deadly error and they would deserve any punishment the Lord might see fit to visit upon them. He cannot conceal his satisfaction when he records that ten years later a cheerful pagan king from Northumbria put a large assembly of the monks of Bangor Is-coed to the sword. In the penultimate chapter of his book 'On the present state of the English nation and the rest of Britain (AD 725–31)' he has some quite nice things to say about the Irish. And even the Picts have a treaty of peace with the English and 'are glad to be united in Catholic peace and truth to the universal church of Rome'. Only the Cambro-Britons are still singled out for condemnation. They have 'a national hatred for the English and uphold their own bad customs against the true Easter of the Catholic Church'. The underlying thesis of his History is to demonstrate that the English are God's chosen people. In order to please God, the dispossessed were called upon not only to respect their oppressors but also to find them particularly lovable.

Gildas and Bede between them have reverberated down the centuries and played havoc with the Cymric imagination. Their writings made the Cambro-Britons mourn a lost paradise which in fact had never been theirs. Generations of clerics seized on the pseudo-history, and a tendency set in to equate the loss of Britain with the Fall of Man. This process laid the foundation of what can only be described as a highly developed national sense of inadequacy and sin.

The theme of dispossession took over any account of Welsh history whether by clerics or by poets. By the ninth century this was coupled with the belief that the Welsh were of Trojan origin, their descent being traced from Brutus, the grandson of Aeneas, the Trojan refugee who founded Rome. This Brutus had been fated to slay his father and mother by accident. For this primeval sin he was driven from Italy and eventually arrived in this island, which took its name from his. These origin myths, recorded in Latin, complemented each other and allowed for much subtle variation and development: just as the fallen man could be saved so the fallen nation could be restored to its former glory. In the weaving of the myth there was a place for political prophecy, bright hope and endless expectation as well as punishment.

The age of the lost kingdoms coincides with the age of the saints. This is hardly surprising. Saints tend to establish kingdoms in the next world rather than in this one. Scholars have shown how important the western sea routes were to the movement of those pioneers of Celtic Christianity who were also responsible for capturing so much of the essence of oral Celtic culture in writing. But the presence of a land corridor from Dumbarton in the north to the Severn estuary through to the south coast of Devon was of equal importance as long as it remained open. Just as the saints could preach and teach, the poets could sing. It could have been possible for an early Welsh-speaking minstrel from the Old North to move south through Rheged and Elmet into Lancashire and the counties of the Welsh border, to Devon and Cornwall and even across the sea singing and reciting stories in early Welsh without ever entering the present borders of Wales. It is in this sense that Welsh tradition is correct in postulating a lost greater Britain, and it is out of this British experience and perhaps a desire to reoccupy a lost world, that so much of the strength and power of medieval story-telling in Wales arises.

In the poetry of Aneurin and Taliesin we glimpse something of the vitality and virility of *Gwŷr y Gogledd* (Men of the Old North): and it is no accident that the names of so many of the knights of King Arthur's court, and indeed the name of Arthur himself, can be traced back to this source. In the beginning Arthur belonged to the bards. In stanza 102 of the *Gododdin*, a warrior named Gwawrddyd is praised for his impetuous ferocity: 'On the castle wall crows feasted on their flesh. He saw to it they had their fill although he was no Arthur.' The poem seems to celebrate a belated attempt to copy Arthurian strategy at a time when Saxon numbers have multiplied to such an extent that his vaunted victories could never be repeated.

As a policy for rearmament, cauldrons of rebirth could never provide a practical solution. As crucibles of myth, however, there can be no question of their efficacy. Cauldrons of inspiration transformed Taliesin into a prophet. He and Myrddin (Merlin), became the dynamic duo of a Cymric resistance that lasted through the centuries until the figure of Arthur was elevated to the position of ideal emperor in most of the literatures of western Europe. In a violent world he was the figure who could show the way to an effective balance between strength and legitimacy. Blessed by the Church, the hero-king could demonstrate on all occasions that might was right. When Henry Tudor snatched the crown of England, the Welsh bards heaved a sigh of relief and reassurance when he named his eldest son Arthur.

History has no claim to be an exact science, but it is always capable of being the most effective propaganda. At no time is this more evident than during the Tudor period. There would appear to be a cultural *droit de seigneur* that belongs to the victor: so much he will annexe, so much ignore, and so much obliterate. Having extracted the vital elements that he needs to preserve and enhance his power and prestige, he has few qualms in proceeding to exterminate the language that was their source and origin: '. . . and also that from henceforth no person or persons that use the Welsh speech or language shall have or enjoy any manner office or fees within this realm of England, Wales, or other the King's Dominion . . .'

The saving grace for our language in that time of crisis was the word 'British'. 'Brytyshe' was a magic formula. As that enthusiastic Protestant William Salesbury put it, 'the Brytyshe language that by continuall misnomer, the recorder of the aunciente hostilitie, is called Welshe . . .' The earliest name for Protestantism in Wales was *Crefydd y Saeson* – the religion of the English. With a combination of scholarship and casuistry men like William Salesbury and Bishop Richard Davies were able to use the writings of Gildas and Bede to turn the propaganda weapon right round and equate *Crefydd y Saeson* with detestable Roman Catholicism. As Davies argues in his 'Epistle to the Cymry':

> That Christianity which Augustine brought to the Saxons did fall short of the purity of the Gospel and the definitions of the primitive church . . . The Britons were distressed to observe such a mixing of this pollution of Christ's religion. Wherefore, when the English took so impure a Christianity unto themselves, the Britons could see no worthy way to communicate with any of them.

At any time in history it seems misconceptions and antipathies have a strange power to fertilize each other. Even as I write, London newspapers are working up an enthusiasm for celebrations afoot in Canterbury to mark the arrival of Christianity. Whatever went on in the Celtic fringe at that time is dismissed as remote and irrelevant. The long arm of the Venerable Bede reaches out once again to inject his version of history into the innocent minds of the category described by the advertising industry as serious readers.

We are of course all of us impressionable creatures. It is possible to imagine that when the figure of Arthur was hijacked by English authority a permanent distortion or at least reorientation occurred in the Welsh mind. For centuries previously, even as far back as the age of the megaliths, the territory of Wales occupied a pivotal position in the cultures and civilizations that flourished along the western edge of Europe. It was the centre of a Celtic sea province and of a provenance of the imagination. When the Tudors occupied the English throne with an heir called Arthur, Welsh eyes were turned with fatal ease to London. The wildest prophecies had been fulfilled. Out of the cauldron of myth that had been kept bubbling by generations of bards down the centuries had sprung a recycled hero. At last the dream had become a reality. The ancient Brytyshe were back at the top of the heap. The power and the glory were there for the taking.

There was, as we all know, a rude awakening: for snorting sleepers there always is. In spite of an increasingly pathetic desire to please, once the Tudors were replaced by the Stuarts, the value of Welshness slid down on the stock exchange index of reputation to bottom out just above the level of derision and contempt. The peaceable pretensions of the Welsh were only acceptable when exercised in the service of an expanding English empire. This attitude of amused superiority remains the hallmark of cultural imperialism. Not so very long ago Jeremy Hooker quoted a metropolitan critic as saying, 'the difficulty of the Welsh language may be hiding from non-Welsh readers the best poetry being written in Wales, but one rather doubts it.' There was a further implication that Welsh poets writing in English, unlike their rebellious Irish counterparts, needed to be mad or bad but not dangerous to know to be worthy of a footnote in the more substantial literary journals.

The fact is we all owe a debt of honour to our senior language. By being more or less irrelevant to power, profit and prestige, it has gone a long way to stockpile a spiritual inheritance to sustain us through a struggle that is far from ended. The vital core remains untranslatable and that is how it should be. Stimulating pilgrimages aim at inaccessible shrines. We may be in many ways double in ourselves, but it will be the poets in the end who will make it possible for us to continue to enjoy the best of both worlds without becoming permanently two-faced. The true source of our being is in a language and a tradition so old that it shapes the landscape in which we live and move. It is this landscape that sustains and inspires us. In relation to the depth of our past we are in the best sense peripheral, and for this reason we need our chronicles and companions. Succeeding generations will have good reason to be grateful to the recipient of this Festschrift. To determine where they are going, at the very least they will need to discover for themselves a clear idea of the nature of their inheritance: a spiritual capital hidden in that mysterious 1.6 per cent.

3

Novel to Play: The Trials of Taffy

JOHN HARRIS

In July 1940 Caradoc Evans framed a brief biographical note for *Welsh Short Stories*, the controversial Penguin anthology edited by Gwyn Jones. Three years earlier he had appeared in another landmark collection, *Welsh Short Stories* from Faber & Faber, compiled on Welsh advice. Between times on Welsh radio the young Keidrych Rhys applauded Evans's fiction as pioneering in every sense, the first genuine expression of a new literary movement in Wales. (Privately he even suggested that *Wales*, his 'militant journal' of this Welsh renaissance, might run a Caradoc Evans special issue.) Such local recognition, though welcome, essentially left Evans unmoved; Wales had treated him appallingly and he would not easily forget it. Besides, the hostility continued: in January 1937 BBC officials in Cardiff banned an Evans broadcast, two months before the National Eisteddfod withdrew its admittedly puzzling request that he adjudicate the Welsh novel competition at Machynlleth. Tersely for the Penguin volume he summarized his writing career: 'Play "Taffy" nearly wrecked a London theatre. Book "My People" banned by police in Wales and burned in many public places.'[1]

The origins of the incendiary *Taffy* go back to 1920 and the close of Evans's banner years: that period between *My People* (1915) and *My Neighbours* (1920) which established him as a literary original, one who worked through narrative and dialogue, through strange comi-tragedy, and through a bold refashioning of language. Yet Welsh establishment hatred countered English critical praise; indeed, was fuelled by it, as it was by Evans's unwavering sense of his own social mission.

'Naturally, I want justice for myself and my book', he wrote as *My People* faced charges of obscenity, 'but a much more vital issue is involved . . . the undoubted right of the critic to pass judgement on the manners and customs of his time.'[2] The critic, who was also an artist, knew that literature is not propaganda, and his moralizing he kept for letters to the Welsh daily press. Here he proved a formidable polemicist, utterly self-assured, and with the happy knack of making his opponents look ridiculous. They in return resorted mostly to personal abuse, though a few tried direct action; Evans's East Sheen windows had once before been broken, and with the appearance of *My Neighbours* came fresh threats of physical violence. The 'neighbours' of this collection were the business London-Welsh, a culturally contorted community who despised the ungodly English yet aped their social ways. With Welsh fury at the book running high ('literary filth' screamed the *Western Mail*), *Punch* suggested that Evans might wish to buy a bulldog.[3] Instead he backed off, professing a tiredness with controversy; he needed a change of direction, a more tranquil literary path.

In turning next to the novel, Evans made good an established intention. Ideas for a larger work had been playing around in his mind, including a treatment of shop life 'bitterly socialistic in feeling and realistic in intention'.[4] Furthermore, by 1920 a novel had become something of a career necessity, if only because a novel invariably enhanced the price of a writer's stories. Against this had to be set the effort that went to novel-making; to what for Caradoc Evans, the short-story writer best over two thousand words, was a hard dry road some forty times as long; and one that might end in the rejection slip or else derisory sales. Money considerations did not bother him unduly, for he enjoyed a regular journalist's income, but as he soon discovered, commitment to novel-writing left little time for anything else. For three years he fell silent. Then in summer 1922 came rumours of Evans at work on a full-length book containing 'no bitterness – or at any rate with a comedy element in it'.[5] The book was *Taffy*; not the projected drapery novel but a lighter, more leisurely excursion through familiar west Wales terrain, capitalizing on the strain of comic fantasy conspicuous in *My Neighbours*. *Taffy*, as it survives,[6] is a tale of warring capellers, and of Marged and Ester, two resourceful younger women determined to advance the fortunes of their parents and their own marriage prospects. In Marged, daughter of Twmi, a rebellious chapel elder, Evans impressively extends his conception of Welsh womanhood. She is a 'depthy' woman (to borrow a Valleys idiom as recollected by Gwyn Jones): shrewd, robust, sensual, the type of clear-eyed female to whom Evans was always drawn. True to comedy, the story ends in all-round reconciliation and an improbable double wedding – though not before the barriers to romantic attachment and good neighbourliness have been fully ventilated.

'The journeyings of the Welsh peasant are short: the man who lives in the heart of his parish is often a stranger at the boundary stone. Our world is the straggling village where we abide . . .' If the tone of the novel is lighter, the social analysis remains unchanged: 'Most of the people of Sion are of the same seed . . . they are governed by the same capel-made laws, which permit cousins to wed cousins, fathers to lie with their daughters, and children to be born out of wedlock.' As the chapel conditions ways of living, so it commands geographic space and annexes the historical past. 'Gwilym Hiraethog, Williams Pantycelyn, Howell Harris, Eynon Davies, Davydd Llwyd George': the Nonconformist lineage adorns the vestry walls,[7] while in the chapel cemetery grey headstones commemorate worthies like Owen and John. Both 'glorified the Big Man'; in John's case 'while driving his wife to Asylum Carmarthen'; in Owen's, 'though his sister made him go with her'. In the assuring words of the narrator, 'Their memorials give strength to the living and promise the righteous a perpetual name on the highway.'

The ironic thrusts are devastating, though generally not sustained by a narrative of commensurate power. No Shadrach Danyrefail dominates, no Bern-Davydd stalks the land. Instead we have Ben Woodenleg, the veteran preacher desperately recycling his sermons, disguising staleness of content by fervour of delivery (his 'zealous fury . . . parted the leaves of ten Bibles in Capel Morfa'). Behind Ben lies Rhys Davies (*Y Glun Bren*, or Wooden Leg), a Congregationalist preacher of the locality who lost a leg at a religious gathering when in an excess of fervour a heavily built enthusiast accidentally trod on his foot ('rough and caustic of tongue, he had a remarkable fluency of speech, especially when praying', adds the *Dictionary of Welsh Biography*).[8] In the novel such fluency is prized, for with doctrinal positions long since established, the challenge is for preachers to enact some pulpit drama. Here Ben believes he has the edge over his rival Spurgeon Evans, the college-trained slip.[9] Older men are positively marked for office:

> it is well-known that in the old days God called His preachers from the coal mine and the plough and the threshing machine. Those who were shy of hearing He maimed so that they were more easily pressed into His service. He hurled a piece of coal upon Ben's leg, thus forcing the man into the pulpit.

Except in matters of money, the minister maintains an appropriate detachment from members of his flock – though 'if one has the ticks, he goes to her with the clippers and the powder' (that 'her' is nicely chosen; Sion's backsliders are usually women). Things are different with chapel elders, and *Taffy* makes plain the interdependence of ministers and deacons. Ben might stoop before his deacon-employer ('Shacob spoke no word. He beckoned with his finger, and Ben felt as if he were a bundle of reeds about to be cut down by a sickle'), yet both know that a successful chapel depends on a charismatic minister. The deacons bear the burden of Evans's ridicule, a village *petite bourgeoisie* of artisans and shopkeepers driven by vanity and greed. The new Capel Split owes less to doctrinal niceties than to personal jealousies and an excess of zinc roofing. Hatred of Church heathens alone unites the capellers, who set aside their warring to turn and face the Anti-Christ. A Resurrection miracle will seal their triumph, transforming Capel Sion into the Big Man's image: 'the walls His frock coat, the two long, narrow windows His eyes, the roof His hair; the double door shall swing cross-wise and will be His lips which will utter judgment.'

Evans had previously essayed the grim humour of a man not being permitted to die before his chapel's new burial ground is ready to receive him, but *Taffy* reveals another facet of the Welsh way of death: the particular gaiety it releases; that 'solemn, joyous moment' when the great misfortune falls on someone else. It is the death of others that sharpens our sense of life:

> We do not ignore death, nor put the thought of him from our mind; we stand at the roadside and show him the way to this or that house, and we have delight in attending to the many ceremonies that are due to him. Death is our enemy when his sting is aimed at us.

Death robs us of the things we love, and in Marged's eyes 'Sion's love is of fields and ditches and hen lofts.' What then of human love? There is sex enough in Sion, about which our narrator must counsel: 'The man who has sinned with a woman must strengthen his wit that he does not fall into her hands; he must trail his gaze on the floor lest he is caught in the trap she has laid for him.' The fool Abel Powell, trainee minister at College Aberhonddu, fatally ignores this advice; he stoops to marrying a pregnant servant girl, even though his Principal has urged that he foist paternity on someone outside the capel – such people are steeped in pollution. As our narrator laments, 'Man will behave foolishly for a woman, though he is commanded to cut off even his right hand if it offends him.' The Sionites understand how in consequence God has dealt with Abel and his low-bred choice; how, denied the prosperity of the Elect, they must 'cast their sweat on eight acres of sandy soil above Morfa'.

Outside his spokesman-of-Sion persona, Evans in the novel speaks directly of the sufferings of women, 'crushed to the glazen dullness of cows by submissive giving, childbearing, and continuous toil . . . you know that a Welsh woman is never allowed to tire, not by day or night, before her man'. Yet *Taffy* is refreshingly free of victimized women; on the contrary, we meet a range of spirited females harnessing their sexuality, some in dubious ways. Shan Gingerbread discreetly offers her body and is well rewarded for her tact; not for her the widow's burden of wool-gathering, or slaving at a neighbour's harvest, or planting out a meagre potato patch. Shan is a striking creation, her powers allied to the supernatural ('of her bread it is said that no woman who ate a piece that had been carried under a man's armpit could withhold herself'), and a quality of folk-tale, of fabulous pastoral bawdy, colours whole stretches of *Taffy*. The communal occasion of harvesting triggers a summer wantonness, upon which 'the old brown woman' (shades of Bertha Daviss!) provides a risqué commentary, prompted by Spurgeon's gift to Marged of his precious sermon pencil: 'Marged turned and lifted her skirt and she put the pencil in the wide calico pocket which hung from her waist.' Spurgeon comes to Marged by way of Ester, Josi Stonemason's daughter, whose transient physical attraction is caught in the image of her breasts falling to the string of her bodice, like 'cats being taken in a sack to be drowned'. Ester has a line in fevered gossip: tales of strange Peggi, who 'liked her tom-cat better than her infant and . . . let her infant perish of hunger so that her cat might suckle her', and of Big Konet ('not the handiwork of the Lord'), a woman to the cattle dealers of Carmarthen but a man to the women of Cwmamman, where in winter he worked in the pits.

From the moment of his arrival the young minister strikes Marged and Ester as a handsome catch, and in a reversal of sexual strategy Spurgeon uses this magnetism, his easy way with women, as a means of social advancement. Neither lust nor love must deflect him from Sion's pulpit – Ester perplexedly wonders 'why a man of so many words did not throw her upon the floor and ravish her'. But Spurgeon bargains without Marged, as do all Sion's men. More than their match in cunning, she becomes their moral scourge. More crucially, she understands the deep necessity of Sion ('Sion, whose other name is life'); religion binds the community; the Capel is law and life; there can be no safety without it (as she reminds her dissident father, only the lonely sinner is stoned, 'like the windows of an empty house'). Chapel religion stirs the sweetest of emotions and guides disturbed longings; she craves the concord of song and 'the hot music of the spoken prayer'; she desires 'to have her passion stirred by the preacher's song sermons'. In Marged can be detected some realignment in Evans's thinking. The psychic roots of nonconformity, its reordering of the emotional life, was something he would explore in *Nothing to Pay* (1930), but the bedrock need of chapel and its imperviousness to criticism were realities newly brought home to him. 'Foolish is the man who kindles his anger against life, for though the flame rage never so hard it cannot scorch even the down on life's garment . . . sooner will Big Pistill go dry than Sion falls.' The passage prompts reflection on Caradoc's own reforming endeavours. He was coming to acknowledge that all his books and press campaigning had had no salutary effect in Wales. Henceforth he would lighten his tone, relax more readily into humour, into fantasy and elements of folk-tale; look critically rather than condemn. So Ben gets his Ester, the deacons fall into harmony, and (to quote Spurgeon) 'God has put a new wick in the sun'.

Evans, for whatever reason, abandoned work on *Taffy*. Possibly he despaired of achieving a necessary evenness of tone; for though much here is inimitable Caradoc (a cold-steel irony, a beautiful lapidary prose), the novel as he left it somehow fails to cohere.[10] Still, its narrative core was salvageable, and late in 1922 he began to recast it in the form of a play. Friends had persuaded him to do so, he told the *Daily Sketch*, explaining how the actual writing had been undertaken on his regular train journey between Mortlake and Waterloo, or else in a Fleet Street pub in the evenings, during breaks from subbing on the *Daily Mirror*.[11] A little sherry eased the labour: 'I like sherry. It makes me feel a *diawl* [devil] of a fellow.' Evans needed the fortification; he might have been a theatre-goer, and a writer who possessed the playwright's instinct for dialogue, but he had never worked in the theatre, and a three-act play was a challenge: 'Do you think it funny?' he asked, arriving for rehearsal with his dog-eared script; 'I don't.'[12] It was as if he had written the piece fifty times before any actor set eyes on it.

Crucially, he did not attempt a dramatic equivalent of his novel; a lover of the commercial stage, he wanted an accessible piece that would hold a popular audience. So we lose the more audacious elements in the novel, as also the device of the narrator, whose dispassionate gaze so informs his stories. The action settles on the preaching match for Sion, the knavery of the Big Heads, and on Marged and Spurgeon, the lovers who come to oppose them. Ester and Ben are correspondingly downgraded and the device of the double wedding rejected; we leave the story at the point of Spurgeon's marriage to Marged, a purposeful act of commitment, not one half of a village event. The two become partners romantically and in their determination for reform:

> Our religion has been made by the ministers, who teach us how they are God's photographs and the Big Heads His Apostles. The minister's god wears a frock coat and heaven is a Welsh chapel where he preaches on the Sabbath in Welsh. The pulpit is a sorry lamp. It keeps us from the Church. It guides us to the polling booth. It turns our joy into sorrow. It gives the right to the bad man to pursue the timid man and the praying man to spoil the maid (*Taffy*, 1924, 82).

Sion must be cleansed; and as it was built by love so by love shall it be remade, by a dedicated minister himself made whole in marriage. The optimism is new in Evans, as is the notion of romantic love as the great regenerative power.

A matinée performance of *Taffy* was the brainchild of H. Dennis Bradley (1878–1934), Irish essayist, satirist and wit, who enjoyed another life as director of Pope and Bradley, civil and military tailors. It was Bradley's unconventional style of advertising that first caught public attention: his pungent mini-essays mixing praise for Bond Street clothes with sharp-edged social comment. Bradley dramatized all his viewpoints, and his strong opinions on the conduct of the war brought him to Evans's notice. 'The wickedest, the most damnable traitor to the country is the food profiteer,' Bradley asserted; 'even with higher wages, the poor can barely get enough to eat, and prices have been allowed to soar to such a scandalous extent that the wives and children of our soldiers, the men for whom we at home are trustees, are robbed and starved.'[13] His words might have been lifted from a Caradoc Evans *Ideas* editorial, and Bradley, so it seems, was encouraged to write for Evans's popular weekly. But he turned instead to the advertising columns of the national daily press, printing pieces at his own expense in the knowledge that advertising copy would almost certainly bypass the censor. In the field of drama, he responded to Caradoc's approach; the English favoured anaemia and artificiality, whereas the Irish painted life as it was, in all its vivid emotion. And Evans had Irish virtues; his *Taffy* deserved a showing. Bradley, himself a playwright and something of an impresario (he had sponsored plays by Rabindranath Tagore) agreed to finance a full production: a single charity performance in aid of the Actors' Association. In casting he managed a *coup*, enlisting Edith Evans at a time when, in the words of her biographer, she was 'scattering gold all over the place'.[14] Bradley thought her the perfect Marged, and around her he and his producer, Miles Malleson, assembled a first-rate cast, the bulk of whom were Welsh. (The producer of Tagore, Malleson was also an actor whose familiarity with Shakespearean comedy gave him a line on *Taffy*.)

The charity matinée of *Taffy* (26 February 1923) drew to the Prince of Wales Theatre an audience no less brilliant than the cast. H. G. Wells took a box; Mrs Lloyd George sat in the stalls, a little in front of Mrs Asquith; Berta Ruck and Augustus John looked on from the dress circle, John having made it known how enormously he admired Evans's talents. Caradoc's friends, the writers Mary Webb, Edwin Pugh and Edith Nepean, were also present (Nepean had designed Edith Evans's dresses), as were fellow journalists Hannen Swaffer and T. W. H. Crosland. In all, more than thirty critics covered the occasion, including James Agate, bright new star of the *Saturday Review*. The theatre was filled to capacity, even the standing areas; in the words of the *Westminster Gazette*, 'the reputation of Mr Caradoc Evans as a satirist of his own people unmatched in English literature since Swift, drew intellectual and artistic London in serried ranks'.[15] Yet not everyone came to praise, as one scrutinizer of the play had anticipated. 'I do not think it is the business of the Lord Chamberlain to interfere with a Welshman's attack on certain of his compatriots and their attitude to religion,' wrote the censor George S. Street, recommending a licence for *Taffy*. 'The play can hardly be expected to make a popular appeal: so far as it is known to them it will naturally be resented by the sort of Welshmen pilloried, but I do not think they are entitled to prevent its appearance.'[16]

The press caught wind of trouble and, sure enough, by 2.30 p.m. on the Monday afternoon a boisterous London-Welsh contingent had crowded into the gallery determined to make their protest. As the curtain rose on the white-washed walls of Capel Sion a rumpus broke out, and each of the play's three acts closed to a chorus of catcalls. Between times, so the *Sunday Express* reported, 'whenever the author got one home on the jaw', the gallery 'booed in a melodious manner'.[17] Cries of 'shame' and 'rubbish' greeted Spurgeon's big speech in Act 3, though applause from the stalls countered abuse from the gods. Occasionally the audience came together in approval (at Marged's denunciation of the deacons, for example), and it was noticeable how on each of her entrances, Edith Evans calmed the tumult (she had been instrumental, it was afterwards agreed, in keeping the occasion largely within the bounds of good humour). Nevertheless, the final curtain descended to shouts of 'traitor' and chants of 'We want Ca-ra-doc!'[18]

> It was a jeer, but they shouted it as though they wanted the author's blood. Caradoc Evans took his call courageously; he looked singularly unperturbed, as the applause of the many well-known people in the front failed to drown the yelling from the gods. 'Who won the war? Lloyd George!' shouted somebody else. 'Three cheers for Lloyd George' yelled another.

Hannen Swaffer thought he saw Mrs Lloyd George crying, while behind her, Margot Asquith's behaviour struck Beverley Baxter as eminently discreet ('she was probably thinking of a Liberal reunion').[19] Backstage an excited Mary Webb warmly congratulated Caradoc; she had enjoyed the whole occasion immensely, down to her interval tea.[20]

After a single theatrical performance Evans awoke a minor celebrity. 'I was greatly moved by it,' wrote Augustus John next morning; 'it was beautifully acted and in every way a success.'[21] Mrs Asquith likewise thanked the author for a most enjoyable play ('tho' I think the 1st act was a little long'), and invited him to lunch at Bedford Square.[22] Within a short time Evans's 'Big Head' phrase, used of the chapel deacons, gained a new currency in the language[23] – all proof that if anything puts an author on the map more readily than a novel, then it must be a play. Words unexceptional on the page can catch fire in a crowded auditorium – witness the comedy of the scheming deacons, often tedious to read, but played to continuous chuckles. And not only words strike home: James Agate instanced Twmi in Act 2 rising slowly from his sick bed to move across the room:

> There was visible, palpable irony in the monstrous spectacle – a mountain of flesh voiding his spiritual rheum in patriarchal accent and gesture, a petitioner of Heaven, cloaked mightily in wide-flung blankets like a terrifying figure of Blake, offering a negligible soul. There was theatre here, something you could see and touch, something which the printed page must have denied.[24]

Agate considered *Taffy* too homiletic for commercial success, a viewpoint shared by the *English Review*, which none the less praised the play as an antidote to the trash that since the Armistice had blighted the West End stage: 'We saw live men. We heard live words. We left more alive than when we entered the theatre.'[25] This response, from the journal that first discovered Evans, might seem a little excessive (others would later talk of *Taffy*'s pasteboard world), yet this again is to discount the dynamics of a particular performance and the vivifying presence of an actress of Edith Evans's stature; 'the masterful and passionate personality of the girl flowed from her with an intensity that dominated the stage' (as for audience hostility, she 'rode the whirlwind and directed the storm').[26]

'There is a chapel on every road in Wales,' Marged warns Spurgeon, who innocently believes that by abandoning Sion he can escape all that the chapel stands for. English roads are likewise marked, reflected the *Nation and Athenaeum*, as are roads throughout the world where men and women live in community.[27] *Taffy*, like all good satire, had a universal application. Understandably, Welsh critics could not manage so detached a viewpoint. 'Everything we hold in reverence, and all that we have ever felt to be sacred, are burlesqued, ridiculed and mocked,' wrote one *Western Mail* correspondent; 'To use our preachers – the finest in the world – deacons, and *yr hen dadau*, as objects for amusement to a London crowd is beyond disgust,' said another.[28] Much was made of the London audience, 'prominent society people and . . . prominent writers, male and female. The cream of England might be said to have been in the theatre, and they were all "taken in".'[29] *Taffy* lent extra fervour to the 1923 St David's Day celebrations. At Cardiff Wil Ifan saw the play as riding on English race hatred,[30] while it reminded J. R. Llewellyn, president of the Barry Cymmrodorion Society, of the bill to flood the Ceiriog Valley.[31] (Llewellyn's hatred of *Taffy* intensified: ten years later he seized a copy of the published play from an astonished Barry Library borrower and threw it on to a refuse cart bound for the local incinerator. Chairman of Barry Council, Llewellyn made good the loss. 'It was my great joy to consign that infernal volume to the ashes of Hades,' he raged. 'If I am obliged to pay the market value of the volume, I will do so, but replace it, never, never, never!')[32] In London a St David's Day dinner for five hundred heard Sir Austen Chamberlain make much of his Welsh connections, but it was the lambasting of Caradoc by Morgan Jones, Labour MP for Caerphilly, that won the greater applause.[33]

Within days Caradoc Evans had issued his response, an article in the *Sunday Express* requiring an editorial statement distancing the paper from his views. Here was Evans at his polemical best, the biblical tone and phrasing suggestive of bedrock truth, or at least of bedrock conviction.

> Jealous of his trust, the preacher has made rules for the salvation of our bodies and souls. Temptations such as art, drama, dancing, and the study of folk-lore he has removed from our way. Those are vanities, which make men puffed up and the collections small. Look you, the preacher asks, do they not cost money? Are they not time wasters? My capel needs your money, boys bach, that the light – the grand, spiritual light – shall shine in the pulpit.
>
> That is the lamp which burns throughout Wales, from Criccieth to Cardigan Bay. It keeps our feet from Church door and public house, and it guides us to the polling booth where we record our votes as the preacher has commanded

us. Be the season never so hard and be men and women never so hungry, its flame does not wane and the oil in its vessel must never run low.

White cabbages and new potatoes, eggs and measures of corn, milk and butter and loaves of bread and money we give to the preacher. We trim our few acres until our shoulders are crutched and the soil is in the crevices of our flesh that our estate shall be a glory unto this awful God. We make for him a house which is as a mansion set amid hovels and for the building thereof the widow must set aside portions of her old age pension. These things we do, for favour of the Lord is obtained by sacrifice unto the preacher . . .

We are what we have been made by our preachers and politicians . . . Our politicians, crafty pupils of the preachers and now their masters, weep and moan in the public places; in their souls they are greedy and very cruel. They have made themselves slaves of the wicked, and like asses their eyes are lifted no higher than the golden carrot which is their reward from the wicked. Of few of us can it be said: 'He is a great man', or 'He is a good man', or 'He is an honest man.'[34]

The last paragraph recalls Evans's 1920 letter in defence of *My Neighbours* ('Dangle before him [a Welsh MP] a golden carrot and he will trot merrily to hell'),[35] while 'Criccieth to Cardigan Bay' alludes to the shrinking domain of his Liberal opponents – in the November 1922 election Liberals lost disastrously to Labour in the industrial south. Yet if *Taffy* reflects Caradoc's optimism at a Welsh political awakening, it was becoming increasingly clear that his brand of radicalism, with its post-*Taffy* talk of fewer chapels and better schools (or more cowsheds even), struck no chord with incoming parliamentarians, some of whom were lay preachers and temperance devotees. Again, Morgan Jones led the charge, denouncing 'the liar of Wales' whose work was 'vile and vicious, sordid and silly'.[36] A prominent Labour whip, Jones explained to *Llais Llafur/Labour Voice*, the Swansea Valley socialist weekly, that Evans's outpourings, whatever his intentions, were now proving harmful to Wales ('in parliamentary circles this [is] quite noticeable').[37] Meanwhile Caradoc's lunch with the Asquiths had proved a gloomy affair ('Asquith drank a bottle of port all to himself . . . I might as well not have been there'),[38] though it fuelled the rumour that Asquith had financed *Taffy*, counting Evans's denigration of the Welsh as injurious to the Lloyd George Coalition Liberals.[39]

A text of the play in book form seems an improbable commercial venture but 'that epic matinée', as Berta Ruck described it,[40] raised a storm of publicity that Evans's publisher was keen to harness. Melrose made the most of *Taffy: A Play of Welsh Village Life* (published March 1924); bound in Oxford blue, its eighty-eight pages bulk large, the last two recording praise from twenty-six theatre critics. A prefatory note explains that the play as printed is 'slightly different' from that presented at the Prince of Wales. This is something of an understatement. Whatever its success in performance, Evans had come to feel that the play was artistically flawed, and he seized on the printed edition as an opportunity for extensive revision.[41] 'There was no coherency in it, and no joining up of the story,' he candidly explained.[42] The psychology of the two leading characters failed to convince: 'I knew why Spurgeon changed his mind, falling from a bad man to a decent man [but] I did not make it clear to the audience.' Accordingly, a revised Act 1 develops Marged as a radicalizing force, a process continued in Act 2 where Spurgeon, correspondingly, becomes a fitter object of her regard (and less a young man on the make). Marged's strength of vision is underscored by one new speech in Act 3, which has her movingly rebuking the Big Heads for betraying their religious inheritance.

> Your prayers will build you nothing. You are men of speech and your sorrow is dry. You have no regard for the first Capel Sion that was Bensha's mud-walled hut on the moor. Every night a candle burnt at the window to guide the folk who came on the narrow path to read the Beybile in Welsh or to seek Bensha to go and read the Beybile to the dying. And however black and stormy the night no one lost his way or went in vain. The Sion that you want to pull down was built by love. Short is the fame of Love. After their day's work women brought timber down the hill and over the valley to make this Sion. And in the night men opened gravel pits and brought up stones from the quarry by the light of a flaming

> fire of twigs and furze. All worked in the sure belief of another God than the God of the English-speaking parson who shot calves and lambs for sport and whose horses trod the corn and tore the hedges. Their love and their sacrifice are nothing to you. Do not the moments of their labour taunt you with shame? You pule and you whine and pluck your garments like a man waiting for a feast for which he has made no provision. (*Taffy*, 72)

Marged's exchanges with Spurgeon lie at the heart of the play, imbued with fresh warmth and feeling, and the revised third act introduces what are perhaps the best known lines in *Taffy*, Marged's lyrical outburst at Spurgeon's declaration of love.

> I have hated you. And loved you. O love made noises in my heart. It stilled the rill of the morning milk as it fell into the pitcher, and at night it chased away the white moss of slumber from my eyes. It stirred the woman within me. (*Taffy*, 85)

This heightened love scene took reviewers by surprise, though they noted how the tenderness and romance were salted by Rhys Shop at the close, urging his hens to gobble up the scattered rice he had earlier sold to the wedding guests.[43] Overall, for one critic at least, the author's stance was clearer: 'He loves Wales with the divine love that chasteneth . . . a love more perceptible than in some of his earlier writings.'[44]

At last from literary Wales came two approving responses. Reviewing *Taffy* in the *Western Mail*, W. J. Gruffydd, professor of Welsh at Cardiff and editor of *Y Llenor* (the newly founded cultural quarterly), was not ashamed to admit that he had thoroughly enjoyed reading the play and that he regretted not having been privileged to see it in performance.[45] Evans's works were not essays in realism; they created their own universe 'lit by a sun other than ours, filled by a deadly air in which normal human beings cannot live'. Close on Gruffydd, and again in the *Western Mail* (30 August 1924), came an appreciation by D. T. Davies, playwright and champion of the Welsh-language drama movement. Surveying Evans's achievement, he felt convinced that 'We have no one in Wales, with the possible exception of Kate Roberts, who has treated the short story so adequately as a literary form.' As to Evans's 'misrepresentations', the truth about Rhydlewis had little to do with the value of his fiction. 'Criticism, a hundred years hence, will be interested in Rhydlewis chiefly as the birthplace of Caradoc Evans, and to the extent that it will shed light on the personality of the author and his work.' By coincidence, Davies's essay appeared the day after a local newspaper review by Caradoc of two of Davies's plays. On his fortnight's annual holiday Caradoc had joined some two hundred and fifty people at a village production of *Y Dieithryn* and *Y Pwyllgor* ('The Stranger' and 'The Committee'). 'Members of the Rhydlewis Company can act', said Evans,[46]

> but they must remember that the actor finds his characters on the plains of reality and not in the wastes of fiction magazines. Truly you cannot put life on the stage; you can put the next best thing: a portrait of life. And one stage portrait is often built with a half-a-dozen life types on the foundation of the author's imagination. That is how one gets into the 'skin' of a part.

Individual actors were commended, at least in part, for 'they succeeded and failed: succeeded in getting their goods well over the footlights and failed to help the three other members of the cast to do so. Team work is essential in all plays.' Still, the performers were more engaging than the plays; *Y Dieithryn*, in particular, seemed 'a sackful of wordy pretentiousness' to Evans's ears.

Taffy, it should be remembered, was not the only play of Welsh village life before the general public. For a decade or more Welsh drama had enjoyed something of a renaissance, evidenced in the mushrooming of amateur companies and the emergence of a group of Welsh playwrights treating of native subjects. Talk of a Welsh National Theatre was in the air, especially in the circle of Lord Howard de Walden, a sympathetic north Wales patron who nourished hopes of a bilingual company with a repertoire of Welsh plays (he had backed such a venture in 1913). Irish parallels (and the achievements of the Abbey Theatre) were inevitably invoked as

English-language plays by J. O. Francis and Richard Hughes gained performances within and outside Wales. Barely down from Oxford, yet emerging as a new organizational focus for the Welsh revival, Richard Hughes believed that the strength of Welsh drama lay in its little companies, from whom (via regional groupings) the stars of a National Theatre would arise. Meanwhile London blandishments must be resisted: was not J. O. Francis's *The Dark Little People* hopelessly mangled by an English company in 1923? Pointedly Richard Hughes, in a survey for the *Review of Reviews*, ignored the existence of *Taffy*, choosing instead to warn against *My People*, a 'cold-blooded and wilful trading on English ignorance, prompted by personal dislike of his fellow-countrymen, and having at most only local application to one or two valleys'.[47] The remark stung Evans, who replied:

> In your last issue Mr Richard Hughes declares that I hate my people . . . This indictment he bases on *My People*, a work of fiction. If an author's personality is to be judged by his fiction, surely the judge should base his judgment on that author's entire output – not on one book. But apparently Mr Hughes wanted a case and got it.
>
> I do not hate my people. I like them well enough to criticize them. I hope my play 'Taffy' proves this.

Evans, like Hughes, was sounded for his views on Welsh drama. The Welsh, he agreed, were naturally gifted but had a fatal tendency to overact. 'They have for too long had the whole stage as preachers. They do not readily give good teamwork.'[48] He saw little encouragement for the future; lacking a core of sympathetic interpreters (the better actors and producers were forced to work outside Wales), Welsh playwrights would increasingly be drawn away from indigenous subjects.

By summer 1925 a revival of *Taffy* had been confirmed, in a production booked for the Q Theatre (Jack de Leon's venture in Chiswick designed to try out new plays), then for a limited West End run. An experienced cast was assembled, with Joan Maude (Marged) and Tristan Rawson (Spurgeon) as leads, and encouraged by this fresh exposure Evans and his producer, Milton Rosmer, set about contriving a more closely knitted play.[49] Another problem lay with the love-making, now deemed too pure to be believable, and especially so in Wales. ('Welsh people don't make love, though they say they do', Evans ventured, in a headline-grabbing quote.) As for possible audience hostility, he hoped that his compatriots would at least have the courtesy to listen to his case. 'I poke no fun at the Welsh because I like the Welsh too much,' he told a startled *Western Mail* reporter.[50]

The first night of *Taffy* at the Q (8 September 1925) was a predictably Welsh affair.[51] The orchestra played Welsh airs as a celebrity audience filed in: Welsh parliamentarians, the secretary of the Welsh Church Commission, the high sheriff of Cardiganshire. Along came T. P. O'Connor, veteran journalist and parliamentarian (and now Caradoc's employer on a literary weekly), eulogizing the production before the curtain went up. Caradoc seemed nervous. That morning he had heard of a possible demonstration and wondered about sitting in the audience. Bruce Winstone (playing Twmi) suggested a nearby pub but, sensing danger in three hours' drinking, Caradoc settled for a room backstage. As it happened, *Taffy* met with general enthusiasm, the cheers drowning the boos, and in answer to repeated calls the author appeared on stage. Smilingly he addressed the house.

> On behalf of everyone connected with the production of this play I thank you for your kind reception. I am grateful particularly to my fellow countrymen for their kindness in leaving their little businesses to come here to witness the truth of the portrayal of the three Big Heads and Ben Watkins. ['Liar!'] We have been behaving ourselves as riotously as men and women do at Welsh prayer meetings ['Liar!' – 'Why don't you produce the play in Wales?'] and having done so, let us depart tonight as men and women depart from Welsh prayer meetings – with new sins in our hearts.[52]

Depart they did, and the policemen waiting in readiness were quietly stood down.

Following its stay in Chiswick (8–19 September), the production transferred to the West End for a three-week run at the Royalty. Rosmer's treatment pleased most reviewers, though the comedy had been played as farce and the pace still dragged a little. Again, as Evans saw it, the fault lay with his text and particularly the final act, which again he tightened. The modifications, though not extensive, are important, for they come at the climax of the play: out went Spurgeon's passionate indictment ('I abhor the righteousness of the capel . . . ', *Taffy*, 82), phrases from which Evans had used in his polemical pieces. Instead we have these lines, spoken by Spurgeon as he turns his back on the dreadful chapel:[53]

> But this Sion is only a bit of Wales. There are in Wales other Sions, where men are not lost in the multitude of their own virtues. Oh, yes, there are fair hearts in the land in which dwell neither greed, nor hate, nor pomp, nor deceit . . . I tune my spirit to the eternal song, and my feet shall company youths and maids in whose minds are stored the streaming glories of our past . . . Yes, I'll pant after the lowly, and cause them to stiffen up with a pride of an ancient people.

Such eager hope, the trust of a man shedding his preacher's garb for the clothes of an honest labourer, echoes Evans's rallying call at Bangor in 1924:[54]

> we are not dead. We have intellect. It is in the coalpits, in the universities, and in the fields. The signs are clear that we are awakening. We have a group of writers and a group of politicians who are marching along; they are not faint of heart; they are marching with dignity and majesty and with great purpose. They and those who will come after them will create a new Wales or a Wales for the Welsh.

The burst of optimism naturally provoked some questioning. 'In Allen Raine, Edith Nepean and Lloyd George you have only one side of Wales shown,' Evans explained to the press; 'No country can prosper on conditions of the Kailyard. The dung heaps must be seen and the causes must be removed. I have been trying to remove them.'[55] Nor was he alone; he discerned 'a new outlook, a new ideal and a new aspiration' abroad in the country. The pulpit stairs were rickety; chapel attendances were falling; people had come to realize that Liberal-nonconformity was not Christianity but 'a wrangle to get people into Parliament and so preserve the vested interests of Nonconformist capitalists'. Significantly, D. T. Davies's plays at Rhydlewis had attracted bigger numbers than six Sunday services in the village combined.

On Monday, 21 September, *Taffy* opened at the Royalty before a packed and largely appreciative audience. Coming forward at the end of the play, Evans faced a degree of barracking but, as at Chiswick, a lively first night had passed off without serious disturbance. Caradoc and Dennis Eadie, the actor-manager who had brought the play to the West End, were quietly satisfied: the revisions had made their mark, a syndicate had materialized with ideas for an American production, and there was even talk of a tour of Wales (assuming Evans could get the all-Welsh cast he wanted). The evening, too, had produced one keen personal pleasure in the appearance of Duncan Davies, Caradoc's 'very argumentative' old friend of drapery days, who after years in Fleet Street was now leaving London for good. Backstage the two men chatted warmly in what was to be their last encounter. (Evans's classic 'Self-Portrait' pays Davies handsome tribute: 'So what schoolin failed to do this young shop-assistant from Lampeter did: educate me.')

Nothing in the first night at the Royalty, or in the two subsequent evening performances, could have suggested what was to come on Thursday, 24 September. The scenes that evening were unprecedented in theatrical memory and greatly served to swell the Caradoc Evans legend.[56] Word of likely trouble went out among the London-Welsh (milkmen and drapers especially) and by the time of the evening performance they had gathered outside the theatre in numbers, chanting the author's name. Evans arrived by taxi and passed through the throng unnoticed, this despite his much-photographed face and distinctive style of dress (his disreputable black hat still a badge of emancipation). Inside the crowded theatre the excitement was palpable but the opening act passed off without serious incident. Then, at the lowering of the first curtain, part of the audience struck up the Welsh National Anthem and the protest began in earnest. Booing and whistling from some three hundred people (almost half the theatre) and cries of 'Judas, Judas' disrupted the second act; twice the curtain had to be lowered so that Joan Maude, the leading lady, could appeal for calm. The third act, it was obvious, would produce some sort of crisis, but against a barrage of noise the players embarked upon it. Once more the curtain came down, allowing Jack de Leon and Tristan Rawson (playing Spurgeon) to appear on stage and plead for a decent hearing, the kind that London gave to any play. The jeering and catcalls subsided, though not for long, and with the curtain once more lowered Jack de Leon urged the audience at least to wait for Spurgeon's closing speech: let them see if they could not approve of the play's final sentiments. Again the noise subsided, but far from converting the critics, Spurgeon's declaration of hope whipped them up anew. Now the drama passed conclusively from stage to auditorium, where summoned policemen moved among the noisiest demonstrators. In the words of the *Western Mail*, 'pandemonium reigned supreme towards the close'. With dialogue scarcely audible and some people attempting to leave, house lights were raised on the scene of disorder. Inevitably some scuffling broke out as half a dozen demonstrators, flanked by their cheering supporters, were marched off to Marlborough Street police station.

Outside the theatre Caradoc regretted the arrests: 'I complain about Welshmen being thin-skinned, and I want to be more tolerant myself than they are.'[57] He put a brave face on the evening; the cast had shown courage under fire in managing to complete the play – only at the very close had some cutting been necessary. There could be no doubt, Evans argued, that the exhibition was pre-arranged; from first to last it had been 'an early closing show'. A spokesman for the protesters agreed; the Thursday half-holiday had given the London-Welsh a chance to show their disgust, not simply at this play but at Caradoc Evans in every guise and the harm he was doing to Wales. Reporting the disturbances, the *Daily Mail* spoke of trouble-makers being 'swept out of the theatre on an alcoholic tide'. Liquor had played its part, as one arrested dairyman made plain in a statement before the magistrate (itself a little drama).[58]

> When I entered the theatre everybody was singing, so I lifted up my voice in the general chorus. Then I was thrown out and somebody pushed me against the constable, and I clutched him before I knew he was a policeman. He let me go, but I fell down and somebody fell on top of me and got me by the throat, and when I came to, the same policeman had me again, and the police doctor said I was drunk in a dim light.

For being drunk and disorderly he and two others were each fined twelve shillings, the money being raised by a collection amongst young supporters.

Some newspapers made much of the evening. During the war, a play or two had prompted protests, but this was the first time a performance had actually been brought to a halt. And the scenes had been ugly, with the police forced to step in. The *Nation and Athenaeum* stood aside from the brouhaha. The playwright had discovered that in Wales, as elsewhere, a measure of godly cant hides a great deal of meanness and greed, and had said so with liveliness and wit. Nevertheless, continued the reviewer:[59]

> It appears that Mr Evans is wrong to suppose that Welshmen are as bad as Zola's Frenchmen in *La Terre*, or as Ibsen's countrymen in *An Enemy of the People*, or as Strindberg's Swedes, or as Mr Theodore Powys's Englishmen, and he cannot make amends by having his young leads as impeccably pure and idealistic as your best American.

The behaviour of the pit was regrettable – it seemed to confirm Evans's indictment of his people – and the *Nation* trusted that the management would stand by the play. This indeed they did, until the end of the scheduled run (10 October) and the prospect of calmer Celtic waters – a revival of *The Playboy of the Western World*.

The lambasting of *Taffy* continued. The president of the London Welsh Literary and Musical Societies' Union saw it as dragging the nation's sacred altars through the mud, for the sake of an English public 'in which the animal instinct is supreme';[60] Ivor Novello, gushing about native talent ('I do not think there is anything more beautiful than Welsh drama, poetry and ballads'), thought the play's whole attitude 'one of unpleasantness',[61] while the high sheriff of Merioneth contented himself with saying that its creator had 'a face like a concertina' – all of which seemed to confirm Sewell Stokes's handy verdict, that Caradoc Evans was 'the best-hated man in Wales'.[62] Once more W. J. Gruffydd came to the defence, remarking how dangerous it was for any Welshman to speak of Caradoc Evans except in terms of execration.[63] Scathingly Gruffydd dismissed those of his countrymen who, about to enter the vast limbo which lay behind Welsh public life ('the resting-place of unfrocked ministers, fraudulent financiers and discredited politicians'), re-emerge into public esteem through 'one great act of atonement': their vilification of Caradoc Evans. Gruffydd would not join them. He had welcomed *Taffy* in book form and was yet more admiring of the revisions. The moral failings it castigated were symptoms of a decayed Puritanism, itself but a phase in the life of the nation, as Evans was right to insist. He was right also to divine a new mood abroad in Wales; and, Gruffydd added, 'if all Welshmen were to agree in thinking thus, our very hopes would create the substance.'

Evans was teasingly vague on those who might be hastening the new order. He would have applauded the political realignment of the early 1920s, even if many of the first-time Labour MPs were cast from the same nonconformist mould as their defeated Liberal opponents. Politicized labour had succeeded in bringing, at least until 1924, an unprecedented share of prosperity to the south Wales coalfield. As Evans put it, 'The men in the pits and the men in the fields are straining at their tethering cords' – the men in the fields less conspicuously, though a flash of rural radicalism lit the immediate post-war years. In speaking of a group of writers intent on creating 'a new Wales, or a Wales for the Welsh', he could only have had in mind W. J. Gruffydd and *Y Llenor*, a journal which, as Evans told Bangor students, 'could stand side by side with the best English reviews'. (Gruffydd, too, had appeared a traducer of his nation, particularly hard on nonconformity – 'a pale shadow of the old way of life, the hollow trunk on which the leaves are all withered and which all manner of vile fungi flourish'.)[64]

Evans's lectures and journalism show how much at this time his sentiments overlapped with Gruffydd's. He spoke of the need to foster a new pride in the nation, and in its language as well:[65]

> The Welsh boast of their language. Yet the first care of many of the town Welsh is to keep their children from learning it . . . I do not say that the Welsh language is of commercial use, but it fits the shape of our tongue; and it is as priggish to forget it as it is to forget one's mother. And if it is worth the while of English and Jewish parliamentary candidates to learn phrases of it for the purposes of electioneering, it is worth our while to keep it green. Our language is our inheritance. It is not a vote catching dodge.

Evans had long lamented the national sense of inferiority, the condition of morbid self-consciousness that had shaped reaction to his writings, and he returned to it vigorously in 1925. Now that he was editing *T.P.'s Weekly*, the popular literary paper relaunched by T. P. O'Connor, some Irish influence seems to have rubbed off; for besides Tay Pay's fitful presence (representative of the Liverpool Irish, he was 'father' of the House of Commons), Evans worked alongside Austin Clarke and Con O'Leary, two Irish writers steeped in their country's past. Certainly, the achievements of the Irish (and indeed the Scots) he set against the dismal record of Wales. Cardiff, he assured readers of the *Sunday Express*, was Welsh only on the map of Wales.[66] There is harmony there – the harmony of master and servant.

> The people of other nations have fought for their own with sharp-edged stones in their hands and with stubborn songs on their lips. The Cardiff Welsh have opened their doors to the invader, saying 'Come you in, boys bach, and rest you here; show us the way and we will follow you.'

Though sounding like a man ripe for Plaid Genedlaethol Cymru, founded in the month of his article (August 1925), Evans could never contemplate the nationalist path. Associating political nationalism with Lloyd George's early careerist moves, he continued to see it as a 'stairway to money-for-nothing jobs', offering Wales little beyond empty talk and mock-heroics. Theatricality was inherent in the Welsh; no other people more easily retreated into rhetoric and a world of make-believe. 'Our whole life is a stage play,' he told an audience in 1924. 'We do not reveal ourselves on our own hearths or on our death-beds, or even to ourselves . . . We have acted so long that we have lost ourselves and are wearing the misty skin of someone that never was.'[67] Evans's male characters are quintessentially 'talkists', hopelessly addicted to language ('You are men of speech and your sorrow is dry', says Spurgeon to the Elders), and peppered throughout Evans's addresses are pithy formulations, not simply of the chapel as theatre ('comedy and tragedy, pathos and farce; each emotion so perfectly expressed that one might have thought the preacher himself believed it'),[68] but of the Welshman's passion for gestures and speechifying in the fit-up world he inhabits: 'the earth is his stage and the lime is his sun'; 'our tongue is our solace; it is never still'; 'we are the real playboys of the Western World'.[69]

Seventy years on, *Taffy* reads as an innocuous comedy with a few happy touches. Clearly it plays better than it reads, but the piece had not come easily and Evans was never wholly satisfied with it. It was writing against the grain, a mixture of indictment and idealism tailored for the popular stage. Even so, it got the author out of his den and into the bustling theatre where he, the most single-minded of artists, deaf to every criticism, took part in rehearsals and collaborated with stage professionals on modifications to his text. If he wrote no more plays, his interest in the theatre remained; during the 1930s he participated, more or less willingly, in Rogues and Vagabonds, the Aberystwyth repertory company set up by his wife Marguerite. He even had a walk-on part in her 1936 production of *Taffy* – by all accounts a nerveless affair received with no murmur of dissent. (Marguerite had her own explanation: the 1925 Royalty audience was not really itself; the Welshman in Wales was a gentleman but in London, in 'his earnest exuberance', he fell prey to Cockney hooliganism.)[70] A 1938 revival supported Marguerite's analysis. Her production at the Grafton Theatre, in London's Tottenham Court Road, enjoyed an arresting set designed by the Swansea artist Evan Walters, several of whose paintings hung in the foyer and along the theatre corridors. Among them was his portrait of Caradoc, famously denied any showing in Wales and now about to suffer beheading: on St David's Day an unknown person armed with a razor slashed it twice across the throat. Caradoc took the incident calmly. He understood his countryman's reaction and his answer was ready-made. 'No one knows how sick he is until he sees his tongue in a mirror,' he said in 1925.[71] So with the Welsh; and when we see our sickness in the mirror of the stage we blame the author of the mirror. 'We imagine that in killing the author we cure our ills.'

Notes

1 Gwyn Jones (ed.), *Welsh Short Stories* (Harmondsworth, Penguin, 1940), 116.
2 *Western Mail*, 15 March 1916, 7.
3 3 March 1920, 179.
4 As reported by Edward Wright, *Bookman* (October 1917), 6–7.
5 *Western Mail*, 10 May 1922, 9.
6 The unfinished *Taffy* is a short novel of thirty chapters, most of which survives in draft (part manuscript, part typescript). Following Evans's death, a portion of the novel went to the National Library of Wales and a portion into the Caradoc Evans papers of Professor Gwyn Jones (since deposited at NLW). The novel is now to be found in NLW MS 20031B and NLW Professor Gwyn Jones Papers, 66/1–2 – from which quotations in this essay are taken.
7 The Revd T. Eynon Davies, temperance secretary of the Congregational Union and a London pulpit giant, was Caradoc's old *Western Mail* adversary.
8 *Dictionary of Welsh Biography down to 1940* (London, Honourable Society of Cymmrodorion, 1959), 147.
9 The youthful preacher undoubtedly owes his forename to Charles Haddon Spurgeon, the immensely popular nineteenth-century Baptist minister who frequently visited Wales and whose writings were widely translated into Welsh.
10 The novel as it survives is by no means in its finished state. It is clear that Evans employed a typist who had difficulty in

reading his handwriting, and that on receipt of the typescript he could still make substantial revisions to his text. What survives at NLW is (1) a portion of Evans's manuscript, cleanly written on ruled paper; and (2) a portion of the typescript (presumably from the discarded manuscript draft), with extensive revisions in Evans's hand.

11 22 February 1923.

12 *Daily Graphic,* 26 February 1923.

13 From an article of June 1917, reprinted in H. Dennis Bradley, *Not For Fools* (London, 1920). Evans, it is worth noting, provided glowing prefaces to two of Bradley's later books.

14 J. C. Trewin, *Edith Evans* (London, 1924).

15 The fullest newspaper report of the matinée performance is probably that of the *Daily Graphic,* 27 February 1923. Berta Ruck, *A Trickle of Welsh Blood* (London, 1967), provides a further eyewitness account.

16 Report dated 12 February 1923, British Library, Lord Chamberlain's Plays: Correspondence, *Taffy* 1923/4723. The licensed copy of the play is also on file at British Library, Lord Chamberlain's Playscripts, *Taffy*, 1923.

17 4 March 1923, 6.

18 *Daily Graphic*, 27 February 1923.

19 *Sunday Express*, 4 March 1923, 6.

20 Edwin Pugh, 'Mary Webb', *Bookman* (July 1928), 193–6.

21 Letter to Caradoc Evans, 27 February 1923, NLW Gwyn Jones Papers.

22 Letter to Caradoc Evans, 27 February 1923, NLW MS 20034D.

23 As noted in *Cassell's Weekly*, 21 March 1923.

24 *Saturday Review*, 3 March 1923, 185–6.

25 April 1923, 350.

26 *The Times*, 27 February 1927. Trewin, *Edith Evans*, 20, has a photograph of the actress as Marged in the 1923 production.

27 3 March 1923, 834.

28 *Western Mail*, 1 March 1923, 6 (letter signed 'D.E.'); *Western Mail*, 3 March 1923, 6 (T. Alun Jones).

29 John D. Lewis, 'Libel on life in Wales', *Western Mail*, 27 February 1923, 6.

30 'Caradoc Evans's "People" ', *Western Mail*, 5 March 1923, 8.

31 *Western Mail*, 3 March 1923, 7.

32 The case was reported in the *Western Mail*, 9 May 1933, 5, and the *Observer*, 14 May 1933.

33 *Western Mail*, 2 March 1923, 7.

[34] 'Do I insult the Welsh?', 4 March 1923, reprinted in John Harris (ed.), *Fury Never Leaves Us: A Miscellany of Caradoc Evans* (Bridgend, Seren, 1985), 156–7.

[35] *Western Mail*, 22 March 1920, 6.

[36] *Sunday Express*, 11 March 1923.

[37] 17 March 1923, 3. Evans abuse continued, near and far. A first leader in the *Cardigan and Tivyside Advertiser*, 2 March 1923, suggested 'a tragedy of a Welsh pervert' not 'a play of Welsh village life' as a suitable subtitle for *Taffy*, while the apoplectic *Druid*, 15 April 1923, mouthpiece of the Pennsylvanian American-Welsh, believed that Evans could be taught a wholesome lesson by a body like the Ku Klux Klan – though if he ever arrived in America on his threatened lecture tour, there were 'enough Welshmen in the anthracite regions to make it so hot for him that he will conclude he has eventually reached the place for which he is destined'. (I am grateful to William D. Jones for the latter reference; his *Wales in America: Scranton and the Welsh, 1860–1920* (Cardiff, 1993) documents the hysterical American-Welsh reaction to Caradoc Evans.)

[38] As quoted in Oliver Sandys, *Caradoc Evans* (London, 1946), 67.

[39] In conversation with the present author, Mrs Anita Arter, whose family comes from Rhydlewis, attests that this was certainly the word in Evans's home locality.

[40] In *A Trickle of Welsh Blood.*

[41] Immediately following the matinée Evans had sent a script to Clement Shorter, in the hope that the editor of the *Sphere* would like it – and that 'you will tell me even if you don't', (Caradoc Evans, letter to Clement Shorter, 2 March 1923, University of Leeds, Brotherton Library, Brotherton Collection).

[42] *Western Mail*, 2 September 1925, 7.

[43] Seemingly another example of Caradoc making use of comments or incidents gathered whilst on annual holiday in Rhydlewis. Attending a wedding in his company, a local resident remarked how someone would be sure to send out chickens to eat up the rice (Mrs Betti Richards, in conversation with the present author, 1986).

[44] *Review of Reviews* (November/December 1924), 457.

[45] 24 April 1924, 9.

[46] *Cardigan and Tivyside Advertiser*, 29 August 1924 (signed 'C').

[47] 'Wales and the Welsh: drama among the mountains', *Review of Reviews* (May/June 1924), 461–6; Evans's reply came in a letter, *Review of Reviews* (June/July 1924), 542.

[48] From an interview, later published in Olive Ely Hart, *The Drama in Modern Wales* (Philadelphia, 1928), 81.

[49] Evidence of the acting version survives in a marked-up copy of the 1924 printed edition used for the Q Theatre production, NLW MS 21624B. Signed by Rosmer and the cast, the book was offered as a gift 'To his friend the ideal Ester (Winifred Evans) from Caradoc'.

[50] 2 September 1925, 7.

[51] See *Western Mail*, 9 September 1925, 7, and 10 September 1925, 6.

[52] *Western Mail*, 9 September 1925, 7.

[53] The text as played at the Royalty is difficult to reconstruct, and these additional lines are taken from a press interview by Evans designed to publicize his changes, *Western Mail*, 10 September, 1925, 6. A text of *Taffy*, based on the marked-up printed copy used for the 1925 revival (and therefore close to the final acting version), is offered in John Harris (ed.), *Fury Never Leaves Us: A Miscellany of Caradoc Evans*, 162–218.

[54] Portions of Evans's lecture at University College, Bangor, 7 November 1923, appeared in the *Liverpool Daily Post*, 8 November 1923, and the *Western Mail*, 8 November 1923. A typescript of the address has also survived, NLW MS 20033C.

[55] *Western Mail*, 10 September 1925, 6.

[56] For reports see *Western Mail*, 25 September 1925, 9; *Daily Mail*, 25 September 1925; *Daily News*, 25 September 1925.

[57] *Western Mail*, 25 September 1925, 9.

[58] *Daily Mail*, 26 September 1925, 6.

[59] *Nation and Athenaeum*, 30 October 1925, 17.

[60] Tim Evans, in an address to the London-Welsh Union, reported *Western Mail*, 5 October 1925, 6.

[61] *Western Mail*, 9 January 1926, 7.

[62] *Personal Glimpses* (London, 1924), 135.

[63] 'Is Caradoc Evans right?', *T.P.'s and Cassell's Weekly*, 17 October 1925, 815.

[64] Ibid.

[65] From the typescript of his Bangor address, NLW MS 20033C. The Jewish reference is to Sir Alfred Mond, the notable Welsh Liberal MP who campaigned successfully for the Carmarthenshire seat in 1924.

[66] 'The captive Welsh', *Sunday Express*, 16 August 1925, 5.

[67] 'The Welsh people', *Faculty of Arts Journal* [London] 4 (1925), 56.

[68] Ibid.

[69] 'The Welshman as playgoer', *Western Mail*, 19 October 1925, 7 (report of an address to the Gallery First Nighters' Club); *Western Mail*, 31 October 1925, 19 (report of an address to the London Spiritualist Alliance); 'The Welsh people', 56.

[70] As reported in *Western Mail*, 31 July 1936, 10.

[71] *Western Mail*, 19 October 1925, 7.

4

The Trouble with Harri: Some Thoughts on Two Writers for Our Time, Harri Webb (1920–1994) and T. Harri Jones (1921–1965)

DON DALE-JONES

Time has been given to eat,
Time for devotion meet,
And time to preach amain,
And time to entertain;
Songs to amuse – at least
The young girls at the feast . . .
(Dafydd ap Gwilym, trans. Tony Conran)

We say, proverbially, of some people, that they are too clever by half. Harri Jones was too clever by one-and-a-half. This quality in him invited bullying at his first school, where his fellow pupils found him 'too mouthy', probably denied him an academic career in Wales and may well have been at the root of the troubles that brought about his tragically early death at the height of his powers as a poet and academic. Of Harri Webb it might be fair to say that he was never quite clever enough; his end too was a sad one. The former moved from north Breconshire to England to New South Wales, became an alcoholic and drowned while drunk; the latter spent most of his life in south Wales, saw his dream of a Welsh republic come to nothing and spent the fag-end of his life watching television and reading reference books. A comparison between them reveals a good deal about the Wales of *c.*1930–80.

We may begin our comparison with Harri Webb's 'In Memory of Harri Jones', originally entitled 'Epynt', written in 1965 and published (in *Poetry Wales*) in 1967. 'I never knew him personally,' wrote Harri Webb in his note on this poem,

> but heard a lot about him as a larger-than-life sort of character who'd had a blazing affair with Rachel Roberts, the actress, when they were contemporaries at Aberystwyth; he lived a very conspicuously *poetic* life up to and, I suppose, including his suicide in Australia.

In a long letter (4 April 1977) to Julian Croft, Australian author of the Writers of Wales monograph, he added, 'I don't think of him as an alter ego, more perhaps as a cousin than a brother.' Harri Jones's death was accidental, but otherwise the brief autobiography is true enough – the nationalist who, in the early 1970s would write to Gwilym Prys-Davies about the need for a blood sacrifice characteristically admired Harri Jones for being, as he imagined (and as was, indeed, the case, though not in the sense he meant), unafraid to go to extremes.

As is normally the case with Harri Webb ('It is important to him to register that the events actually happened as described,' writes Brian Morris in his Writers of Wales monograph), we know the exact occasion of the poem: on 29 July 1965, Harri Webb and John Howell, another leading member of Plaid Cymru, made the journey which is here described, through Harri Jones country: Llywelyn the Last was killed on the banks of the Irfon (near Builth Wells, where Harri Jones went to secondary school); the Chwefru flows through Llanafanfawr (where he was born). The poem defines an Anglo-Welsh dilemma: Harri Jones did well to 'get out of / This hole in the middle of Wales' (for which Harri Webb would later invent the memorable phrase 'the Green Desert'), he was 'perhaps lucky / Not to come back to this land', but, for a Welshman, 'there is nowhere else / Anywhere'. The dilemma is no less that of Harri Webb: he left his homeland for only a short time (though he did, in the 1950s, apply for a post in Australia), but he was frequently exasperated by it and saw 'all his dreams, all his political thought and work . . . come to nothing' (Brian Morris, p.108): 'All nationalists are idolaters,' he said in the *Western*

Mail interview of 1985. 'They offend against the Second Commandment . . . (it was the Seventh that caused so many of Harri Jones's problems). They place their country alongside God. But when you look around for alternatives, *there aren't any*' (my emphasis).

We seldom know the precise *occasion* of a poem by Harri Jones, but for most of his poems (every one of the 402 written between 20 May 1950 and 26 September 1964) we have the almost exact date. This is because in 1949, when John Glanville sculpted the well-known bust of the poet, his wife, Delia, who was studying bookbinding, presented Harri Jones with the volume bound in black leather which he called the Black Book, an allusion of which I am sure Carmarthen will be proud when it becomes known there, where he made fair copies of his poems as they were completed. This (as far as I know unique) treasure would be in the National Library if they could find the funds to make an appropriate offer for it.

On 14 January 1964, Harri Jones copied into the Black Book a poem entitled 'Back?' which might have affected Harri Webb's elegy, if he had read it. It was not published, however, until 1966 (in the posthumous *The Colour of Cockcrowing*). 'Back?' is dedicated to R. S. Thomas, whose life and work are a demonstrably valid answer to the 'trouble' of both Harris, but who probably never noticed this and would not have been particularly honoured if he had – he is drily dismissive of his admirer's work. In a poem which Harri Webb presumably had seen ('Land of My Fathers' in *The Beast at the Door*, 1963) he had referred to Wales as 'the old country that sings and kills'. In 'Back?' he attributes the 'question' to 'the curlew's wing' and 'the strong sides of the salmon', resonant metaphors both, and answers it, in part, by setting side by side the attractive and unattractive aspects of his native land: 'the narrow path, the sheep turds', the 'old, thin bitch . . . writhing her lank belly with memories', the 'chapel, and a charade / Of the word of God', the 'ingrowing quarrels' and 'the shamed memories of Glyn Dŵr / And Saunders Lewis's aerodrome' on the one side, and 'the birded language' (which, unlike Harri Webb, he never learned to speak), and 'a match at Swansea' (rather inadequately) on the other. His overt answer is:

Of course I'd go back if anybody'd pay me
To live in my own country
Like a bloody Englishman

but there is a covert one in the poem's final lines:

But for now, lacking the money,
I must be content with the curlew's cry
And the salmon's taut belly

And the waves, of water and of fern
And words, that beat unendingly
On the rocks of my mind's country.

His best poetry explores countries of the mind and depends upon an imaginative absence from Wales, Harri Webb's upon a disgruntled political presence.

The central character of *Outside the House of Baal*, J. T. Miles, a Calvinistic Methodist, might well have been born in the same year as Llewelyn Morgan Jones, Harri's father, and, like him, has a son who becomes a university lecturer. Emyr Humphreys's acute exploration of the Welsh response to the challenges of the twentieth century embraces the lifetime of both poets, and his definition of the Welshman of the period touches on a phenomenon in which I am particularly interested as a 'Gog' who left Wales (involuntarily, let it be said), and returned, contributing a tribute to a native of Trefforest who remained:

> As soon as he gets away from the Welsh condition he becomes a different animal . . . Outside Wales, you have a positive individualist, a leader, a man with all his abilities liberated, a pleasure to watch; a Bevan, a Lloyd George. Inside Wales a guilt-ridden negative man with no initiative, weighed to the ground by a sense of cosmic doom, bent under a load of dead-wood tradition.

It is hard to read this without feeling an uncontrollable desire to telephone its author and burst into argument with him. It might be said that what we have here is the special pleading of an invented character, not the considered opinion of a distinguished author, but that does not matter. Literary cases in point fly immediately to mind – Caradoc Evans, Emlyn Williams, Gwyn Thomas (and where exactly would Dylan Thomas fit in, not to mention R.S.?). Confining myself with some difficulty to my chosen two, I have to say that the author (or his character) has got it more or less upside down: Harri Webb stayed at home and was 'a positive individualist', no question of that; Harri Jones got away (voluntarily, but under the compulsion to find a job suited to his abilities), but, a Calvinistic Methodist by heritage, found 'all his abilities liberated' (he produced twelve poems, six of them translations from the Italian of Roberto Sanesi, in 1958, the year before he sailed for Australia, and a hundred and twenty in 1961, when he had established himself in New South Wales). He was 'a pleasure to watch' (celebrated as much in Australia for his poetry-readings as Dylan Thomas had been in the USA), indubitably 'guilt-ridden', emphatically not 'negative', but definitely 'bent under a load of dead-wood tradition'. ('The religion of my people took an unfair revenge on me for my sins and for my sin,' muses the semi-autobiographical hero of the unpublished story 'These Rooms, This Bed, This Woman'.)

Less than fifteen months separate the birth of Harri Webb (September 1920) from that of Harri Jones (December, 1921); their places of birth and their ancestry exemplify two broadly opposite but essentially interlinked environments. Harri Webb was born in Swansea (he thought of himself as a Swansea Jack and insisted on returning there to die). His father, a Pennard farmer's son, was a power-station employee married to the daughter of an estate worker. Harri Jones was born at Cwm Crogau, a small hill-farm in north Breconshire, his father a hill-farmer's son and his mother the daughter of a cockney–Welsh union in the Rhondda. (I must acknowledge at this point my debt, throughout this essay, to Dr P. Bernard Jones's unpublished thesis, 'Taffy was Transported: The Fictions of Home in the Work of T. H. Jones', and thank him also for his helpful suggestions.) William Webb had lived in Australia and fought, during the First World War, with the Anzacs at Gallipoli; Llewelyn Jones had served in Egypt, Palestine and France. The formative years of both sons would be affected also by the Second World War, during which both served in the navy in the Mediterranean theatre – a profoundly disturbing experience for Harri Jones, one of whose finest and most substantial poems, 'Lucky Jonah', was composed when the sea voyage to Australia brought vividly to mind the appalling images of the Malta convoys.

Harri Jones's paternal grandparents were Welsh-speakers, but because his mother spoke only English, that was the language of his home, as it was of Harri Webb's. Harri Jones had a sense of guilt about his inability to speak his native language. At least, he professed, or seemed to profess it – a central problem of interpreting his work is to distinguish truth from 'a little artistic manipulation, just a little sweet lying' ('A refusal to write biography', unpublished, *c.*1952): 'all my poems lie', boasts the reminiscent 'Builth Wells' (2 February 1964), and a projected volume of short stories, most of them apparently autobiographical, was to have been titled 'Holy Deceptions'. He made no attempt to learn Welsh, but for more than half his life he was an exile in England and Australia, where there was no incentive to do so.

Harri Webb's childhood and schooldays were passed in Swansea. Like Vernon Watkins and Dylan Thomas he experienced the nearby unspoiled country and seaside, notably of the Gower. He attended Oxford Street National School and Glanmor Secondary Boys', where he took no interest in games, art, metalwork or woodwork and showed some talent for acting, but none for any aspect of mathematics. His aptitude was for English and modern languages, and he was a diligent student of what he fancied. In 1938 he obtained an open scholarship to Magdalen College, Oxford, the first pupil ever to do so. The only aspects of this that appear to have significance for his adult life are the acting, the linguistic ability and the habit of keeping a substantial diary, which began early and was ingrained by the age of sixteen.

For Harri Jones the same period was a series of epochs. He attended Llanafan Church School and Builth Wells County School, boarding out in the town during the week, and both his rural home area and the urban (albeit small-town) context of his adolescence were deeply significant for his work in poetry and in prose. A series of short stories (some of them yet to be published) written in the 1950s follow the development of 'Gwilym' from childhood (home tensions, a close relationship with his grandfather, school, chapel) to adolescence and young manhood in London.

Harri Jones, like Emlyn Williams, was a performer from an early age, both at eisteddfodau and in school plays. He performed on the rugby field also. While Harri Webb's creative activity was confined to his diary, Harri Jones was publishing poems, stories and prose pieces in *The Wyeside*, Builth County School's magazine, and was co-editor of it as a senior pupil. In 'Builth Wells', he looks back with wholly disingenuous nostalgia on these years:

> A picture of a town beside a river:
> Schoolcaps, girls' knickers, French letters,
> And French teachers, beside the sylvan Wye:
> How beautifully my memories lie.

But it is a prose piece, 'The Welsh Hills', written in his seventeenth year, which defines already the landscape of the mature poetry: 'seas of greenest fern', 'buzzard . . . above Cwmchwefri Rocks', 'a fox will slink' and 'badger dens'. This is the 'garden beginning' ('A Welsh poet finds a proper story') – the Serpent waits in the wings.

Harri Webb published no poems anywhere until he was nearly thirty years of age. 'Poeta nascitur non fit', says the Latin tag ('for publication', added Ezra Pound), but Harri Webb was a made poet (out of admiration for Hugh Macdiarmid and conscious political commitment), where Harri Jones was a born one in the tradition of Dylan Thomas (though it was Harri Webb who would become Wales's *Bardd Gwlad*). This shows in their respective responses to the work of Dylan Thomas, a major problem/touchstone for poets of their generation. As far as Harri Webb was concerned, his fellow townsman might not have existed, but for Harri Jones he was an influence to be followed (in the short stories, especially 'A Day at the Seaside', and in such early poems as 'In my Returning', 1947), challenged ('The Enemy in the Heart', 1946), toyed with ('Poem Dedicated to the Memory of Dylan Thomas', April 1954) and, with some help from Auden, Eliot,

Yeats and Wallace Stevens, escaped from. Harri Jones's characterization of himself, in Australia, as 'the poor colonial's Dylan Thomas' is a measure of his success in coping with an influence which remained compulsive for lesser poets.

Very different early experience, then, and very different responses to university. Harri Webb, like Gwyn Thomas, made nothing significant of Oxford, where he read modern languages, wrote no diary, made no friends, and whence he departed without any significant impressions. It is hard to imagine this, let alone explain it. It cannot have been working-class background alone – Emlyn Williams is only one Welsh working-class student who demonstrates the contrary. Perhaps it was an intuition about his future, perhaps a combination of humble background, a particular kind of temperament and the historical circumstances – he graduated in 1941 and was immediately called up to serve in the navy.

Harri Jones went to Aberystwyth in 1939 on a county exhibition scholarship and made virtually everything of it: by January 1940 he was secretary of the Labour Club, he regularly sold the *Daily Worker* in the town until he joined up, took a prominent part in demands for a charter of student rights, became treasurer of *The Dragon* and secretary of the Boxing Club, met Alun Lewis and heard Vera Brittain, fell in love (for the first of many times) with a bank manager's daughter who sent him a 'Dear John' letter in 1944, led a vigorous social life in and around the public houses and won the Inter-Collegiate Eisteddfod prize in 1941 with the astonishingly mature essay, 'Visions', before his studies were interrupted by his volunteering for war service.

On his return as a mature student in 1946, and in spite of experiences that lacerated his dreams for the rest of his life, he wrote a great deal of poetry, including the Yeatsian verse play *The Weasel at the Heart* (for Rachel Roberts – he was married by this time, but that was never an impediment to his pursuit of the White Goddess), was published in *Life and Letters* and the *Welsh Review*, was further involved in left-wing politics, edited *The Dragon*, took a first-class honours degree in English and followed it with an MA on the imagery of the Metaphysical poets. His future must have appeared obvious – university teaching combined with writing (mainly of poetry), membership of the Welsh Academy, three years in the chair at the Literature Committee of the Welsh Arts Council, a professorial chair (at Aberystwyth) and a series or two on TV. As clear as that Harri Webb, washed up, as it were, on the beach at Largs in 1946, with only the navy and a third in modern languages behind him, was destined for (or is it 'doomed to'?) 'emergency training' and the classroom. In both cases, fate, with a certain amount of assistance from character, decreed otherwise.

Harri Webb had been very happy in the navy. He had not suffered the Malta convoy nightmare, had risen to the rank of petty officer, and spent the final year of his service at HMSs *Nile* and *Hannibal*, base ships at Alexandria and Trieste respectively, in intelligence work: 'The formula was simple – A roomful of pretty girls to spend the working day with, a mess of boon companions to spend the evenings. Willing hands on all sides for dalliance or drinking' (Harri Webb, unpublished diary). It would be some time before he could recapture such bliss, but if Meic Stephens's picture of him as Herbi Watt in the short story 'Election Fever' in the *New Welsh Review*, 34, is approximately accurate, eventually he managed it:

> Herbi Watt, the Party's own poet, who had made himself scarce all day while the canvassing was in progress, was now holding court in the main bar, making bardic utterances about the state of the nation for the benefit of some girl-students from Aberystwyth who were plying him with drinks.

On being demobbed he was 'full of the most bitter gloom', but a tour of the Highlands brought 'the first breath of the new life of freedom. And too of reality' (Harri Webb, diary), and he returned to Wales to live there the life of a writer and political activist for Welsh independence. He took a course in administration at the Swansea Technical College, learnt Welsh in three months, and, after working as a sales representative in the offices of a manufacturer of jewellery cases, as a grocer's clerk discharged for inefficiency, and commissionaire at the Capitol Cinema in Queen Street, Cardiff, was employed by Keidrych Rhys at the Druid Press, Carmarthen, became editor of the *Welsh Republican* and found, from 1952, safe and regular work as a librarian, which lasted him until his retirement.

Harri Jones had married Madeleine Mitchell in December 1946. He obtained his MA in 1948, and his first daughter, Siân, was born in the same year. From 1948 to 1950 he was in London, living in squalor in a bed-sit over an off-licence in Asylum Road (an irony which the lover and poet must have found hard to appreciate at the time) just off the Old Kent Road, doing a regular pub crawl of the Spaniards, Cheshire Cheese and Prospect of Whitby, teaching English to foreigners and publishing reviews, poems and stories wherever he could. He kept trying to obtain a university post, but there were few on offer, and even his own professor, Gwyn Jones, was unable to help.

The nearest he got to a university post was to be almost on a short list at Manchester. Madeleine left him to join her sister in South America, Siân was with his mother at Llanafan, he detested London and soon tired of Fitzrovia: the post-naval depression had been postponed for a year or two in his case, but by now he must have felt even fuller of 'bitter gloom' than Harri Webb four years earlier. When he and Madeleine were reconciled, he lowered his sights, applied for teaching posts and got one at the Royal Naval Technical College, Portsmouth – they told him that he was over-qualified, but as he was ex-navy and unemployed, he could have the job if he really wanted it. The wrong man, in the wrong classroom, he began work in 1951 and remained for nine years.

The next problem – no small one for Anglo-Welsh writers in the 1950s – was to get his poetry published. His first success had been in 1946, when Gwyn Jones published his challenge to Dylan Thomas, 'The Enemy in the Heart' (a poem so complex in technique and imagery that half a dozen pages of critical exposition are insufficient to analyse it) in the *Welsh Review*, but that magazine was short-lived. Between 1946 and 1957, when R. S. Thomas's publisher, Rupert Hart-Davis, published *The Enemy in the Heart*, his first collection, he placed work in *The Dragon* (he was still doing this in summer 1949), *Life and Letters*, the *Dublin Magazine* ('You, and your magazine, will always be remembered with honour by us, the Welsh who write in English', he wrote to Seamus O'Sullivan in May 1949), *Dock Leaves* and the *Western Mail*, and managed to get a few poems broadcast by the BBC.

Dock Leaves, established in 1949, was the only literary magazine reliably available for Anglo-Welsh writers (the *Welsh Review* ran only from 1944 to 1948, and *Wales* from 1958 to 1960) until it was joined by *Poetry Wales*, and Anglo-Welsh writers had to do the best they could in Dublin and London. Harri Webb was luckier in that the beginning of his career coincided with his employment by Keidrych Rhys, the *Welsh Republican* gave him a platform from 1950 to 1957, and he survived to benefit from *Poetry Wales* (founded in 1965 by his friend Meic Stephens), the Triskel Press, of which they shared the founding, *Planet* (1970), television patronage and the whole apparatus of support developed by Meic Stephens as literature director at the Welsh Arts Council from 1967. Harri Webb's collections were published by Gwasg Gomer, a Welsh publisher in Wales, one of those encouraged by the Arts Council money which also ensured the continuing health of *Dock Leaves/Anglo-Welsh Review*, *Poetry Wales*, *Planet* and the Welsh-medium journals.

The most significant developments to take place during the lifetimes of these two Anglo-Welsh writers (Harri Jones emphatically remained such in spite of his transplantation to Australia) have had to do with the increasingly popular movement towards Welsh cultural and political independence. For Anglo-Welsh writers in particular, this meant changes in the way they related to, and in their work embodied, the national consciousness. It was much easier for an outsider such as Raymond Garlick, a slightly younger contemporary, to develop his 'myth of Wales' than for writers who grew up in pre-war Wales and attended the 'Welsh' schools of the period. One of the successes that should have cheered the declining years of Harri Webb was the great change in attitudes and even syllabuses, at secondary level in particular, which makes this no longer true. Raymond Garlick was able to make a conscious choice unimpeded by preconceptions, some of them hardly at the conscious level even for a poet, developed (in some cases inculcated) during childhood and adolescence (and not only in the classroom).

I have no knowledge of the attitudes which prevailed at Oxford Street National School and Glanmor Secondary Boys' School in Harri Webb's time, but, thanks to the work of Dr Bernard Jones, a great deal of information is available about Harri Jones's school experience. At Llanafan Church School, the speaking of Welsh was discouraged under his first headmaster, a bully whose measure of educational achievement was good handwriting; the bully's successor was merely indifferent to the language, but there were 'lots of hymns' (Ethel Lewis, quoted by Bernard Jones) at assembly. The nine-year-old Gwilym (the Harri figure) of the short story, 'A Day at the Seaside' buys himself an English dictionary and a notebook at Aberystwyth and in 'Lucky Jonah' we find 'A small boy in a small Welsh school' dreaming of going to sea. And that is all – but at home there was contact with Uncle Daniel Jones of Bwlchciliau, the last *Bardd Gwlad* of Llanafan, who knew a great deal of Welsh and English verse by heart, and his paternal grandfather, 'Old Crogau', who enjoyed reciting poetry and coached the Jones children in their (English) recitations for local eisteddfodau.

The headmaster of Builth Wells County School, P. G. Davies, appointed in 1929, had considerably reorganized the school. He introduced the termly magazine, *The Wyeside*, a dramatic society and a school eisteddfod, and greatly improved academic standards. Harri Jones thoroughly enjoyed himself, as soon as he had settled down, and developed rapidly, playing rugby with enthusiasm, acting, taking part in the eisteddfod and doing particularly well at English, French and history. He could always be relied on for a contribution to *The Wyeside* and he contributed (for a country schoolboy) a surprising range of writing, humorous and serious, in prose and verse.

P. G. Davies was a Welsh-speaker, and an enlightened educationist for his time, but as far as being prepared to become a citizen of a developing Welsh Wales was concerned, Harri Jones might just as well have been at a grammar school in the Home Counties. Any stimulus he got for becoming a post-modernist poet came from his own initiative in reading as widely as the school library permitted and from his friend, Donald Jones, who lent him books not available there, rather than from any of his teachers. As far as the teaching of poetry was concerned, Palgrave's *Golden Treasury* was the inevitable text, and of this he wrote, in 'A refusal to write biography': 'Why, the title's a downright lie! . . . the name Palgrave and all golden books make you sick for the rest of your life.'

Since neither of our writers (except perhaps in some negative sense) received from his schools any help in developing a sense of Wales, it is interesting to discover where this sense came from and how it grew. In 'A Refusal to Write Biography', Harri Jones consciously begs the question: 'it is probably being Welsh that started it all – the song in the blood like a known, comforting disease, the history of defeat, the proud awareness, the ineradicable culture, the sense of inferiority, and the virility and aggressiveness.' His capacity for political commitment was exhausted before he left Aberystwyth; Harri Webb's was central to his life. Not, however, in 1946:

> He is not, at this time, strongly conscious of his Welsh nationality, and he seems to have had very little in the way of political convictions of any kind. Although he was fluent in several European languages his knowledge of Welsh was rudimentary and unexercised. He had not studied that language at school . . . (Brian Morris, pp.10–11)

After his demobilization at Largs, he spent some months wandering, unemployed, about Scotland and in the process came across the works of Hugh MacDiarmid, that fiercely patriotic, left-wing controversialist and writer of nationalistic poetry, the Saunders Lewis of Scotland. Brian Morris suggests that Harri Webb may have visualized a future for himself as the English-medium Saunders Lewis. Harri Webb's diary account of the Scottish experience records that 'I had . . . carefully immunized myself against the attacks of meaningless Wordsworthian mysticism' – certainly consistent with such an interpretation. On returning to Wales he proceeded in a straightforward and methodical fashion, securing a qualification that should enable him to support himself, and learning Welsh immediately. His pertinacious attendance at National Eisteddfodau was a further self-schooling for the chosen role.

In April 1948 he took his first two steps, a letter to *Wales* – 'A Welsh theatre is necessary to reveal us to ourselves . . . Why should the Arts Council [be] peddling Priestley in those quaint places whose names they probably can't pronounce?' – and membership of Plaid Cymru. In 1949 he started working for

Keidrych Rhys and discovered Welsh republicanism (it had taken him no time at all to become 'disenchanted by the tameness of Plaid Cymru' (Brian Morris, p.21) and from 1950 to 1957 edited the *Welsh Republican*, writing a large part of most of its issues. His first published poems, 'Triumphal Entry' and 'Anial Dir' (nos. 23 and 24 in the *Collected Poems*, edited by Meic Stephens) appeared in *Wales* in 1949. Brian Morris writes that 'they are about the landscapes of Wales; they are not very good', but this is misleading. They certainly keep the promise to avoid Wordsworthian mysticism, and contrasting lines from them reveal the authentic Harri Webb(s):

> Tongwynlais is a gateway gleaming with pearl
> Tongwynlais has banners and battlements and songs
> and the Taff at the feet of the last hills sings
> her green redemption to the nightingales
> ('Triumphal Entry')

This is your heroical/lyrical, which I do not like because it so often turns out inflated/sentimental, though not in a poem like 'Dyffryn Woods':

> And now as in the long green ages
> The Dyffryn trees stand full and tall,
> As lovely as in exile's memory,
> Breathless, a breath before the fall.

'Anial Dir' is the authentic *saeva indignatio* which Harri Webb shares with Jonathan Swift and Saunders Lewis:

> The gritty shitty bitter waste
> Of hovel-homes run up in haste
> Now rotting to their last decay,
> And the young men have gone away.

It is not quite true that, to paraphrase Groucho Marx's famous joke, Harri Webb would never have wanted to belong to a political party that would have him as a member – to be fair, he kept chopping and changing because he could not find one that was as radical as he was. He abandoned Welsh republicanism in 1953 for the Labour Party (distance – he was living in England at the time – must have been lending enchantment), abandoned the Labour Party for no party at all in 1958, and rejoined Plaid Cymru in 1960, editing its magazine, *Welsh Nation*, from 1962 to 1964. In 'Whose Funeral' (1965) he wrote of Winston Churchill as 'a great man . . . a good enemy' (perhaps with a view to arousing some of *Welsh Nation*'s sleepier readers from an imagined complacency?). He was a member of the New Nation movement and signed their Remonstrance of December 1965, and he was Plaid Cymru candidate for Pontypool in the general election of 1970.

In March or April 1972 he wrote a long letter to Gwilym Prys-Davies in which he asserted that bloodshed as advocated by the Irish Republicans was 'ABSOLUTELY NECESSARY to redeem the Welsh from shame' and added that personally he was 'quite psychologically prepared for anything'. Brian Morris believes that he was, at this time, genuinely prepared to die for Wales, but unlike Gwynfor Evans later, he took no practical steps in that direction. Instead he made plans to 'swan off to Canada, at the expense of the Welsh Arts Council' (Brian Morris, p.77) in the hope of finding 'a little alcoholic refreshment . . . boon companions . . . pretty girls'. I agree with Brian Morris that this was not hypocrisy, but I prefer Walt Whitman's riposte to his explanation:

> Do I contradict myself?
> Very well then I contradict myself,
> (I am large, I contain multitudes).

For it is impossible to dislike the man who could write 'My Budgie' ('This futile bird, it seems to me / Would make a perfect Welsh M.P.'), 'Synopsis of the Great Welsh Novel', 'The Stone Face' and 'I have seen a group of Yorkshire colliers stand rivetted in admiration before [Augustus John's] drawing of a whippet in the Barnsley Art Gallery' and

> Dic Penderyn received Christian burial in the graveyard of St Mary's Church, and the Mother of God took into her keeping the son of another mother who, like her own, had met his death at the hands of evil men for the great love he bore his people.

Harri Jones's 'myth of Wales' is more complex. He was already moving towards a definition in the descriptive essay, 'The Welsh Hills', which he wrote at the age of sixteen about the landscape around Cwm Crogau. The essay concludes:

> Always, when we talk of Wales, we come back to those hills. Simple, yet strong, kindly and smiling, yet filled with the mystery of antiquity, beautiful in all seasons, and full of wonder for the simple soul of the countryman. They are the very heart of Wales and the Welsh.

This is the derivative, genre writing of an apprentice supplying his audience with what they expect: the essay contains hardly a hint of the physical reality of scraping a living – 'Torn timber lugged down cold and bleeding hillsides, / Wet, ravaged barley ripping the skin beneath the skin' ('Welsh Pastoral Elegy', 30 March 1963) or the mental/spiritual terrors inflicted by an ingrained Calvinistic religion whose god manifests himself in a creation red in tooth and claw, swoops and strikes like a buzzard and kills the predestinately damned ten-year-old as exultantly as the boy kills a rabbit ('Cwmchwefri Rocks', 22 September 1962). No hint, either, of the Welsh countryman's taste, shared by the poet from a surprisingly early age, for beer. Harri Jones's developed picture has nothing to do with kindness and smiles; his Welsh hills are an arena of torment: 'Never shall I escape from the hills of my childhood . . . The hills overshadowed my birth, and nursed and thwarted my childhood and youth. They are my bones and my flesh' ('A Refusal to Write Biography').

There is no further evidence until 1946, when 'Poem for Wales' was published in *The Dragon*. Five years' experience of a wider world had allowed time for reflection, and this poem, of six sixteen-line stanzas with a complicated rhyme-scheme is a self-consciously bardic performance. Addressed to the 'Dark hills for whom I feel this chemic love', the 'Epi' (significantly not 'Pro') thalamium 'I sing today' celebrates a union which has already taken place, nothing less than holy matrimony between the poet and his motherland. After confessing 'My weakness, my lost faith', it characterizes his ancestors as 'proud and violent and passionate' and pledges him to revive, maintain and advance the 'splendour of your ancient name'. He will strive to ensure that 'in your sons shall your great fathers live', so that: 'when I die I may with honour say, / Dark fathers, O in me you have not died.' Harri Webb could hardly have done more – in a sense, never did quite as much, and although it might well have occurred to *him* to seek female assistance:

> But when I lie in proud and perfect peace
> With a dark-haired woman of my race
> Whose raven eyes will never cease
> To lighten my hell-murky earthly place . . .

he would certainly not have mentioned it in a poem.

Like Harri Webb's profession of readiness to die for his country, this perfervid bid for the bardic supremacy of UCW Aberystwyth resulted in no commensurate practical activity. Harri Jones was never a nationalist, let alone a republican – the reference in 'Back?' to 'Saunders Lewis's aerodrome' is perfunctory and not particularly accurate – he was always, self-consciously, the poet, and anything he writes about Wales is to be taken metaphorically. He writes poems 'about' Wales, and poems of sexual love, and because love is sinful (originally and when it is the fornication his religion vainly warned him against) and because his own original awareness of this occurred in Wales and transformed the paradise garden of 'The Welsh Hills' into the 'hell-murky earthly place' of the mature poetry, sex and Wales will often come together. It appears that some kind of neurosis, yet to be critically explored, led to the compulsive drinking and promiscuity that destroyed him; perhaps the origin of this lay in his sense of guilt at surviving when better men were killed, and the fact that it was during the horrors of war that he was jilted by the first woman with whom he had fallen in love.

'The Anglo-Welsh' (*Dock Leaves*, Summer 1953) completes the process. As I owe my information about the origin of this poem (during Harri Jones's London period) to Bernard Jones, I will give it in his words: 'The poem . . . recalls a specific . . . Fitzrovian night' and is part of a debate with Aneirin Talfan Davies about the 'contention that only through the Welsh language could one communicate the true experience of Welshness'. 'Remembering among the unlovely London voices' Aneirin's accusation: 'You live upon your grandparents' memories', Harri is:

> vexed and despondent; where my unruly heart rejoices
> I am tongue-tied, having not gratitude enough
> To speak in my own language or to hold my peace.

In language reminiscent of the 'Poem for Wales' ('Ancestral summonses to a more splendid cause'; 'defeats and triumphs my fathers sung'; 'ancestral piety and pride') he explores the possibility of abandoning 'the beautiful alien tongue', and learning 'the ancient intricate laws' in order to become 'the resonant laurelled son / Of those who fought and laboured and undoubting died'. His conclusion is the bardic one – that the 'guilt and heresy' with which he is 'shackled' as a Welshman writing about Wales in English is a necessary 'struggle of self with self', a 'war' essential to his poetry. Yeats's famous assertion that out of the argument with ourselves we make poetry and out of the argument with others, rhetoric, does not quite neatly distinguish Harri Jones (who admired him and learned a great deal from him) from Harri Webb (it *is* true, however, of much of Harri Webb's work) – it is impossible to write seriously about the poetry of this generation of the Anglo-Welsh without reference to Yeats.

Harri Jones's answer to his 'keen scholarly' inquisitor is first an assertion: 'Even here I see the dragon's splendour in the air; / Even here a mighty singing breaks upon my dream', and finally the Yeatsian rhetorical question: 'What have my ancestors or I to do with peace?' ('Was there another Troy for her to burn?').

The conclusion is prophetic too: Harri Jones found peace neither literally in Wales (he never lived there as a mature poet), nor in the Wales of his mind, nor in love. Had he been able to live and work in his own country, it is possible (though not at all likely) that he might, like Harri Webb, have compromised, learned Welsh and written some good poems in it (a 'Colli Iaith' for example) to go with the better ones in his first language. Instead, as early as 1950, exile had turned the beautiful bride, the 'loved, remembered land . . . / Dear hospital of hopes and the sweet light' of 1947/8 into a 'maggot murdered Eden'. It was in the Australian exile that the finest poetry was written, and most of it brings together Wales, the Paradise from which Adam/Harri has been cast out because, in his pride, he has refused obedience to his Old Testament god, and sexual guilt (Eve/his current lover tempted him to disobey):

> The world was all before them, where to choose
> Their place of rest . . .
> They hand in hand, with wandering steps and slow
> Through Eden took their solitary way.
> (*Paradise Lost*, xii, 646–9)

In 'A Welsh Poet finds a Proper Story' (4 October 1964) the 'proud and perfect peace / With a dark-haired woman of my race' has turned to:

> In a garden beginning he finds a proper story
> And lets the paper bellow, bark and build it
> For him while he cradles in the treetop in Wales
> His silence and the serpent and the woman
> And all that glory.

In 'My Country, My Grief' (1 January 1964) we find his final variation on 'What have . . . I to do with peace?':

> Anguish is my country.
> I would not recognize
> A land where only fair winds blow
> And the sun shines.
>
> But the land where every wind
> Is the breath of guilt
> Is home, and let the loud seas lash
> Wherever I have slept.
>
> My paradise will be despair
> And the cold winds that blow
> About the rocks, about your hair
> And the grief I know.

A central aspect of nationalist as of contemporary feminist thought has been the rediscovery and reinterpretation of history. Harri Webb's first publication, *Dic Penderyn and the Merthyr Rising of 1831* (1956) was a notable contribution. I have already quoted an elegiac passage from this pioneering study, which is appropriately adversarial in tone (the substitution of 'Rising' for the conventional (English) 'Riot' foregrounds its reinterpretive intent). It is both indicative and encouraging that 'later historians have relied' on this work (Brian Morris). In *Our National Anthem: Some Observations on 'Hen Wlad fy Nhadau'* (1964) Harri Webb defends Evan James's poem against Saunders Lewis ('the most lying anthem in Europe'): what is important, he points out, is that 'it was written, rapidly, by a poet of the working class, set to music by his son . . . arises from a real situation and . . . belongs . . . not to the . . . crachach . . . but to the gwerin' (Brian Morris, p.55). It is enough to say of Harri Webb's historical poetry, at its best, that it memorably celebrates Welsh history and sometimes cogently reinterprets it.

Harri Jones can occasionally sound very much like Harri Webb:

> I was always defeated
> My dad died at Camlann
> And his dad at Catraeth
>
> But I walked Sarn Elen
> And helped to make Blodeuedd
> And was Nest's lover
>
> I was not absent from Glyndwr
> Or the last Llewelyn
> Or the bloody-minded Tudors . . .

he writes in 'Welsh Bastard' (26 January 1964), dedicated to David Jones. The marriage celebration, 'Poem for Wales', is heavy with history of a conventional kind, and in other poems an impeccable pedigree is claimed: 'My fathers laboured for three hundred years / On the same farm, in the expected legend . . .' ('Difference', 1950); but Bernard Jones has pointed out that Harri Jones's ancestors were in reality immigrants from west Wales. As far as the poetry is concerned it does not matter whether the historical roots are real or emblematic. As always, the difference between these two poets is that Harri Webb's Wales is a real place, susceptible to change through appropriate political action, Harri Jones's an archetype.

As Wales has moved closer to independence, an obvious issue has been its relation to Europe. There has never been, among Welsh people, the kind of nonsense over 'sovereignty' that is heard in England – Wales has had no such thing for seven hundred years, nor has there been any Welsh imperialism to encourage delusions of grandeur. Indeed, like the rest of Europe's minority cultures, Wales has, for a very long time, been part of somebody else's empire. The increasing development, in recent years, of (for example) twinning arrangements between towns in west Wales and Brittany indicates popular interest in the cultures of other European minorities.

An interest in Europe is common among Anglo-Welsh writers of the Harri Webb/Harri Jones generation (Raymond Garlick is a notable example) and a natural characteristic of Welsh nationalism. Harri Webb read Romance languages at Oxford and was fluent in French and Spanish; his *Collected Poems* contains thirty-four translations, most of them from French or Spanish, but including also translations from Catalan, Galician and Breton. It was to the Salzburg seminar of 1958, where he made a very strong impression, that Harri Jones owed his recruitment by Norman Jeffares into the Australian university system. He met the Italian poet, Roberto Sanesi, there and translated eight of his poems (seven of them were published in *Songs of a Mad Prince*, 1960), and the Black Book contains a number of poems in French. In Australia Harri Jones's interest necessarily switched from European poetry to that of the USA; Harri Webb's did not alter. It is seen in 'Wendenabteilung Fair':

> Meic Stephens, Meic Stephens, lend me your great book
> (In the name of George Steiner and Noam Chom-sky),
> For I'm stuck for a word and I must have a look
> At Friulian, Galician, Jurassian, Alsatian, North Frisian,
> Aostan,
> And the Flemish of Westhoek and all . . .

(a characteristically playful tribute to *Linguistic Minorities in Western Europe,* 1976).

The Swansea Jack lies buried near the cliffs of Pennard, within sight of the land his ancestors farmed. The poor colonial's Dylan Thomas was cremated in Australia and his ashes scattered in the churchyard of St Michaels, Brynpabuan, near the track which leads to Cwm Crogau ('Always . . . we come back to those hills'). In their different and similar ways they exemplify what it was to be Anglo-Welsh in their time. Their lives and their works set stations along the Via Dolorosa of literary, social and historical development which has closed the rift between the Welsh and the Anglo-Welsh and is healing the wounds of the Welsh language and moving Wales towards independent nationhood within a united Europe. It is too early to say what history will make of them. Harri Jones, second only to R.S. and Dylan Thomas among Anglo-Welsh poets of this century, and the finest Welsh poet of sexual love since Dafydd ap Gwilym is, as I write, forgotten in Wales – and we call the English insular!

5

Bed, Farm and Map: Three Responses to the Troubled 1930s

JAMES A. DAVIES

This essay examines three works published during the late 1930s: Glyn Jones, *The Blue Bed* (1937), Geraint Goodwin, *The White Farm* (1937), and Dylan Thomas, *The Map of Love* (1939).[1] It is concerned with understanding these texts as products of and responses to particular social and historical circumstances. Through such understanding, similarities between these texts emerge that may well throw some light on the nature of Welsh writing in English.

Glyn Jones's grandfather was an insurance agent and noted Welsh-language poet. His father, prevented by illness from becoming a schoolteacher, worked for the post office; his mother *was* a schoolteacher. The superb autobiographical chapter in *The Dragon Has Two Tongues* describes a comfortable, cultured, chapel-going upbringing. After grammar school Jones qualified at St Paul's teacher-training college in Cheltenham, then settled in Cardiff (where he lived until his death) and spent his teaching career in some of the city's poorest areas. He was later to write: 'My life during the thirties . . . was of course very greatly influenced by the Depression and left-wing politics, and also by the pacifist debate and the fear of war.'[2] He became a member of the Peace Pledge Union and, later, a conscientious objector.[3]

Geraint Goodwin's father was a rate collector and assistant overseer for Newtown parishes. He was a much-respected man, a pillar of chapel and community. He died when his son was eight. The writer's stepfather was a prosperous bacon and provision merchant. At the age of thirteen Goodwin left Forest

Villa, his happy and comfortable family home in Newtown, to become a boarder at Towyn County School in Merioneth. He became a journalist on the *Montgomeryshire Express* until 1923, when, aged twenty, he began a successful career in Fleet Street with Allied Newspapers. In 1929 he was sent to Wiesbaden to report the withdrawal of allied troops from the Rhineland. By 1936 he felt, as he wrote to Edward Garnett, that 'the international situation lies on one like a load. What artist can think of work when, at the sound of a drum, all life as he knows it may be blown to smithereens.'[4]

As is well known, Dylan Thomas's parents were the children of railwaymen. Thomas's father – a complex and unhappy man who lived a life of tension between bourgeois achievement and working-class inclination – became senior English master at Swansea Grammar School, where his son enjoyed a career mainly of spectacular academic failure. He left in 1931 to become a journalist on the local paper, before departing for London and literary bohemia in 1934. Glyn Jones helped foster the myth that Thomas's work was 'quite unconcerned with social, political and industrial problems';[5] Thomas took a very different view. In 1938 he wrote indignantly to Henry Treece:

> . . . surely it is evasive to say that my poetry has no social awareness . . . that you actually consider me unaware of my surroundings, out-of-contact with the society from which I am necessarily outlaw. You are right when you suggest that I think a squirrel stumbling at least of equal importance to Hitler's invasions, murder in Spain . . . [there follows a long list of 1930s phenomena] . . . but I am *aware* of these things as well.[6]

Even such brief and simplified biographical summaries emphasize two points. Firstly, the three authors were products of what in Wales can be regarded as the new middle class that emerged from increasing educational opportunities.[7] In England, possibly, the immediate antecedents of two of these writers, perhaps of Thomas also, would, at best, have been considered *petit bourgeois*. In the between-wars Wales of Merthyr, Newtown and Swansea, they were certainly middle-class. Even ever-modest Glyn Jones regarded himself 'during rare moments of delusions of grandeur even perhaps as lower middle class'.[8] The bourgeois sensibility, the middle-class stance, it can be argued, is, in any case, a relative matter, particularly in Wales. The three grew up in families set apart socially from the mass of the working class, and cushioned financially against the dreadful social, financial and cultural deprivation of the times. This made them – in their work, at least – very conscious of class difference and protective of familiar social positions and distinctions. In Jones's case these factors led to an approach to working-class life that combined anthropological curiosity, fascinated distaste and a reproving subtext; in Goodwin's to a concern with class distinction and with characters, so often female, who value social comfort and/or traditional values above what the heart might want and the feelings try to dictate; in Thomas's to the attempted control of fantastic events by means of suburban transformations furthered by tight literary structures. Implicit in gestures that can seem radical is, in each case, a profoundly bourgeois, deeply conservative outlook.

Secondly, it cannot be sufficiently emphasized that all three were alive to the ever-increasing dangers and problems of the period: the rise and spread of fascism, the Spanish Civil War, futile attempts at appeasement, the slide towards the Second World War. All three – Glyn Jones, in particular, because of where he taught – were well aware of the economic depression that was devastating south Wales. This is not to say that all was dreadful: for the three writers the 1930s was the decade of marriage, in two cases of children and, in all three cases, of literary success. Yet even such happy events may have intensified their sense of vulnerability and heightened awareness of terrible threats to their very existence. This would certainly have been so for Goodwin, whose health deteriorated in the last years of the decade, leading to his death in 1941.

The Blue Bed and Other Stories is dominated by the novella, 'I Was Born in the Ystrad Valley'. The narrator, Wyn, the son of a collier, educated at an English university, embodies two common attitudes towards the less privileged. One is guilt at having advanced culturally and socially (he is an art lecturer in Cardiff). This makes him contemptuous of his education: his 'charming middle-class professors', he believes, took him for 'a real and complete sucker . . . one of their very nicest little doctored toms, a collier's son with the outlook of a French aesthete' (pp.19–20). He is convinced that 'art [including literature] is no concern of the working-class man . . . I believe that the nature of the working-class is to remain inarticulate and that the working-class man should express himself only through action and the class struggle' (p.23). Wyn's other attitude is Christ-like identification with human suffering, seen when he helps at a boys' club in Cardiff and has occasion to visit a poor family in appallingly squalid circumstances.[9] The love and pity he feels for them is such that 'I understood for the first time in this upper chamber, love, and the cross, and the washing of feet' (p.36). Such hubris, viewed uncharitably, can remind us of the 'bleeding-heart liberalism' practised by so many 1930s intellectuals, evident, for example, in Spender's 'An Elementary School Classroom in a Slum' and Auden's 'A Communist to Others'. The ease with which links can be made between Glyn Jones's narrator and those two public-school, Oxford-educated poets, should alert us to the fact that, in their Welsh way, Wyn's attitudes (even the second, with its assumptions of superiority) are quintessentially bourgeois.

Glyn Jones cherished a belief in the indifference to social class of most Welsh people,[10] but this novella is much concerned with that very topic. 'I Was Born in the Ystrad Valley' is an account of a working-class revolutionary movement that is 'organized and completely carried out without the help of middle-class money, organization or philosophy' (p.56). It is a movement that fails. That failure is described from a determinedly middle-class authorial standpoint.

For the reader is made to evaluate events from the author's point of view, which is not the same as that of the first-person narrator. One example is Wyn's view of art and the working man, which was hardly Jones's. Another is the presentation of Alun Vaughan, the journalist from rural west Wales, who befriends Wyn and recruits him for the revolutionary movement. His liking for 'erotic and bawdy stories', which makes him, in Wyn's opinion, 'a pleasant chap enough to know' (p.51), is of a piece with his contempt for Cardiffians, for 'empty clichéists and windbags like the local communists' (p.56) and for Welsh nationalists led by 'a pale intellectual with wadding in his ear' and with their 'summer schools for spooners' (p.56). Given such lack of humane regard, it is no surprise that, for Alun, the end chillingly justifies the means. A workman's body is fished out of the river: ' "He was fond of children," said Alun, "but he couldn't keep his trap shut." He grinned over the report of the inquest he was writing for his newspaper' (p.58). Such attitudes disturb us, not least because they so clearly echo the period's Fascist excesses.

They do not, however, disturb Wyn or affect his regard for Alun. When they part after the revolution's failure Wyn feels that 'knowing Alun had loved me was very sweet and as I walked back along that country road through the night I felt for the moment happy and almost triumphant' (p.105). Such moments, which also gesture towards the homo-erotic, dramatize the limitations of his moral sensibility. We also notice that, in important ways, Wyn is like his friend. He is without Alun's ideological callousness but, though working-class in origin, Wyn has also come to occupy a superior middle-class position, judging, evaluating, patronizing. Thus he notes of the cell leader in Ystrad: 'He was easy for me to love, he spoke with the violence of a bewildered child enraged at an injustice at the hands of someone it has tried to satisfy' (p.62). On another occasion Wyn demonstrates the arrogance of the too-consciously virtuous: 'I sorrowed with her proudly', he writes of an unknown weeping woman he passes one night, 'I bore for a moment in anguish one corner of her cross' (p.106). His assessment of his own father – 'a meek dignified man with too much pride it seemed to me for complaint or resistance' (p.63) – is revealing in a different way. Wyn admires that 'meek . . . pride' because it is potent with anti-revolutionary force. Both his father and an old shepherd who prays for Wyn's safety ignore the workers' movement and so draw from Wyn responses rooted in conventional middle-class approval.

After the dismal failure of the revolution Wyn flees for his life to west Wales. But, after a short stay with Alun, who then leaves the country, he returns to the Ystrad Valley feeling that, despite the dangers of arrest or of being shot, that is where he belongs. But he gets no further than

> the brim of the valley I was born in, and as I stand on the mountain above it the lights far below come out, frequent and beautiful, burning calmly under the water of darkness . . . after everything I am still alive, a man, living flesh, but all the suffering I had beaten off in months of action descends upon me, and my body is down; this huge carrion strewn across the mountain tops is my dying flesh. The big birds circle over it between the sheer cliffs of my soles and my molten hair, each seeking a place to set down his dripping foot. Stonecrop breaks out like green fire along the folds of my flesh . . . From the marches of my loins the starlings rip themselves in a flock . . . Small creatures, the curlew and the gorcock find my brow and my hands . . . Naked headed heavy birds snarl from their cruel slate-hooks, they beat with their raw wing-bones against my bitten face . . . And now at last the vultures lift their beaks out of my eaten eyes. (pp.107–8)

Tony Brown comments: 'Thus the story ends, with Wyn metaphorically, indeed mystically, at one with the valley where he had been born.'[11] But this is too positive and not wholly accurate. Wyn does not return to 'the valley where he had been born'; he gets no further than 'the mountain above it', seeing 'the lights far below'. On that mountainside he becomes 'carrion', then, seemingly still conscious, a part of the harsh natural setting, until, finally, he is attacked with vicious cruelty by wild birds. The suggestiveness of this ending is not wholly controlled or clarified. As Jones himself suggested, Wyn's fate is linked to that of warriors fallen in battle and preyed upon by birds, familiar in early medieval Welsh writings. As such – and keeping in mind Jones's pacifism – the image is one of waste through force failing. We might also keep in mind Jones's enthusiasm for Shelley and find a reminder – a bourgeois version – of the Prometheus myth: Wyn punished for his radical presumption in trying to wrest from authority what he believes rightfully belongs to the people. In both readings he ends his life in suffering and in exile from his community; both readings are complicit in the bourgeois text's rejection of revolution as the way to proceed against the established social order, even one demonstrating manifest unfairness.[12]

This bourgeois spirit is evident throughout the volume in the homogeneous tone and language that can suggest to the reader that all the stories are told by the same authoritative narrator. It may also be evident in the stories' fascination with the physically grotesque and repulsive. One example, from 'Wil Thomas', can stand for many:

> His hair was white and cut short, and for a nose he had a hook like a large soft beak, big and fleshy, constellated all over with small equally spaced blue black-heads like pencil dots. His heavy jaw, wanting a shave, was like white velvet, and his eyes were noticeable, being khaki – his eye, more like, because he had only one. The place where the other had been looked sore, the raw lids hanging loose, the flesh all round red as though the eye-hole had been cut in his skin with a scissors. (p.152)

Such description can be linked to the emphasis on gross physical behaviour – belching bakers, preachers with running noses, dying miners with gangrenous legs – and to strange and exotic activities in most of the short stories. These last include shifts from a kind of realism into surrealism or fantasy, the dead coming back to life, as in 'The Kiss' and 'Wil Thomas', or the living seeing their dead selves, as in 'Eben Isaac', or meeting God, as in 'Cadi Hughes', or a man turning into a tree, as in 'Eden Tree', or, in the same tale, digging up tears, excavating a cross.

This fantastic world is solidly working-class, a world of colliers, ironworkers, small village shopkeepers, plus their slatternly wives. It is observed by a secure, confident, occasionally patronizing figure, the third-person narrator (in the first-person novella, the implied author) in his anthropological role, or, almost, as naturalist equipped with eager net and sketch-book, two classic middle-class roles.

The narrator is also an intruder; Wyn apart, he is an invisible intruder into a world that is, itself, one of constant, sometimes shocking intrusions: the dead into life, the living into death, God into a miner's cottage, a miner digging into the unknown, man into nature. In 'The Blue Bed' the gardener enters a woman's house and seizes a baby; in 'Porth-y-Rhyd', the volume's final story, Tudor, seemingly the only man alive, runs into the hostile bay, a strange woman enters his house, a ship comes in on the tide. Even 'Knowledge', a sensitive realist exploration of a marriage, is structured in a similar manner: Penn, the husband, feels out of place at the chapel prayer-meeting where his wife prays emotionally; his wife feels the same when she enters her husband's garden.

Invariably, Jones's intruders are disruptive, sometimes menacing or alien, occasionally beguiling. Thus God violently strikes Cadi aside as he takes away her husband. The workman in 'The Kiss', seemingly back from death and concerned to demonstrate compassion for his brother, shows scant concern for their mother. She first appeals to her son not to unwind his brother's bandage and then, when he ignores her:

> she had fainted without his noticing it, and she lay in her chair before the fire with her face inverted and her hair hanging out of her head like a soft root and a vein gulping uneasily along her throat.
>
> Very tenderly, with tears running down his face, he bent forward and kissed the putrid flesh of his brother's hand. (p.129)

The positive effect of this gesture is to a great extent undermined by the son's indifference to the mother that gives even this Christ-like tenderness a callous edge. In 'Wil Thomas' the returned dead minister forces one-eyed Wil to take into his hand an offered eye: 'it was . . . slimy like a peeled plum, heavy and moist as an egg-plum with the skin pulled off' (p.165). Yet, in 'Cadi Hughes', Ifor is glad to go with God; in 'Porth-y-Rhyd' the strange woman and the ship with father and son mean death, to which Tudor runs eagerly.

Indeed, it is surprising that all do not run with alacrity when terminal possibilities beckon, given that the worlds intruded upon are so lacking in love and joy. Glyn Jones offers a bleak vision of marriage and relations between men and women. Wyn breaks up with his rich Cardiff girl-friend because she lacks a developed social conscience; the gardener in the title story beats the empty bed with a branch in a paroxysm of frustration and violent, quasi-sexual despair; Penn and Gwyn, in 'Knowledge', maintain their relationship only by not infringing on the different worlds – respectively, of nature and religion – to which they are most deeply drawn. Eben Isaac is henpecked by his wife Keziah, 'a loud-mouthed blowzy woman' (p.172), later described as a squalid grotesque; Cadi Hughes 'had nearly killed [her husband Ifor] with her bossiness during the twenty years of their married life' (p.197); Wil Thomas and Mari have stepped out of an Andy Capp comic strip in which marriage is guerrilla warfare. These are strange, often asexual relationships; strong sexual charges are rarer, and invariably frustrated by grotesquerie, struggles for power, and helplessness.

Glyn Jones's is a patronizing and troubling view of working-class life. When he writes of Mari in 'Wil Thomas', 'She put some steak and onions in the oven and then went out wearing comfortable things, house shoes and a shawl and one of his old caps on her head' (p.154), we know we are in the bleak land of south Wales Valley stereotypes. Indeed, the whole volume reflects the essential bleakness of Jones's vision, so apparent in the central symbolism of 'Porth-y-Rhyd', the final story:

> In front of him was nothing except a laddered sea-sun on the sand, and the stones shagged black and white with weed, and stretching over him a thin white sky-skin with a crazy sun in it; when he turned to the shore, that too was empty in the distance and completely desolate . . .
>
> He stood in a warm pool and wept with his hands bloody over his face and the bleeding wounds of his feet sending out red growths into the water. It was bitter, knowing no man and being entirely alone on the earth. His life crumpled up and went dry and shrivelled, like a membrane. And then he felt the heat getting more than he could bear, and his tongue became like an earthy pebble in his mouth. (pp.235–6)

T. S. Eliot's influence is very evident in this powerful evocation of the world as a waste land. What is unique to Jones is the rendering of the natural scene, of the man's wounds, and of his life, in terms of the disfigured, the wounded, the cancerous; the effect is of a dreadful affinity between man and nature, both ugly, drying, wasting away. When the tide returns it brings the black ship of attractive death. The scene – like the volume for which it provides a conclusion – all too aptly conveys the individual's vulnerability in an increasingly threatening world.

The White Farm and Other Stories is a strange and sad book about the border country in and around Newtown, Powys, where Goodwin had been brought up. As we might expect, some of the stories make use of some of the possibilities of the border setting. Thus the title story describes an English husband accompanying a Welsh wife as she revisits the hill-farm where she spent her childhood; other examples of similar cross-border clashes include 'Saturday Night', in which an Englishman takes his Welsh girl-friend to a local performance of Gounod's *Faust*, and 'Janet Ifans' Donkey', which concerns a wealthy Englishman in a small Welsh town who has designs on the daughter of a local family.

But Goodwin's borderly interest is not simply, or simplistically, in national differences. 'The Trial of Shoni Bach', for example, is about a man 'come up from the South, where he had been working in the pits' (p.58), a man with a mysterious, troubled past who struggles with the demands of being a publican in a strange and potentially violent place; in 'The Auction' a small, ferret-like man from 'somewhere farther North' (p.110) thwarts a farmer's plans to buy sheep from the latter's fiancée's farm-sale; the main male character of 'Into the Dark' is from 'somewhere "down South"' (p.116) and is rejected by the daughter of a wealthy family. Goodwin's concern is more with what might be called the border version of Glyn Jones's intrusion – a permeating sense of invasive difference, in its social, or psychological, or non-nationalistic cultural manifestations – than with the relationship between the Welsh and the English.

He shares with Glyn Jones a concern – here, almost, an obsession – with social class. Certainly, in 'Janet Ifans' Donkey' that invasive difference is explored in such terms. Thomas Williamson is a port-sipping 'chairman of the Bench' (p.70) and the wealthiest man in the district. But money cannot buy him everything. As the incoming mill-owning son of a Midlands business man he is better than *nouveau riche* but not quite top drawer. He meets Miss Vaughan, whom he wishes to marry, at the 'county' dance: 'He was not "county" but it was the first year of his mayoralty and he was very wealthy, and he was let in on sufferance' (p.79). She is 'the youngest daughter of a Welsh squire – they were as poor as church mice' (p.80), but much respected. When old Janet Ifans is in his courtroom to account for the damage caused by her donkey, the old woman's behaviour makes Williamson seem ridiculous. The case degenerates into farce before Miss Vaughan, present as a curious observer, takes charge; the uproarious gallery falls silent 'as though at a command' and old Janet immediately defers to her: 'The Vaughans were a very old family and one of themselves. And the old lady became as docile as a lamb' (p.95). The confrontation, as Williamson sees all too clearly, is between 'the aristocrat and the peasant' (p.96). Class conflict is also at the centre of 'Into the Dark', in which Alys, the doctor's daughter, home in her high-hedged house from a Swiss finishing school, has a hopeless love affair with Shoni the southerner, for whom wood carving and British Legion charity provide subsistence living.

Even when class divisions are less obvious Goodwin is quick to establish confrontational distinctions. 'Come Michaelmas' explores the social hostility between the poor farmer's wife come to market with substandard geese, and the mill girls, cheapjacks and bargain hunters who refuse to buy at a price that becomes, for the woman, an assertion of social identity. 'The Auction' not only crackles with social antagonism – which is the main concern – but also with sexuality, both combined in the reaction of the woman selling her animals to Wili Morris, the 'little man' who outbids her fiancé:

> . . . if he as much as laid hands on her, she told herself, she would thrash him with her crop. But again she was not so sure. And the sight of him, with his little red ferret head, and the lifted curl of the nose, and the thin, savage little face, drove her to a frenzy. She would like to strike him where he stood. (pp.110–11)

Here is another version, less extreme in terms of social division, of the aristocrat and the peasant, with Goodwin, here as elsewhere, reserving physical ugliness for those with less – though, here, only a little less – social status.

Such, to repeat, class-obsessed stories are also the product of the deeply conservative vision – the desire to conserve and retain – that may well be a central charactistic of the bourgeois sensibility. Both 'Janet Ifans' Donkey' and 'Into the Dark' end with the rejection of lower-class claims. In the former, Williamson is humiliated by his lack of social authority. When he meets Miss Vaughan for the last time, in the almost empty courtroom, 'he knew that she was sorry for him – sorry in her heart. And he knew, too, that she had always been sorry for him' (p.99). In the latter story, Alys bows to her mother's fierce insistence on the unsuitability of the match, and to her own feeling that leaving home for Shoni would be too difficult; she rejects him absolutely in favour of 'the old familiar things' (p.143), the comfortable world she knows. In doing so she has 'a sense of shame' (p.147), but the honesty with which she examines her motives, the story's insistence that to follow her heart would be a step into the dark, and Shoni's abrupt ultimata, make us sympathize with Alys and the claims of her world.

We find the same kind of rejection in 'The Old Folk in the Dead Houses' and, particularly, in 'Saturday Night'. In this last story Len, the Englishman, is a clerk with pretensions to style and culture, whereas Megan's father 'was only a "ganger" on the railway and her mother was dead and she had care of the family' (p.35). Their night out at Gounod's *Faust* ends in small-town farce when the scenery collapses over the singers. Megan laughs with the hysterical audience, which offends Len: ' "Why did you?" he implored. "Like them!" he jerked a finger over his shoulder' (p.49). The relationship ends as a gulf opens between them. In 'The Flying Hours are Gone' the narrator, who left home for London to become a lawyer, then a successful journalist, recalls Ceri, the poor girl he inevitably left behind.

The conservative nature of Goodwin's vision is underlined not only by his in-built preference for the bourgeois point of view and the social status quo, but also through the locating of basic values. The volume's title story illustrates this last statement. Goodwin writes of the Welsh wife and English husband:

> They were not drifting apart so much, as they *were* apart. And was it his fault? It was not that they had ever been together – her little world was like herself, so small and

> tender and wisp-like: for ever proof against his loud and obvious heartiness. It was like hammering on a closed door and blustering on the step: and there, beyond, was the quiet and the mystery. (p.16)

In this contrast of fragile and robust, of sensitive and blundering, there is no doubt where our sympathies lie. The story as a whole clarifies the wife's 'little world', the 'quiet and the mystery' of her sensibility, phrases that refer to all that the white farm represents:

> *Pant-y-Pistyll* – the Hollow of the Spring. Always the drifting mist, for ever lifting, and the noise of the water, the sharp tinkle to the deep, harsh earth-flooded roar of the winter: the green earth, the smell of peat and the high blue crust of the mountain – that was her home, her father's home, and that was where she belonged. She let it all possess her, gave herself up to it, as to a lover. She had gone away from herself, far, far away. Now she was – only now she was: never before, perhaps never again, but now she was. (pp.25–6)

The woman recognizes the need for roots, her sense of her own, her desire to return to them, her love for them. This is the volume's central passage and, perhaps, the central passage in Goodwin's work as a whole. And, to repeat, the ideas it endorses are, here, deeply conservative: they include rurality, living within the natural cycle, within a family tradition, possibly within the Welsh language, to which 'the old *hiraeth*' (p.26) – the phrase used in the story and elsewhere in Goodwin's work – beckons the feeling being.

Here, in a sense, is a version of Abercuawg, that *locus classicus* of reversion;[13] another can be glimpsed in 'The Trial of Shoni Bach'. Shoni, troubled and tormented by the demands of his work and his uneasy relationship with Marged, drinks most of the night, sleeps drunkenly, then, when dawn breaks, goes outside 'into the still dripping quiet and set his face towards the mountain':

> The soft washed green turf of the foothills smelt very fresh. The heavy smell of the earth came up to him from below.

> He stood there, waist high in the wet bracken, feeling the life drip back to him like a cistern filling. His body came loose about him: the strength of him cried out.
>
> Then, with a shout, he slipped off his clothes with the quick deft movement of the collier, and flung himself down on the wet earth.
>
> When he went back he was singing. (p.68)

The influence of D. H. Lawrence is strong here, as it is so often in Goodwin (and, indeed, in Glyn Jones). It is not a beneficial one. Shoni moves beyond the demands of violence, sex and drink, to nature's revivifying purity; the story moves uneasily, unconvincingly, from precise realism to a far less precise quasi-mythical, quasi-symbolic mode.

The climax of 'The Flying Hours are Gone' is more successful. The narrator, the successful London journalist and unhappy middle-aged bachelor, observes the cottage that is now the home of the girl he left behind him:

> the top of the house with its curl of smoke climbing over the trees, I can smell the peat, that smell which *is* the mountains to us who have been bred there. I can see a man trimming the hedge . . . it must be her husband. I can hear the dog barking and the cheep-cheep of the young turkeys and someone stepping across the cobbled yard and then the slamming of a door and then a child crying . . . (p.194)

The comforts of home, roots, family life, tradition, the rural setting: all this contrasts with the narrator's restless, unfulfilled life in London.

Goodwin offers a further impressive treatment of these ideas in 'Saturday Night'. After the farcical opera, her relationship with Len now over, Megan walks home through the beautiful autumn and nocturnal landscape. When she arrives home her father is out on a spree and she sings her young brothers and sisters to sleep with Welsh folk-songs:

> her heart full to brimming. Her breasts had gone out in the flood-tide of her emotion and the old *hiraeth* came up in her throat: her eyes were half-shut in the longing, and her

> beautiful contralto voice, clear and low, went out with an infinite tenderness. (p.53)

The scene, with its music, is carefully contrasted with the tawdry opera performance and Len's pretentiousness and, as such, is a reminder of the care with which Goodwin structured his stories. The depth and sincerity of feeling, the appeal of traditional Welshness, are certainly set against the shallowness of English Len. But that appeal – and the accompanying risk of nostalgic sentimentalizing – is lessened, in this passage, by suggestions of sexual longing in the reference to her breasts, and by the story's ending:

> As she tucked up the little one for the night he said, half awake:
>
> 'Our Meg . . . ?'
>
> 'Hush.'
>
> 'You're . . . not going to go away?'
>
> 'There's silly!' she whispered.
>
> 'Fine and nice,' he said turning over drowsily, the songs still with him.
>
> That was to be her recompense. (p.54)

Withdrawal has its price, though, even here, the very last word does not lose all its positive force.

Throughout Goodwin's stories the old world calls to the new, a constant presence in the sensibilities of many of his characters. They often turn back to that world with a sense of the inevitable. We see this in 'Come Michaelmas'; we see it in 'Late Spring', the volume's final story. This concerns a young married woman having to leave her boy-friend at a fair to return to her husband on their mountain farm: 'Overhead, the bronze haze moved and lifted, and beyond that was the thin blue vault of the sky, very still and distant, and the first bright glitter of the stars. Around about lay the mountains, sombre and fearful' (p.288).

So the volume ends with a strong sense of foreboding, of 'visionary despair', as one reviewer put it.[14] Goodwin's stress on invasive difference, consistent with his social conservatism and emotional commitment to traditional values, moves in parallel with a despairing view of human relationships. These last are too often the fraught expressions of violence or hatred: the fierceness of the quarrel in 'Saturday Night'; the humiliation felt by the woman in 'The Trial of Shoni Bach' as the husband turns from her to the whisky bottle; Shoni snarling and jeering at Alys in 'Into the Dark'; the unhappiness of the relationship in 'The Old Folk in the Dead Houses'; the violence of husband to wife in 'The Young Bull'. In the volume's last two stories, the wife murders the husband ('The Coroner's Officer') and the final exchange between the lovers in 'Late Spring', as the man prepares to leave, is:

> 'No stoppin', Jack,' she pleaded.
> 'Ah. Thee bitch!' he said, raising his hand. (p.287)

The superb 'The Picnic' brings together Goodwin's main ideas. On one level this story is about a man and a married woman, sweethearts long ago at Aberystwyth, who meet again and take an afternoon drive to a lonely mountain lake where the man will go fishing. They leave the comfortable valley and drive up through the mist past long-disused lead mines, stop at a lonely pub kept by an old woman, find the lake in the mist, go out in a small boat, which springs a leak, strip to swim for it, though without hope of survival, only for good luck to bring them close to an island. With a great effort the man grounds the boat and lies exhausted on the shore:

> He lay there, face to the earth, and got the feel of it; slowly his belly began to move within him. But still he lay there.
>
> Then he crept up through the rim of trees and listened, his head cocked, the savage ancient face tilted . . .
>
> From somewhere within he heard her laugh – a shrill, high defiant laugh – then the white gleaming shape went flitting into the shadows. With a bound he plunged into the darkness. (p.164)

The couple have moved away from the 'pretty picture' (p.149) of ordinary life, away from the recent, more prosperous past of lead mines and 500 miners living it up at the old woman's pub, beyond their personal pasts of lost romantic opportunities and the uneasy tension of their reunion, to the world before lead mines and miners, the world of the 'old mountain' (p.154). It is a primitive world beyond the known and the civilized, a world of basic values, of instinct and feeling, of unaccommodated man and woman. Here, in the mists on the lake, the man rowing for his life, his 'savage ancient face' and predatory sexual plunging, is a version – different in degree, perhaps, though not in kind – of the world of the white farm, of Megan singing folk-songs and of the observed cottage in 'The Flying Hours are Gone'. Unexpectedly, perhaps paradoxically, at the heart of a bourgeois vision that, in one manifestation, insists on preserving social hierarchies and returning to traditional values, are laughing, naked, chasing lovers invading a dark wood.

In the sixteen poems and seven short stories of *The Map of Love*, Dylan Thomas's world is unashamedly middle-class, as a topographical composite makes clear. In 'The Enemies', for example, the Revd Mr Davies reaches the Owenses' bungalow, their 'little house with a garden' and

> saw a young man with a beard bent industriously over the garden soil; he saw that the house was a pretty picture, with the face of a pale young woman pressed up against the window. And, removing his black hat, he introduced himself as the rector of a village some ten miles away. (p.18)

This scene is a surprising combination of 1930s country-cottage life, latter-day Trollopiana, even a domesticated Pre-Raphaelitism. It is part of a world that includes suburban gardens and men in deck-chairs listening to the wireless, whilst from a first-floor bedroom window a young man sitting at his desk stares at a private girls' school close to a park. The asylum in 'The Mouse and the Woman' has grounds like that very park, with flowers and gravel walks where 'Children in print dresses might be expected to play, not noisily, upon the lawns' (p.74). A good place for a picnic, perhaps, like that in 'The Orchards', with the white cloth, thinly cut bread and 'pruned, transparent hedge' (p.48) that, as I have written elsewhere, suggest 'ineffable gentility'.[15] Even the asylum building 'had a sweet expression, as though it knew only the kind things of life and the polite emotions' (p.74). Elsewhere the houses are grander, as in 'The Tree', with its gardener, potting shed and tower. Within such a house is, doubtless, 'the clean glittering of the kitchen, among the white boards, the oleographs of old women, the brass candlesticks, the plates on the shelves, and the sounds of kettle and clock' (p.76), and the front parlours where stuffed animals rehearse the pastimes of the gentry. In the poems, lovers lie on the sand, part of the bourgeois world of 'a white child in the dark-skinned summer' (p.71), released from 'nurseries' (p.72) in (to return to the fiction) homes visited by clergymen who are surprisingly and invariably Anglican.

Into this world come strange intruders: Callaghan in 'The Visitor', who may well represent death, battles with Rhianon for the dead or dying Peter, then carries him off into the 'corrupting night' (p.29) on the Jarvis hills; the good but bewildered clergyman, the Revd Mr Davies, in 'The Enemies', stumbles into a world whose respectable façade conceals 'the secrets of darkness' (p.18); the girl and boy, in 'The Map of Love', initially embarrassed by a world of tropical fecundity and uninhibited sexuality, move shyly yet eagerly into the aqueous world of sensual pleasure (this last in a story which, despite moments of extreme surrealism, has strong affinites with Glyn Jones's 'Porth-y-Rhyd' and Goodwin's 'The Picnic', in that all three are about a world governed by basic and compelling instincts that seem only to exist outside social limits). The idiot in 'The Tree', the woman's lover and the writer himself in 'The Mouse and the Woman', the madman in 'The Dress', have similar roles. To return to a recurring point: all seven stories are structured in terms of intrusion, of what has been called invasive difference, so that we see why 'The Visitor', with its suggestive title, opens the 'Prose' section. The same is true of many of the poems: the young narrator enters the harsh peasant world of 'After the funeral'; Thomas's first child, Llewellyn, is the 'saint about to fall' into the world from a heaven of sorts; the compassionate foetus of 'If my head hurt a hair's foot' worries about entering life; Thomas himself, in 'Twenty-four years', crouches 'in the groin of the natural doorway' (p.81), preparing to enter and to advance – or decline – through life.

The entered worlds are, to say the least, unwelcoming. Callaghan, in 'The Visitor', battles with the caring Rhianon for Peter's dead or dying consciousness; the Revd Mr Davies is afraid and feels 'an old god beset by his enemies' (p.20); the idiot in 'The Tree' is crucified by the boy in the garden; Beth Rib and Reuben are drawn to and submerged in a sensual world dominated by the old and seductively virile; in 'The Mouse and the Woman' the lover goes mad possibly through sexual guilt, whilst the writer is an all-powerful destroyer; the madman in 'The Dress' returns to his mutilated wife and asks, it seems, for affection and/or forgiveness; Marlais, in 'The Orchards', finds only a burned landscape, sexual disappointment and the world he thought he had left.

The stories are as full of difficult relationships as those of Glyn Jones and Goodwin. To be sure, we find more sexual joy, more love, in this volume – as is evident in Peter's feelings for Rhianon in 'The Visitor', the surrendering of the girl and the boy to each other in 'The Map of Love', or the initial exchanges between the lovers in 'The Mouse and the Woman' – but it must also be noted that the relationships in Thomas's world are often destroyed by death or socially induced inhibitions, or lead to jealousy and sexual failure, as in 'Not from this anger', or to the warring absence of the famous poem.

Valentine Cunningham points to the prevalence in the decade's literature of 'the threshold . . . the border, the frontier, the doorstep, the railway station, the bus station, the dockside'[16] and, we might add, the class border. Cunningham's comment establishes Goodwin, through the accident of birthplace, as the archetypal thirties writer. But all three are, not least because of their obsession with social class. In their writing, relationships between men and women so often not only lack warmth and love but invariably exist within the range of emotions from hostility to violence. For, even though personal circumstances – such as the Thomases' tempestuous marriage – may well have been influential, it is surely no accident that those relationships seem microcosms of the decade's wider hostility, violence and death. Further, the recurring intrusive presences – intrusion as a structural principle – noted in the three volumes, reflect the most significant activities of the period: the invasions, intrusions and penetrations, carried out by successful Fascists, bewildered refugees and the mobile unemployed desperate for work.

But though all three volumes are permeated by the period, shaped by its social and political tensions and structures, *The Map of Love* is different in degree, perhaps in kind. Glyn Jones, in *The Blue Bed*, struggles for wider significance through myth or allegory. His attempts to transcend the particularities of realism too often strain into incoherence, as in the ending of 'I was Born in the Ystrad Valley' or in the allegorical difficulties of 'Eden Tree'. And, though 'The Picnic' moves seamlessly from realism through social symbolism into a mythopoeic insistence on persisting atavism, other stories – such as 'The Trial of Shoni Bach' – venture less successfully along the same path. In any case, most of Goodwin's stories are localized explorations of individual actions, fine in themselves but in which little effort is made to widen the range of reference.

Dylan Thomas, on the other hand, has a discourse for an age in which larger historical events impinged more and more directly on individual action. Invariably his stories and poems move effortlessly into wider symbolic statements. In 'The Tree', for example, the gardener's influence on the boy – stemming from the former's obsession with the Crucifixion – has much to say about indoctrinated cruelty leading to atrocities against the helpless that was only too relevant in the decade before the Second World War. 'I make this in a warring absence', a poem of 1937–8, charts the movement of a marital quarrel through thoughts of retaliation to a desire for reconciliation appropriate for the age of appeasement. Only Thomas, in the line, 'And a stranger enter like iron', (p.79) in 'A saint about to fall', and the phrase 'your iron head' (p.80) in 'If my head hurt a hair's foot', can link birth and the firing of a bullet or the dropping of a bomb, the intimate moment with the violence of the age.

Throughout *The Map of Love* is a recurring apocalyptic note. It is present in the fires that burn in 'The Orchards', in the massacre of the cattle and sheep in 'The Visitor' and, with chilling prescience, in 'The Map of Love', the title story of 1937: 'There was a spirit in the valley that would roll on when all the hills and trees, all the rocks and streams, had been buried under the West death' (p.110). It is heard again in

'Because the pleasure-bird whistles', as the recent past is recalled as 'an old year / Toppling and burning in the muddle of towers and galleries' (p.67), in the burned cathedral overwhelmed by a new deluge in 'It is the sinners' dust-tongued bell' and in the volume's recurring violent imagery. It is even present in the beautiful love poem, 'We lying by seasand', in which the lovers

> wish for wind to blow away
> The strata of the shore and drown red rock;
> But wishes breed not, neither
> Can we fend off rock arrival . . .

As Tindall notes,[17] this is a poem reacting to T. S. Eliot, a poem in which the beach becomes a waste land, but the 'red rock', divested of Eliot's initially welcome shade, is in Thomas's poem a disturbing and intrusive presence – a further example of that ubiquitous invasive difference – as the lovers wait for the inevitable end of the 'golden weather'.

Above all, Thomas's apocalyptism and the shaping force of the 1930s are apparent in 'A saint about to fall', the poem of late 1938 written for the birth of Llewellyn. As is well known, this poem was first entitled 'In September', the month in 1938 when war seemed imminent, the British navy was mobilized, and Chamberlain foolishly proclaimed 'peace in our time'. When first published in February 1939, the title was changed to 'Poem in the Ninth Month', which links birth and the historical moment.

In one sense the poem gestures towards the Wordsworth of the 'Immortality' ode: the birth is described as a fall from a better place. But whereas Wordsworth's child comes from a heaven that remains a positive point of reference throughout his earthly sojourn, Thomas subverts that idea by describing heaven as devastated by the loss of the child-to-be. That devastation is described in terms all too familiar in the late 1930s: 'The stained flats of heaven hit and razed . . . / Wind-heeled foot in the hole of a fireball'. Here is a place of 'chucked bells', a desecrated Eucharist, the Christian message overwhelmed by 'flames and shells'. Less than a year after the atrocity heaven is another Guernica.

'The violence of birth is a foretaste of violence on earth', suggests Tindall. 'Glory cracked like a flea' as the newly born left heaven. The birth itself is described as courting disaster, as the foetus 'Lurched through [the] scuttled sea' of the womb. The baby encounters unhappiness: 'the squawking shores . . . a bed of sores'. The world it has entered is faced with a new deluge – 'the sour floods / That bury the sweet street slowly' – and war's violent atrocities: 'earth is barbed with a war of burning brains and hair.'

In such a world the womb is an asylum, at once refuge and transit point for those mentally disturbed by thoughts of what awaits them outside. This last is conveyed by imagery that suggests a new massacre of the innocents involving bayoneting children ('As their blade marches in'), ideas of the primitive, the physical stress of childbirth seen as an expression of general woe, birth, as has been noted, described in terms of the entrance of a bullet or a bomb, and the world as a 'thundering bullring', a troubling reminder of the Spanish Civil War and the Guernica bombing.

The central invasive occurrence, and the merging of private and public so that nothing escapes the dark *Zeitgeist*, are profound comments on the historical moment. They are supported by the poem's dialogism, and this concept, as Bakhtin has reminded us, involves the exercise of power.[18] The latter can be experienced in several ways. The dialogue that this poem sets up with the 'Immortality' ode, forcing the earlier poem to the margins of relevance, in itself speaks for the power of events of the 1930s. Within the poem there is an actual dialogue between the poet and his newly born son that can be understood in terms of mood. The imperative weakened by the apostrophic in the son's interjection into stanza two, the five lines that begin with 'O wake in me in my house in the mud . . .', is set against lines, the rest of the poem, in which the opening subjunctive modulates into the indicative, and is changed utterly into the imperative that reacts to the new child's interjection and dominates a final stanza in which, briefly, the poet echoes the infant's apostrophic gesture ('O wake to see, after a noble fall').

That imperative, suggesting both bourgeois authority and the decade's authoritarian force, dominates but does not absorb, for example, the baby's plea to remember heaven as it was, and the tenderness of 'Cry joy' and 'you so gentle' in life's 'rough seas'. For this poem, truly dialogic, whilst suggesting kinds of authority also refuses the reader a sense of its unity. This last point is partly made through syntax: the accumulated power of the first stanza's single complex sentence is abruptly halted by the short, almost curt, opening line of stanza two, by further shorter sentences and, in stanza three, by the sharp series of imperative clauses. As for the rhyme-scheme: it is defined in stanza one but, after the first eight lines of stanzas two and three, offers increasing variations as rhymes are halved or consonantal, or the sequence changes. Paradoxically, reminders of order hint increasingly at the disintegrative or fragmenting possibility, which describes not only the poem but also the 1930s.

The relationship between text and context in Thomas's work, poetry and prose, is infinitely more complex than was dreamt of in Glyn Jones's or Geraint Goodwin's philosophies. The three titles emphasize this. To highlight a bed – even though offered, in the title story, as a site of sexual frustration stemming from social division – is to centre a defining symbol never wholly dissociated from origins – sexuality, birth – and withdrawal. Goodwin's farm, as has been suggested, is a place of basic, conservative values to which the characters return. Both symbols are essentially reversive. Further, 'blue bed' and 'white farm' are phrases in which realist objects are motioned through colour towards puzzling symbolic suggestiveness, at once indicating the volumes' limitations and their sources of literary achievement. Thomas's map is very different in its suggestions of wider horizons and the exploration of new territory. In itself, it is also a realist object, but a 'map of love', the two nouns united by the cadence, points to the persuasive modulating of realism into penetrating symbolism that is one of the most impressive characteristics of Thomas's volume. To indicate the scale of his achievement in this way is not to deny the high quality of the other two works. All three are penetrating responses to troubled times.

As the references to Lawrence, T. S. Eliot and Wordsworth indicate, they are writings that relate to an English literary tradition. That they are also examples of Welsh writing in

English is, in part, because they are creatures of their upbringing. Even though we must have reservations about a too simple or too direct relationship between life and work, our three writers were demonstrably affected by uniquely Welsh class divisions and ideas of the bourgeois. It might also be argued that the pervading invasive trope found in all three works is intensified in works by the Welsh because, even though they shared with all other Britons the felt force and consequences of nations moving through small wars, both military and social, to the cataclysm of 1939, their experience of economic disaster and the peripatetic unemployed was probably greater than most. And there is little doubt that reacting against the confines of social realism offers itself as a defining characteristic of Welsh writing in English. To make this last point in a different way: it may well be that both Glyn Jones and Geraint Goodwin were positioning themselves within a young literature profoundly shaped, during formative years, by Dylan Thomas's commanding literary presence.

Notes

1 The three volumes were published in London, *The Blue Bed* and *The White Farm* by Jonathan Cape, *The Map of Love* by J. M. Dent. In the case of the first two volumes, page numbers included in the text refer to the editions of 1937. Quotations from the poems and stories first published as *The Map of Love* are taken, respectively, from Dylan Thomas, *Collected Poems 1934–1953*, ed. Walford Davies and Ralph Maud (London, J. M. Dent & Sons, 1988), and *Collected Stories* (London, J. M. Dent & Sons, 1983). References to these editions are also included in the text.

2 *The Dragon Has Two Tongues* (London, J. M. Dent & Sons, 1968), 31.

3 For biographical information on the three writers see: Leslie Norris, *Glyn Jones*, Writers of Wales (Cardiff, University of Wales Press, 1973); Glyn Jones, *The Dragon Has Two Tongues*, ch.2, *passim*; Sam Adams, *Geraint Goodwin*, Writers of Wales (Cardiff, University of Wales Press, 1975); Paul Ferris, *Dylan Thomas* (Harmondsworth, Penguin, 1978).

4 Rhoda Goodwin, 'The Geraint Goodwin–Edward Garnett letters', *Anglo-Welsh Review*, 22 (1973), 128.

5 *The Dragon Has Two Tongues*, 173.

6 *Collected Letters*, ed. Paul Ferris (London, J. M. Dent & Sons, 1985), 310.

7 The authors' dates are: Glyn Jones (1905–95), Geraint Goodwin (1903–41), Dylan Thomas (1914–53).

8 *The Dragon Has Two Tongues*, 24.

9 Glyn Jones's concern with Christlike behaviour is explored in Tony Brown, '"Praise . . . in my pain and in my enjoying": self and community in the short stories of Glyn Jones', in Belinda Humfrey (ed.), *Fire Green as Grass* (Llandysul, Gomer, 1995), 65–81.

10 *The Dragon Has Two Tongues*, 15–16.

11 'Praise . . . in my pain', 67.

12 In correspondence with Tony Brown, Glyn Jones linked the ending of his novella with medieval Welsh poetry. He recalled that when he wrote it he was also translating work by Llywarch Hen and Heledd, in which there are several references to birds feeding on the bodies of warriors fallen in battle (See T. J. Morgan and Glyn Jones, trans., *The Saga of Llywarch Hen*, London, Golden Cockerel Press, 1955). I am grateful to Tony Brown for this information and for subsequent discussion of the passage.

Jones's explanation is compelling but, in my opinion, need not exclude Promethean connotations, probably derived from Shelley's *Prometheus Unbound*. We keep in mind Glyn Jones's enthusiasm for Romantic poetry (see *The Dragon Has Two Tongues*, 27).

13 See R. S. Thomas, '*Abercuawg*', *Selected Prose*, ed. Sandra Anstey (Bridgend, Poetry Wales Press, 1983), 155–66.

14 Quoted in Adams, *Geraint Goodwin*, 71. The reviewer was Humbert Wolfe (*Observer*, 14 March 1937).

15 'A Picnic in the Orchard: Dylan Thomas's Wales', in Tony Curtis (ed.), *Wales: The Imagined Nation* (Bridgend, Poetry Wales Press, 1986), 63.

16 *British Writers of the Thirties* (Oxford, Oxford University Press, 1989), 9.

17 *A Reader's Guide to Dylan Thomas* (1962; repr. New York, Octagon Books, 1981), 153.

18 See Lynne Pearce, *Reading Dialogics* (London, Edward Arnold, 1994), *passim*, for valuable consideration of this point.

6

Like Foolish Boys: Some Thoughts on the Poetry of Two Cousins

R. GERALLT JONES

It is probably inevitable that poets born and brought up in materially deprived conditions, in poor and subjugated countries, should be much concerned with landscape. That, and the language in which they write, may well be all that they can claim as their own. Landscape, in such circumstances, can become an entirely dominant influence, overwhelming for those trapped within it, a constant magnet for those alienated from it. It has been so in varying degrees for many Welsh poets, but was so in a quite unique and frightening sense for two remarkable cousins born in the shadow of Snowdon at the end of the nineteenth century.

I have lived for many years with the poetry of these two and I am at present engaged in attempting a literary biography of one of them.[1] The nature of their relationship with the very earth upon which they walked, indeed with the gift of life itself, was so intense and at the same time so ambivalent that one is tempted at times to extrapolate wildly and to say that all poets are so obsessed with earthly mortality that all poetry exists only as a desperate and doomed attempt to fly free. Such extrapolation would offer a nice gloss on Shelley's 'To a Skylark', for example, but I will resist the temptation, and restrict my comments to my attempts to grapple with this elusive pair, for the relationship between the two of them, arguably the finest Welsh-language poets of the century, was at least as ambivalent as their relationship with the land around them.

In adulthood they were known as Thomas (or T. H.) Parry-Williams and Robert Williams Parry. Both their names had suffered by then, however, from middle-aged spread because the former was christened Tom, not Thomas, and was known as such throughout his childhood, while the latter was simply known as Bob Parry until the 'Williams' crept into regular use at some point during adult life. It may not be over-fanciful to suggest that Bob Parry's 'Williams' was in fact a quite deliberate ironic inversion of his by then more eminent cousin's genuine double-barrel. Bob Parry actually wrote a piece of light verse latish in life, commenting on the inflated nomenclature of Welsh literary figures, including that of his cousin and himself. The puckish, partly self-directed, satire exemplified in that poem was not untypical of a man who, obsessively reserved and withdrawn though he became in later life, had been brought up in a working-class community that would use constant verbal sniping to make sure no one grew too big for his boots.

Born and brought up within a few miles of each other, they knew each other well as boys. Bob was the elder of the two by three years and was in many ways Tom's boyhood hero. The extended family, according to another member of it, was what he termed 'distant' and the three sons by different wives of the one grandfather, Thomas Parry, rarely met. Bob though would quite frequently cycle up from the valley to where Tom's father, 'Uncle Harry', was headmaster of the primary school at Rhyd-ddu. In one of the many meditative essays that he later wrote, Tom describes his cousin '. . . visiting us, a lively and mischievous lad, singing songs to his own accompaniment at the piano, the life and soul of the company at table, performing acrobatics on his bicycle. I would take part with him although I was younger . . .' Bob was clearly the leader, the gifted elder brother that Tom never had, who crossed his horizon occasionally to show what riches life could offer. But there was another side to the young Bob which was to affect Tom even more deeply when he came across it: '. . . once I felt my smallness dreadfully; I overheard this lad discussing the strict metres (*cynganeddion*) with my father, when I never even knew what *cynganeddion* were. I was excluded from the company of two on that occasion.'

As they grew up, their lives moved apart, and Tom drew inexorably ahead. And yet there were constant parallels. Bob went to the local secondary school at Penygroes and lived at home, but Tom, having been awarded a scholarship, was sent off to Porthmadog to the grammar school there, and to lodge away from home, a traumatic move that affected him all his life. Both went to university, but while Bob left school at fifteen and spent some years as a pupil teacher before entering the college at Aberystwyth in 1902 to follow a two-year teacher's course, Tom swept into the same college in 1905 on a continuous wave of academic expectation, a wave that owed its initial momentum to his outstanding success in the scholarship examination. Having obtained his teacher's certificate in 1904, Bob went back to elementary-school teaching, but, pressed by his father as Tom was by his, continued his studies, and by 1907 was ready to return to university to complete his degree. But he did not return to the college at Aberystwyth. He went instead to Bangor. Why? It could hardly have been coincidental that his young cousin Tom was by now threatening to sweep all before him at Aberystwyth.

Both graduated in 1908, Tom with a first in Welsh, Bob with a pass degree in Welsh and English. Both had won bardic chairs at their respective college eisteddfodau, but whereas Bob was satisfied with winning his chair in 1908 for a highly regarded *awdl* on 'Cantre'r Gwaelod' and going back to the classroom, although now persuaded to take a post at the local grammar school, Tom swept the board with eisteddfod prizes at Aberystwyth, both in 1907 and 1908, before going on to Oxford, Freiburg and the Sorbonne on a high-flying tour of some of the most highly respected academic philologists in Europe.

While Tom, much advantaged by his father's familiarity with European professors, was pursuing glittering academic prizes, Bob, frustrated by a lack of either financial or academic support for his own research ambitions, sought poetic success. In 1909 he came second to the awesome T. Gwynn Jones for the National Chair for a romantic *awdl* on the theme 'Gwlad y Bryniau'. And finally, in 1910, he not only won the chair himself, but won it with an *awdl*, 'Yr Haf', which was to go on record as one of the poetic turning-points of the century. Bob would be known from then on as 'Bardd yr Haf', and it was as such that he was eulogized by many when he died in 1956, unsuitable though such an epithet was long before then. Was it as a result of Bob's new-found bardic fame that Tom interrupted his academic studies to win both the chair and the crown – a previously unheard-of feat – at the National of 1912 and then, having returned to Aberystwyth as a lecturer, to win both again in 1915?

Bob was not beaten yet. Following his eisteddfod triumph and subsequent bardic fame, he returned to university to work for an MA degree. Having achieved it, however, he took up a post as headmaster of a small rural elementary school at Cefnddwysarn, near Bala. This was so unusual in those days that it merited a local newspaper headline: 'M.A. at a small country school'. It was now Bob's turn to face parental pressure and he was soon persuaded by his father that such a position was not suited to a man of his abilities. He applied for and was appointed to an English post at the grammar school in Barry in south Wales where, in direct contrast to his sense of peace and fulfilment during his single year at Cefnddwysarn, he was desperately unhappy. He was in a sense rescued from the obedient pointlessness of Barry when he was recruited into the army and spent even more fruitless years as a private soldier, most of the time as a member of an anti-aircraft detachment based at Billericay and guarding the London skies against Zeppelins. He never went to France or saw direct action, but he could hear the guns of Flanders from over the Channel as he waited for the Zeppelins and wrote a poem about it.

Tom, meanwhile, was running into difficulties in Aberystwyth. His experiences in Germany, and especially his revulsion against the feverish militarism he had found among some of the German students at Freiburg, had generated in him a strong anti-war feeling, along with a deep and abiding suspicion of the concept of patriotism. He registered as a pacifist, suffered a good deal of personal antipathy as a result, and at the end of the war his academic career suffered a severe, if temporary, set-back. There was a strong feeling in some quarters in Aberystwyth that 'the boys' who had gone to war should not, at the very least, be placed at a disadvantage *vis-à-vis* those who had been allowed to stay at home by calling themselves 'conshies'. A virulent dispute arose, largely as a result of this feeling, regarding the award of a chair of Welsh for which Tom was the obvious candidate. No appointment was made, and Tom, deeply wounded by the whole affair, abandoned, not only his lectureship, but his literary studies in general, and went off to study medicine. In view of all this, it might be thought that he would not have been too impressed by Bob, the reluctant soldier, bemoaning the boredom of army life and the unpalatable nature of army food.

After the war, Aberystwyth relented, and Tom got his chair, but never again, as he said openly, did he take up a public position on any controversial social or political issue, although he was often supportive of those who did. When, after his marriage many years later, in 1942, he returned more and more to public life, it was as a kind of national icon and a central pillar of the Welsh establishment, for which he was showered with honours, both lay and academic. He eventually received a knighthood, the honorary presidency of numerous Welsh bodies, including the National Eisteddfod, honorary degrees from various universities, the gold medal of the Honourable Society of Cymmrodorion. Fêted and revered as he was, however, he maintained a reserved and very private lifestyle, protected by a highly capable wife, but he remained charming, courteous and unfailingly helpful to all who sought his assistance, whether in literary or personal matters.

Bob, on his release from the army, initially went back to a 'suitable' teaching post in Cardiff. He soon discovered his mistake, but it took him two years to act upon the realization, when he once more secured a rural primary headship, this time at Oakley Park near Llanidloes. He had been there only two terms when he was offered a somewhat uncertain position on the staff of the college in Bangor, part-time as an assistant lecturer in the Welsh department and part-time under the Tutorial Classes Committee, later to become the Extra-Mural department. He took up the position, went to live in Bethesda, married a girl he had met while in Llanidloes, never received any significant academic preferment, retired early in 1944 and died in 1956, in many ways a sad and disappointed man and one who, in his last years, was not in full possession of his faculties.

It is clearly not my intention, in a brief essay, to present full parallel biographies of the two cousins, but I have attempted to relate the life of the one to the life of the other in a thumbnail sketch because I believe that, even from afar, the one was a lifelong influence on the other in a far more crucial sense than is usually recognized, and also because, however different their ways of coping with life may have been, there is, in my view, a quite striking similarity between them, a similarity that is sometimes concealed by the superficial differences in their poetry. The obvious differences are easy to itemize. Bob's verse, fluent, lyrical, sensual and deeply emotional, is easy to categorize as Romantic, and it surprises no one that one of his early influences was Keats. Tom's verse is spare, laconic, unadorned and intellectual; he is often referred to as a pioneer of modernism in Welsh. Both styles were, in my view, careful constructs which concealed a naked, underlying truth, a truth which had much to do with the relationship between man and the earth itself, that is, between individual men and the place which gave them being, and which was also much concerned with cruelty and violence between creatures, humans and animals alike.

But the underlying driving force which threatened them both was more primal than any of this; it was a terrible and inescapable sense of the fearful, incomprehensible and destructive nature of life, which sometimes has them both teetering on the edge of nihilism, and which indeed may have driven Bob over the edge before the end, but to which, by and large, they both reacted with a powerful stoicism tempered by a childlike and enduring wonder. In Bob's case it was a Wordsworthian sense of wonder at creation itself which, in those rare moments and places when it was unspoilt by man, could possess a beauty that seemed almost immortal. Only seemed, however, for it always faded and was always spoilt, and furthermore always had lurking within it that terrible destructive force that lay at the back of all things. In Tom's case, it was a more intellectual wonder at the vast, aesthetic complexity of the cosmos, in which man was an inconsequential atom. In both, however, the sense of wonder was a saving grace, as was their deep compassion for all innocent and simple creatures, whether man or beast, beaten and destroyed by cosmic injustice.

But we run ahead of ourselves. Some evidence is required for my belief that, in both Bob and Tom the poetry was a construct, its creation a therapy which enabled them – always with the caveat that it may have failed Bob before the end – to cope with a mortal condition that, in reality, was too terrible to cope with, which created a deep insecurity in them both; and landscape, however ironically, was a convenient vessel within which to frame such a construct, although we need to be clear at the start that we are talking about two very different landscapes.

I said that they were brought up within a few miles of each other. They were, but the few miles were crucial. Tom, as everyone who knows anything about him knows, embraced the barren mountain country around Rhyd-ddu as his natural habitat; although even that, as we shall see, is a less straightforward embrace than it is sometimes thought to be. Bob's country was a softer, lowland landscape, in the Nantlle Valley; in fact, he feared and disliked Tom's mountains, as he feared and disliked anything big and powerful. This fear is openly expressed in the sonnet 'Diddanwch':

> I don't find solace in the sea
> So much as in the mountain. In the mountain either
> So much as in the gorse-strewn hillside by my door.
> For I never walk the great bare mountain
> Without leaving ajar behind me
> The mountain-gate; nor the uninhabited shore
> Without being driven by its long grief into the bosom
> Of that homely woodland where my fosterbrothers dwell.
> Headlands of sea and sky! Not for me.
> Who loves the sweet blackbird's neighbour wood,
> The grey seagull's wanderlust over the ocean
> And the still pine-trees beneath the perfect stars.

That is clear enough, and the appealing image of the gate which separates the safety of the familiar from the danger of the great mountain being left ajar in case he should suddenly wish to dash back expresses no more than simple truth.

Tom, one might say, was made of sterner stuff. And indeed, in many ways, he was. He had something of the stoic's capacity to face ultimate truths head-on. But only briefly, and only after entering caveats. He was not so different from Bob.

In 1923 and 1924 he wrote two poems, the first of which, 'These Bones' is a grim farewell to mortal love, and the second, entitled 'The Lie', is a continuation of the same theme. 'The Lie' contains these lines:

> Weep that we should be put on this bit of a world
> Hanging in an expanse that is all crooked,
>
> Set to tread paths
> That can't be trodden – and trying to live;
>
> Then left to limp, step by step,
> Between sin and death without knowing why.

Read in the original jolly jingling rhythm, this is even more terrible than in a halting translation. But having penned such a stark challenge to a harsh and perverse creator, he then attempted to moderate the impact by subtitling the first poem 'A momentary fancy' and the second 'A dark hour'.

When I wrote a monograph on T. H. Parry-Williams in the Writers of Wales series some years ago, Lady Parry-Williams, who was then alive and had been gracious and co-operative in all other aspects of my project, took me seriously to task for lending these poems any credence and pointed sternly to the caveat subtitles; the construct was to survive beyond the grave.

And yet, as I said, he was made of sterner stuff than Bob. For he accepted the fact, as he saw it, that he had been formed by the landscape that surrounded him in childhood. He accepted it, but he did not, as some people assume, welcome it. In a famous sonnet, he expressed his oneness with the bare mountains: 'The ancient forms of these mountains pressed closer / Until the bareness entered the essence of my being.' But elsewhere, as in a revealing essay entitled 'The Little Wood', he showed that the bareness, in the landscape and in himself, was in fact a burden rather than the mark of belonging that he welcomed. 'The Little Wood' was an isolated outcrop of stunted trees, a rare place of hiding and shelter in the huge exposure, a magic play area for Tom and his brothers:

> I don't know how to describe the magic among the trees and in their shadow. The land around was so bare and poor that

> we could imagine, when we were in the wood, that we were in a high-roofed tropical forest . . . and although the trees were but thin dwarfs, they appeared to be tall, powerful columns to us little ones. The great thing was to be secret and out of sight beneath the trees enjoying, unbeknown to us, the most mysterious delight that man can conceive of . . . that pagan-sacred communion between man and trees above all . . . I grew up and I lost much of that gift to feel the magic of the presence of trees . . . The deadly bareness of that place has weighed more and more heavily on my soul.

'The deadly bareness of that place' makes it pretty clear that Tom did not regard the barren expanses of Eryri as in some way virtuous; they were what he had inherited, what he had to live with, and perhaps an indication of some lack within his own genetic make-up.

As for Bob, he too was unhappy with his environmental heritage, on two very different counts. As Bedwyr Lewis Jones pointed out in his monograph on Robert Williams Parry in the Writers of Wales series, the opening poem in his second and much more significant volume, 'Cerddi'r Gaeaf', is dedicated to a meadow on the valley floor near his home where, according to the celebrated medieval legend of Math, Pebin and his daughter Goewin had had their home. It is now a huge tip, comprising the waste from the nearby Dorothea Quarry, once famed as one of the largest man-made holes in the world. But the whole of the Nantlle Valley is in fact redolent of the Mabinogi. The very name, Nantlle, is a corruption of 'nant Lleu' – Lleu's valley – and Lleu also figured largely in the story of Math, he being the unfortunate husband of the faithless Blodeuwedd. For Bob Parry, this was his Nantlle, the land of ancient pagan legend, where man lived in true communion with nature, where trees and meadows and rivers and green slopes sheltered innocent creatures.

But now the magic had all gone. Life had become cruel and corrupt, and all that had worked together for good in the natural order of things had been overlaid by two complementary, if contradistinctive, cultures: the commercial values of industry and the grey puritanism of nonconformist religion. Both had conspired to remove the magic from the land and those who lived on it, and had left for him in his generation a heritage that was a pale memory of what it had once been, and even that memory was inaccessible to most of those living there.

Most of Bob Parry's poetry, placed within this context, forms a coherent whole; it deals with wild creatures, hunted and persecuted, with creatures tamed by man who have lost that sense of risky freedom in their natural state that wild creatures should have, with glimpses of the ancient magic gained at special times and in special places, with the role of the poet as the voice of the natural order, with his sense of his own terrible inadequacy and with good, straightforward human beings badly done by in a corrupt world. It was quite clear that his calling was to be a poet, and his vacillations in regard to the proper way to earn his daily bread were caused in the main, at least in his early days, by parental pressure. In truth, he wanted to live as near as possible to that natural order he revered and to be free to be its poetic voice.

Bob Parry, however, was nothing if not a vulnerable and fallible human being, and, as time went on and as the university failed to recognize his services, even by regularizing his position, he laboured under a huge sense of grievance and even, at one time, refused to have anything to do with Welsh literary or academic life, outside the strict requirements of his work. He was regarded, it is true, as the greatest of living poets by the nation at large (and the Welsh, at that time, were a literate people who knew their poetry), but poets, as he wrote in a scathing satirical poem, accounted for little, compared with 'chwilotwyr' (rummagers, or, more kindly, researchers), 'For are not fishermen / Greater than the little fish?' This sense of grievance, amounting to outrage, in regard especially to the nature and behaviour of the university, was not limited to its treatment of himself. He was moved to mount powerful poetic attacks on the university in respect of its treatment of Saunders Lewis, and his progressive sense of disillusion eventually led to his retirement in 1944 and his final disappearance from public view.

What of Tom during all this time and what of the relationship between them? We know that Tom too, afflicted, or gifted, by the same hypersensitivity, had also had his periods of withdrawal and rejection of society. Nor was this a one-off response to his treatment during the First World War, something he could put behind him in order to get on with his life; moods of deep depression occurred more than once in later life. The death of his parents one soon after the other in 1926 and 1927, after painful illnesses, were clearly part of such a period, as was the death of his sister in 1933. But Tom had more positive ways of dealing with self-doubt than Bob. It is not coincidental that he embarked on long sea-voyages in 1925 and in 1935, 'to come face to face with himself in places far distant from the piece of earth where he belonged', as he explained in an unguarded moment. Nor was it coincidental, if even more radical, that he made a second, but abortive, attempt to abandon a life of letters and turn to medicine, also in 1935.

For a long time, nevertheless, his life was, in the main, limited to a hard-working and highly conscientious attention to his academic duties, and, as he had promised to himself, an avoidance of any involvement in controversy, even literary controversy, of which Welsh literary life had no shortage, then or at any other time. It should be remembered that this was a man who in youth, had been most actively involved in literary controversy of all kinds, a powerful iconoclast and a mean debater.

I believe it to be the simple truth in regard to this matter that he had found the quarrels surrounding his wartime stand, and the hostility he had endured as a result, to be so disabling and personally agonizing that his very survival as a properly functioning adult, let alone as a university professor, meant avoiding a repetition of such experiences at all costs. It was not that he no longer held strong views; it was that he could not afford the repercussions that would follow their expression. In both Bob and Tom, however differently they might choose to deal with the problem, artistic sensitivity, allied to a compulsive honesty, was a heavy burden to bear, and it grew no easier as life went on.

It is worth noting at this point that conventional religion was a source of solace for neither of them. In Tom, the involvement of ministers of religion in recruitment during the First World War, and the part persons of a religious persuasion had played in his own persecution, had certainly accelerated a rejection of conventional belief which he never regained. In Bob, the hated characteristic of hypocrisy was inextricably linked with the Chapel and he would have nothing to do with it.

During the war, Bob was called upon to write many elegies – *englynion* in the main – to young men killed in battle. He would always oblige, but, although these poems would be inscribed for ever on tombstones in localities where religious observance was still very much the norm, not one of them contains a grain of Christian hope for an ultimate resurrection. Death was a tragic and terrible end, especially for the young, and especially for those whose remains were buried in some alien plot rather than their own earth, but it was the end. It is not surprising that the Bob Parry who felt an almost mystical link with his own Nantlle could find some consolation in a situation where the soldier had at least been brought home:

> But the earth of Cefnddwysarn
> gently was laid upon him,
> and the birds patter
> around his grave as they visit him.

He could not offer the same consolation in his celebrated sequence of *englynion* to the poet Hedd Wyn, killed at Passchendaele and buried in France:

> It was a hard and bitter thing to drive
> a gentle one from the solace of his books:
> hard to place his earth in earth,
> hardest of all to die far away.

And the common thread running through all these elegies sounds as clearly as a tolling bell in this final couplet of an *englyn* to a lad from Blaenau Ffestiniog: 'Grieve, companions all! / A beautiful boy is motionless dust.' Both Tom and Bob, however, found it easy to distinguish between good people who were associated with religious life, and religion itself. Bob wrote many poems in praise of people who committed themselves to the religious life, in particular ministers of religion who had served ungrateful congregations for years for a pittance. And Tom could write movingly and enviously of those who retained a simple and honest religious faith. For if religion as such could offer them no solace, or reason for living, the friendship of good men could. In this too they were remarkably similar. There is universal testimony to the fact that both flourished in the company of close friends. In such company, the witty, sparkling, mischievous Bob Parry that Tom had known in childhood would return. But they both disliked the company of fellow poets and writers, and, worse still, fellow academics. They preferred the company of men close to the earth, far removed from literature and learning, engaged in day-to-day rural activities. In Bob's case it seems to have been the sedentary delights of conversation, practical jokes and the playing of indoor games that would engage his interest, while Tom, throughout his life, loved to be active and to use his hands. He writes of visits to his uncle and aunt on a farm above Beddgelert, where he would be given the run of the farmer's workshop and while away the day in carpentry. He also, throughout his life, continued to engage in the country sports taught to him by the locals in Rhyd-ddu and he was no mean shot with a twelve-bore. In this, of course, he was fundamentally different from Bob, for whom the killing of any wild thing was anathema, but I have no record of this being a cause of friction. The important fact is that neither Bob nor Tom was a natural recluse: neither was a loner by choice. The exigencies of life and some fundamental insecurity within them had driven both, in different ways and for different reasons, to employ survival techniques not natural to them.

In the event, for all Bob's pre-eminence in early youth, it was clear that Tom possessed resources and survival techniques not available to Bob, not least of which was his formidable intelligence and the inner compulsion to put his intelligence to work in the rational analysis of situations. It would appear that he possessed the rare capacity to rationalize even his own uncertainties and complexities, and to act accordingly.

It may not be out of place here to say a word about Tom's father and to suggest that, in his father, Tom possessed a notable asset that Bob never had, although there is an ambivalence underlying even that simple fact.

Harry Parry-Williams was the intellectual and formally educated member of a working-class family who, though gifted in many ways, were not otherwise schooled beyond the elementary stage. Bob's father, a deacon and a leader of the community, was a checker-clerk at Nantlle Station, looking after the loading of slates from the quarry on to the railway; his mother was the daughter of a well-respected local minister. Bob was brought up deeply in the shadow of the two social influences he was later to detest, but it was not an intellectual upbringing. (The third son, who was to father another distinguished academic, Thomas Parry, later to be principal of the college at Aberystwyth, and, like Tom, also knighted, still lived in the family home in the nearby village of Carmel.) Harry, as headmaster of the village school, was an important figure in the locality. But he was more than that. He was highly thought of in wider educational circles for his progressive teaching methods, and was regarded as an expert in language teaching. So much so that European experts in the new academic discipline of philology, and in the fashionable study of Celtic languages, came to Rhyd-ddu to learn Welsh from Harry and to be smothered in Welshness.

This was the atmosphere in which Tom grew up, and this was the Uncle Harry that Bob as a young lad rode up from Nantlle to discuss *cynghanedd* with before Tom knew what *cynghanedd* was. His father had clearly instilled intellectual curiosity in his son very early in life, but he also generated much grief and bitterness in him when he sent Tom off to grammar school in Porthmadog and to live in lodgings. Tom could have gone, like Bob, to the new secondary school down in the valley, but Porthmadog had a stronger reputation, and Harry wanted his outstandingly gifted son to be removed from undesirable distractions in Rhyd-ddu, so that he could concentrate on developing his considerable intellect.

Many feel that it was this early separation from his childhood land that created the legendary Rhyd-ddu that Tom was later to incorporate in his poems and essays, and that was to serve as his spiritual retreat and place of safety for ever after. I have no doubt that there is much truth in this, but I also have little doubt that the existence of such a spiritual retreat might not have appeared nearly as important to him had the second trauma not occurred, namely the events at Aberystwyth during the First World War.

It is time to look more closely at the ultimate literary stature of the two cousins. Bob published two volumes of verse only, *Yr Haf a Cherddi Eraill* in 1924 and *Cerddi'r Gaeaf*, after much prodding and prompting, in 1952. They are very different, the first volume Romantic in nature, Keatsian in its sensuality, and with the famous *awdl* as its centrepiece. It also contains some fine elegies and war sonnets. That it did not satisfy the poet himself, and was in fact published at a point when he had in a sense outgrown it, is indicated by the fact that it also contained a late inclusion, a skilful and witty parody on his own 'Summer' *awdl*, entitled 'The Duck' and dealing with a tragic and fatal love affair between Lady Duck and Sir Fox. It was the sensuous Romanticism of the volume which sealed his fame as a poet, however, and when his second volume appeared, much sparer and sharper both in style and content, many reacted against it and one reviewer begged leave to doubt whether this could indeed be the work of the poet of 'Summer'. It is on this volume nevertheless that his status as a poet rests, and poem after poem in it succeeds in linking his magical gift for verbal music with his central themes of simplicity and innocence and the fundamental corruption of modern society. A series of sonnets, bringing together these two themes in stark contradistinction, are among the finest poems in the language.

Tom did not possess Bob's supreme and seemingly effortless ability to weave verbal tapestries – and the harder and subtler weave of the later volume is as consummate musically as the richer tones of the first. I think Tom knew this well enough and, indeed, from the earliest days of their acquaintance recognized Bob as the superior poet. I am not sure that Tom was naturally a poet at all, in the sense that there was a compulsion in him to create verbal music; I have a feeling, although there are many who will take issue with this, that he might never have written verse had Bob not been there ahead of him, in a sense egging him on. We must revisit that thought, but before we do, we should review Tom's literary achievements.

As one might imagine, he did not rush into print. Having more than matched Bob's early triumphs stroke for stroke, he then held his fire and did not publish his first book, which was not in fact verse, but a collection of essays, until 1928. His first volume of poems followed in 1931, and from then on he produced seven books of verse and prose, judiciously spaced out, finishing with a final volume in 1966. Both his verse and his prose are carefully considered constructs; one might almost say that Tom was quite deliberately creating T. H. Parry-Williams, the poet and essayist, ensuring that he would be unmistakably different from any other literary figure. As far as his published verse is concerned, it contains only two poetic forms, one of which is adopted from other languages, namely the sonnet, while the other, a rhyming couplet stanza, was only previously used in Welsh as a vehicle for light verse. With great skill and control, and with a thoroughly modern spareness of expression and a wide use of vernacular and even invented vocabulary, he made both vehicles serve his purpose, namely a search for the nature of meaning, within a context of doubt which, at one extreme, is almost nihilistic and at the other exudes a mystical sense of the numinous. The choice of such unusual verse forms, allied to the fact that he published no poetry at all in the strict metres, ensured that he had the field to himself. (It is significant that he did exactly the same thing as a scholar, choosing areas of research where there were effectively no rivals.)

The poems undoubtedly represent an intellectually powerful and painfully honest journey of discovery, but it is not always realized that the construct is a composite one, and that the poems and the essays are not separate bodies of work. They complement each other in a way which is certainly unique in Welsh literature and for which I know no close analogy elsewhere either. The essays are in a sense prose-poems which perform multiple functions, one being to serve as a kind of treasure trove of crucial and oblique autobiographical revelations, and the other to act as subtle elucidations and parallel commentaries on themes dealt with differently in the poems. The whole *œuvre* unquestionably sets Tom apart from any other writer and, taken as a whole, brings us into the presence of a piercing and wide-ranging intellect, again and again throwing subtle and tangential light on the problems of being. And yet one has to be reminded, as one moves through his work, of a perceptive comment made by one of his father's European visitors, Dr van Hamel of Utrecht, writing from Rotterdam in May 1914 and addressing his letter in Welsh (the letter itself was also written in Welsh) to Mr H. Parry-Williams, The Celtic Academy, Rhyd-ddu. Dr van Hamel had, of course, heard of his son Tom's eisteddfod triumphs and he had been sent his work by the proud father. 'Tom's genius', he wrote, 'is very philosophical, and his poetic devices are more rational than sensitive.' We can hardly doubt Tom's sensitivity, but the impression we, like Dr van Hamel, have, in his work as in life, is that he held that sensitivity under a formidable intellectual control. Poor Bob could not, and that perhaps, for all their many similarities, was in the end the difference between them.

And yet that too is probably too simple. If control there was, it was not easily achieved. After his marriage, to a wife who had an impressive presence and who sheltered him faithfully from all ills, there is no doubt that Tom grew in confidence and performed his myriad public functions with dignity and *gravitas*. And yet . . . my memories of him in such situations, once off the official stage, were of a man ill at ease with public attention. In the milling busy-ness and manic social exchanges that go on all day at the back of the National Eisteddfod pavilion, the small man in the far corner, learning his speech by heart, alone and unnoticed, would be Tom; the same Tom who once beheld with awe the cavorting of his cousin Bob on his bicycle and at the tea table, entertaining all and sundry with his jokes and stories. And I recall a personal anecdote, told me by my wife. It was at another National Eisteddfod, the one held at Ammanford in 1970. I was myself engaged in some public performance in an outlying chapel and she, having returned to the eisteddfod car park after delivering me there, was walking our small children towards the field itself when she spied a familiar figure, complete with his trilby hat, sitting alone in a tiny car. She went towards him, worried that he might not be well. He explained that the only place where he could find some peace at the eisteddfod was in the car park and having paid courteous attention, as ever, to the children, went back to his catnap and his peace.

There remain many questions unasked, but let us satisfy ourselves, for the purpose of this essay, with asking just one more. What of the relationship between the eminent Tom of late middle age and the sad and embittered Bob? Were they close? Did they meet often? I cannot think that they did. For all the elegant and moving tribute to him that Tom penned on his death, my feeling is that they had become estranged. And there are at least some scraps of evidence to support this view.

In all the voluminous, if admittedly incomplete, correspondence relating to Tom in the National Library of Wales, there are very few letters from Bob. And of the few, two are revealing. They both note briefly that Bob has heard of Tom visiting Bangor in the recent past; he points out that he still lives in Bethesda. And when Tom was awarded the medal of the Honourable Society of Cymmrodorion in 1951, it was intended that Bob too should be honoured at the same time. He sent a polite note of refusal, explaining that he was not a suitable person to be honoured in such a way; surely the hurt on both sides as a result of such a refusal must have been immense.

And then, when *Cerddi'r Gaeaf* appeared in 1952, there is a preface of thanks from 'RWP' to three people who aided the publication. Two were known to be intimate personal friends, Gwilym Evans and J. O. Williams. The third was his other cousin, Thomas Parry, then professor of Welsh at Bangor. Would one not have expected Tom to be associated in some way? Well, perhaps not, perhaps the relationship was, after all, too private for letters and too personal for public recognition. Rather than ask any more questions, the best place to leave these two, two of the finest poets in the language, is with part of Tom's official goodbye to his boyhood hero, one who, to his mind, had been granted some rare gift that he himself, for all his great abilities and obvious success, did not possess:

> And so he has gone after languishing a long time; we had indeed 'lost' him years ago. When I saw him last some time ago, he was there, but without being with us. I hope, for the sake of Wales, that Wales realises someone and something remarkable has gone away.
>
> We have lost from among us some indefinable treasure, some elemental essence that only dwells among human kind once in the course of many years, if indeed it ever happens more than once in quite the same way.

The gift, naked and uncompromising, had destroyed Bob. Tom was the one who survived.

Note

1 As a result, this piece is written, in the main, from the point of vision of cousin Tom, T. H. Parry-Williams. Those familiar with the Welsh language who would be interested in pursuing their early relationship further, but in the main from cousin Bob's viewpoint, should turn to a parallel piece by Bedwyr Lewis Jones in *Taliesin*, 74 (Summer 1991).

7

Outside the House of Baal: *The Evolution of a Major Novel*

M. WYNN THOMAS

One evening in the early sixties, while driving his elderly mother back to her home after a family visit, Emyr Humphreys was greatly struck by an innocent remark she made as she gazed through the car windscreen. It was bad luck, she flatly assured him, to look at the moon through glass. The comment made him realize she was a survivor from an earlier 'horse and buggy' age, whose picture of life had been significantly different from his own. He suddenly saw her as the personification of historical change and as yesterday's fragile witness. Out of his consequently urgent impulse to explore aspects of the disappearing past his mother had known, came in due course *Outside the House of Baal* (1965), Emyr Humphreys's most impressive attempt not only to describe but also to calibrate the changes that had drastically refashioned Welsh society during the first sixty or so years of this century.

Appropriately enough he found that important features of this socio-cultural transformation were conveniently focused for him in the history of his mother's family. His maternal grandfather, who had been widowed relatively early, owned a prosperous hill-top farm within comfortable cycling distance of Emyr Humphreys's boyhood home in the village of Trelawnyd (then called Newmarket), a few miles inland from Rhyl. Like Pa in the novel, this grandfather was an old-style, philoprogenitive patriarch, puritanically stern and somewhat of an autocrat. In their own adult lives his numerous children found various pragmatic ways of modifying the tenets and practices of his brand of high nonconformity – which had been heroic and hypocritical by turns – to suit the spirit of a new, secular and complaisant society. Like Lydia in the novel, Emyr Humphreys's mother was in her youth a free spirit, lively, strong-willed and unconventional, who eagerly embraced marriage to a schoolmaster as a convenient escape from a claustrophobic home background. The marital tension that predictably ensued may well have given rise to scenes similar to the one in the book when the little boy Ronnie, returning from school with a friend, is aghast to hear his parents quarrelling loudly, and tries to cover both the noise and his confusion by raising his voice and banging the gate. He ends up – perhaps like the future novelist himself – wretchedly taking refuge in books.

In an earlier scene in the novel Ronnie is warned by his mother to hide his war-comic under a cushion before his father returns from chapel. Emyr Humphreys's own father bore in general very little resemblance to the minister J.T., but he had seen service at the front in the First World War, spent the rest of his life suffering the after-effects of poison-gas, and was so reluctant to recall his war experience to mind that he absolutely forbade his sons, when they were children, ever to play at being soldiers. Partly in consequence, the First World War has long exercised a powerful fascination over Emyr Humphreys's imagination. At its simplest, this can be seen in his attempts in *Outside the House of Baal* to enter this potently secret, forbidden territory of paternal experience by sending the central character, J.T., to the trenches. Then again, at its most complex, this fascination with war – and related forms of violence – is an active element in the creed of pacifism, to which both J.T. and Emyr Humphreys are lifelong adherents. After all, the pacifist is, paradoxically, fixated on war because it is the principal evil in terms of which he defines himself morally and because it offers the ultimate challenge to everything in which he believes. Finally, and in a sense most importantly, the First World War marks, for Humphreys, a turning-point in recent Welsh history, and it is treated as such in *Outside the House of Baal*. Born in 1919, he has repeatedly attempted to reconstruct, in his fiction, the conditions of life of his parents' pre-war generation, as if seeking an explanation, in the very strangeness of that period, for the bewildering historical changes he has himself lived through.

Outside the House of Baal, unquestionably his major novel, is perhaps most centrally about the decline of Welsh nonconformity, which can be conveniently dated from, and may partly be attributed to, the First World War. Indeed, in an interview Humphreys has gone on record as describing this as an unqualified cultural catastrophe, since he believes that, in its spiritual prime, nonconformity provided the basis in Wales for a 'civilization', as he has put it, of outstanding value.[1] The novel, of course, tells a somewhat different story, and is compelling precisely to the extent that it problematizes the issue, locating the character of the Calvinistic Methodist minister J.T., for instance, at the exact point where different judgements come most hauntingly into conflict. And it is here, in the complexity of his treatment of one of the central components of Welsh culture, that Emyr Humphreys most significantly, and most successfully, departs from established practice. For upwards of fifty years before his novel was published, Welsh authors writing in English had by and large contented themselves with reproducing a crude identikit picture of the Nonconformist: cunning, lecherous, avaricious and of course invariably hypocritical. Caradoc Evans, a bilious genius, had first devised and patented the picture in 1915, using it to inspired effect in the propaganda war he waged in his fiction to liberate Wales from chapel 'Prussianism'.[2] Later writers, however, from Dylan Thomas to Gwyn Thomas, inherited from him a crude stereotype which made it next to impossible for them to engage meaningfully with one of the most powerful and subtle aspects of their own culture – powerful not only in terms of the institutions it controlled, but also because the moral climate it created affected every aspect of social and political life.

Emyr Humphreys's altogether more complex approach to this whole subject may be due in part to his being that rarity in twentieth-century Wales, a convert (of sorts) to nonconformity – although in his case the 'conversion' had a cultural as well as a spiritual provenance. He was raised an Anglican, his upwardly mobile parents having moved away from a nonconformist background they associated primarily with the social backwardness of Welsh-language culture. It was therefore perhaps inevitable that when the young Humphreys, inspired by the militant cultural and political nationalism of leading Welsh intellectuals during the thirties, began to learn the Welsh language, he should also begin to follow in reverse the path his parents had taken. This process was no doubt accelerated when, in 1946, he married the daughter of a minister with the Annibynwyr (the Welsh Congregationalists, or Independents). It was many years, however, before he was able to translate his growing understanding of and qualified sympathy with Welsh nonconformity into fully effective fictional terms. The eight novels he published before *Outside the House of Baal* include occasional examples of a fairly superficial treatment of the subject, and the new complexity of approach that is one of the most outstanding features of this novel may be due in no small part to the fact that for several years before it was written Humphreys's father-in-law had been living permanently with him and his family.

The period spent apprenticed to a blacksmith before entering the ministry; the eventful journeys from north Wales to preach in the strange and turbulent mining valleys of the south; these and other episodes in J.T.'s fictional life had their origin in the facts of the Revd Jones's actual career. Much more importantly, however, Emyr Humphreys encountered in his father-in-law's principled mildness of character those aspects of the nonconformist heritage that were to him most attractive and most admirable. They were also, it should be noted, the antithesis not only of the stereotyped picture but also of what nonconformity had largely, in actual historical fact, become by the time – around the last quarter of the nineteenth century – it had indisputably developed into the established religion of Wales. By then the chapels had become the Liberal Party at prayer, social institutions that facilitated the triumphant rise of the Welsh bourgeoisie. Pa's fear, in the novel, of the foundry workers; young Kate's scorning of Maldwyn Birch, a mere carpenter; the irritation of Lydia and Dan Llew with the striking miners; all these are signs of the difficulties many of the chapel-bred had in coming to terms with the experiences of the new working class, particularly in the industrial areas.[3] When Lloyd George, the darling of the chapels, became the great war-leader in 1914, many of the leading ministers used their awesome cultic power to mobilize their congregations, and proved to be deadly effective recruiting sergeants.[4] Both the jingoistic atmosphere of the time and the 'Christian' arguments used to justify the war are captured by the novel, in scenes that include J.T.'s argument with the principal of his theological college and his courageous (or foolhardy – one has to double one's terms, it seems, whenever one assesses his actions) protest in the eisteddfod against the pro-war rhetoric spouted by the Lloyd George-like figure on the stage.

There was, though, another strain of nonconformity that shows in J.T.'s character, as to some extent it did in the case of Emyr Humphreys's father-in-law. Broadly speaking, it can be described as Nonconformist in the root sense of that term: radically dissenting, both in spirit and in actual social practice, from the comfortably established order of things. In the case of some major nineteenth-century issues, like parliamentary reform, the land question, the anti-tithe campaign and education, this progressivist brand of nonconformity quickly blended into mainstream political activity. But this was not so in other cases that most famously included Samuel Roberts (S.R.)'s concern with 'public witness by the individual conscience, with peace, free trade and the limitation of the power of the state'; Michael D. Jones's attempt to set up a new Welsh homeland in Patagonia; and of course Henry Richard's tireless work to ease international tension, which earned for him the sobriquet of 'the Apostle of Peace'.[5]

After the First World War, nonconformity, its moral authority virtually destroyed by its indirect participation in the carnage, tried to regroup spiritually on the ground of its radical first principles, and at least one of the fascinating leaders that then emerged later influenced Emyr Humphreys's portrayal, in *Outside the House of Baal*, both of the central figure J.T. and of the minor character Bayley Lewis.[6] George M. Ll. Davies was a charismatic, if controversial, personality during the inter-war period. A strikingly handsome man of impeccable integrity, he was imprisoned as a conscientious objector during the First World War, thus embarking on what he was later to call a lifetime's 'pilgrimage of peace'. His denomination, the Calvinistic Methodists, disapproved of him as much as they did of the fictional J.T., refusing to let him be ordained until his pacifism had become socially acceptable. He went on to play a leading part in the work of the Peace Pledge Union – an organization Emyr Humphreys himself joined in the late thirties. Davies was as opposed to class war as he was to actual war, and in 1932 he joined the settlement of Maes-yr-Haf which the Quakers opened in the Rhondda in an effort to improve the plight of the mass unemployed by other than militant political means. A gentle, other-worldly reconciler both by instinct and by conviction, he turned his outrage at the social dereliction in the south Wales Valleys during the thirties into an exhausting labour of non-denominational Christian love for the people, but in the process laid himself open to the very charges – of naivety, presumption, self-deception and ineffectuality – that the seasoned political agitator Bill Mabon wittily levels in the novel against Bayley Lewis.

In the opening sentence of his autobiography, George M. Ll. Davies quoted Emerson's remark: 'we are always hoping to get settled down. There is only hope for us so long as we are unsettled.'[7] It is precisely this 'selfish' and 'irresponsible' spirit of unsettledness that irritates both Lydia and Kate, in their different ways, about J.T. He, in his turn, is made restless by Davies's vision of the way in which 'the ancient paganisms, the worship of Mammon, Mars, Demos and Eros still survive under highly modern names, while persons become workers, or conscripts, voters, or film addicts.'[8] In short, modern society lives all too cosily, J.T. believes, in the House of Baal. As for the novel, it refuses to take sides, preferring to dwell in what E. M. Foster once called 'the twilight of the double vision'. In so doing, it is true to the creative spirit of uncertainty that informs one of the jottings in Emyr Humphreys's working notebook: 'Geo M LL D – an idiot busy body . . . or a saint?'

The drafts and working notes for *Outside the House of Baal* throw interesting light on the development of the novel from its inception in early summer, 1963, to its completion almost exactly a year later.[9] Most of the main characters, spanning three generations, are there from the beginning and the network of relationships that connects them is already fairly clearly defined. Governing the whole enterprise from the outset is what one note calls the 'thesis' of the novel: 'view of life of two – J.T. and Kate – in their seventies – the life of the last 70 years – the feel of human effort struggling to be trapped in that semi-detached house.' The sympathetic, yet unsparing depiction of old age in all its crabbiness of spirit and its painstaking, often laboured, physical movements, is there in the original opening, which concerns Kate rather than J.T. Also recorded early is the intention to ensure that the novel covers four distinct historical periods – 'before War I; between wars; War II; after War' – the difference between them being summed up as follows: 'What will you die for – c.f. 1914, your country; 1930s, the workers and Spain; 1941, civilization versus Hitler; 1960, Wales.' But although the main features of many of the leading characters are established from the beginning, the exact course of several of their lives remains to be fixed. There are plans, for example, to allow Lydia to have affairs, and to let her leave J.T. and settle in London. In particular, the fates of Ronnie, Vernon and Thea remain undetermined – and remain in the balance, since the death of both brothers is canvassed as a serious possibility – until quite late in the process of composition, although a socially significant contrast between the characters of the two brothers is planned from very early in the writing.

Indeed, the elaboration of contrasts is consciously adopted by Emyr Humphreys as a fundamental method of construction. Sometimes he scribbles down antitheses that are, one feels, to be operative throughout the whole novel: 'It's sin that makes the world go round. It's love that makes the world go round.' 'All is meaningful: all is meaningless.' At other times he has his central pair of opposites – Kate and J.T. – specifically in mind: 'she can't believe, he can'; 'J.T.M. – failure and fear: Kate – no faith and [is] content. Purpose – survival'; 'In action she is useful. In repose his spirit moves – he is the useful one – balance.' This last contrast is later translated from idea into motif, with J.T. associated primarily with the head (as in the opening phrase of the first paragraph in the published novel) and Kate with the hands (as in the second section). Such open identification by the author of one of the secret motifs – whether they be physical gestures, or objects such as J.T.'s collar, his Gladstone bag, or the photograph of Ma – that provide the novel with its texture as well as its infrastructure, is however a rare occurrence in the manuscripts.

'Events every time – ideas in background', says one of the memos Emyr Humphreys wrote to himself. It is partly a reminder of the importance, to him, of story, a point he underlines elsewhere in his notes: 'story animates, therefore events, it is true, must be described in detail; but the story must hook you compulsively & animate the entire functions of the . . . imagination. This is essential.' At the same time, however, he suggestively speaks of his wish to 'hold the story like a face that turns slowly to keep in the sun'. Although the metaphor mentions one face only, it actually highlights, and in a sense explains, the multifaceted structure of a novel in which attention seems to fall upon different objects, different locations, different characters, different events, almost as impartially as light (so Whitman put it) 'falls about a helpless thing'.

This effect of serene, lucid impartiality is, the notes show, one that Emyr Humphreys consciously aimed (and strove) to produce. 'I am absent and I do not pass myself on to you', he tells himself, and an imaginary reader, in one entry. Another time he admonishes himself sharply: 'don't presume to know what they [i.e. the characters] think. The intimacy of their own thoughts.' Write, he instructs himself, 'without claiming infinite knowledge', and in one striking manuscript passage he seems acutely aware of having evolved what is for him a new kind of writing, whose 'grace of accuracy' (to borrow Robert Lowell's phrase) marks it off from the style of his previous novels.

> Late in life I took upon myself the burden: to say what is true. That is wrong. I always knew that the primary element of the beauty of a saying was the 'yes indeed that is so' element. What I had not reckoned with until now was the discipline involved in sustaining 'the saying' over a book of 100,000 words. So it is that I wake up compelled by the spirit of dedication, living as this book lives, and my dreams are dominated by physical effort.

As the very earliest drafts show, however, Humphreys did at first find it difficult to resist the temptation to trespass on the consciousness of his main characters. In its original form, the opening section describing J.T.'s slow awakening to the day included passages like the following, which register his mental reactions to the sound of Kate's busyness downstairs:

> It was always necessary to keep in touch with the woman's movements . . . The fall of the lavatory seat after the chain pulling. And the ultimate sweet but final warning of the tinkling of tea cups. Whether he could or he couldn't, that was the time to start moving.

The very next paragraph cuts, without warning, back to the time, half a century earlier, when J.T. was a youngster apprenticed to Isaac Dafydd the blacksmith (see chapter 4, section 3 of the published novel.) It therefore seems that Emyr Humphreys did not start out with the clear intention of setting up a twin-track narrative, one devoted to the past and the other to the present, and each proceeding at a different pace.

The notes also allow us to pinpoint one of the sources of his new spare style of writing. In 1958 he had been introduced, by his friend Walter Todds, to the philosophy of Ludwig Wittgenstein, some of whose familiar gnomic utterances are recorded in the notebooks for *Outside the House of Baal*. 'What we cannot speak about we must pass over in silence' was one ascetic remark that motivated Emyr Humphreys to aim at a chaste integrity of expression.[10] At the same time he was fascinated by the wealth of meaning which Wittgenstein had stressed every word, however humble, possessed. 'To utter a word', the Austrian had written, 'is as if a note were struck on the keyboard of the imagination'; and Emyr Humphreys briefly entertained the idea of entitling his novel 'The keyboard'. In fact, the final title of the novel emerged quite late in the day. Much of the writing was done under the working title of 'Of the event', and among other ideas entertained were 'Where is now?' and 'A Welsh dream'.

Two more of Wittgenstein's aphorisms are to be found in the notebooks. 'Not how the world is, is the mystery, but that it is', he wrote in the *Tractatus* (6:44),[11] and, particularly in relation to the laboured, painfully deliberate movements of J.T. and Kate in their old age, Emyr Humphreys is able to bring out the power and the pathos of the sheer mute existence of objects – what one writer has recently called 'that terse epiphany of the things in themselves, which already results from the poetry of their names'.[12] Central to Wittgenstein's philosophy was the realization that 'The limits of my language mean the limits of my world', and central in turn to the novel is the perception that profound historical changes are accompanied by fundamental shifts in the language of people's understanding.[13] J.T.'s religious language of sin and forgiveness is virtually unintelligible, for instance, to the self-made man Dan Llew, to his miserably cuckolded son Norman, and to members of the younger generation in general, whether they live in Wales or America. Even the importance to J.T. of the Welsh language itself is something which is essentially incomprehensible to someone like Ronnie, who is intent on social advancement. But virtually from the beginning of his ministry J.T. himself, of course, speaks a language of faith which is scandalously different from that traditionally used by his theologically conservative denomination. Hence his reluctant emergence, in the novel, as the leader of the 'new', and politically progressive, wing of Calvinistic Methodism in opposition to the reactionary views of Machno Jones and his followers. As the notes for the novel remind us, this liberal outlook continued to gain ground within nonconformity after the Second World War, up to the very time when *Outside the House of Baal* was being written, thanks partly to the impact of the posthumously published writings of Dietrich Bonhoeffer, who advocated a 'religionless Christianity' of the kind that manifestly appeals to the ageing J.T.[14]

'Time after all is the chief character in a novel' is one of the observations Emyr Humphreys makes in the notes, and the way in which time is managed is one of the outstanding features of *Outside the House of Baal.* Of its twenty-six chapters, ten are set in the present and sixteen in the past, but the latter are given four pages to every one of the former. In the first quarter of the novel there is a regular pattern of alternation between past and present, but thereafter the arrangement is irregular, with the maximum disparity occurring after chapter 18, when there are four chapters in succession dealing with past events. Most striking of all, perhaps, is Emyr Humphreys's success in devising techniques for distinguishing between the pace of living during youth and vigorous prime, and the slowing down, not only of physical movement, but of the very metabolism (so to speak) of consciousness itself, that is part of the ageing process. Life, and all the contents of living, seem to take on a greater specific gravity in those chapters that deal with Kate and J.T.'s time in 8 Gorse Avenue.

As one would have expected, the manuscripts show that some of the original sections and chapters had to be rearranged in a different order before the present convincing pattern emerged. For example chapter 1 was at first followed by a chapter (now chapter 8, section 2) describing how Kate was most embarrassingly up to her elbows in soapsuds when the young auburn-haired J.T. first called at Argoed. Dramatically effective though this juxtaposition was in one way, it had the disadvantage of forcing the author from the very beginning into a non-chronological treatment of early events, which is presumably one reason why it was abandoned. And when this episode was eventually transferred to chapter 8 it took its place alongside other sections, scattered through chapters 7–10, which had previously been tried in different locations and in different permutations.

There are also one or two other differences worth noting, between the first version in manuscript and the text as published. As has already been explained, Emyr Humphreys originally drafted episodes hinting at Lydia's extra-marital affairs, but the subsequent omission of this material may have necessitated the addition of two scenes which underlined by other means the tensions within the marriage. The first is the opening scene of chapter 19, which concludes with Lydia begging Jenny Leyshon not to tell J.T. about the money she has had to borrow in order to make ends meet; and the second is section 2 of chapter 20, in which Lydia shocks the young doctor by tearfully announcing that she cannot stand her husband and that, had she but the money, she would leave him tomorrow. In addition, the manuscripts provide interesting examples of phrases and sentences added, particularly at the conclusion of sections, for incisive effect. So, for instance, chapter 13 originally ended with J.T., nonplussed by Kate's tart reaction to his sorrow at hearing of his old friend Ifan

Cole's death, limply holding up for inspection the letters that have just been accidentally soaked in sardine oil. In its published form, however, the chapter concludes with a splendidly climactic and combative one-liner: ' – What if we all just lived for ourselves, Kate said.' Such changes emphasize the distinctiveness of the 'scenes' of which the novel is composed. In their compression of meaning, and with their heightened air of significance, they resemble short stories more than they do casual vignettes.

The notebooks mention actors and actresses of the post-war period, with whom Emyr Humphreys had worked and aspects of whose personalities helped him construct the character of Thea. There is also abundant evidence of the effort Emyr Humphreys put into historical research for the novel, including references to newspaper articles, to *cofiannau* (biographies of eminent ministers and the like), and to theologians from Augustine to Bonhoeffer. But one entry puts all this material into perspective, and reminds us, as it was intended to remind the author, where the main burden of interest consistently lies: 'Y thema yw bywyd J.T. a K.[:] peidio colli golwg ohonyn nhw yng nghoedwig hanes. [The theme is the life of J.T. and K.: not to lose sight of them in the forest of history.] In the dark forest of history I saw two white figures stumbling through the trees.'

Several versions survive of the opening paragraph of the novel, and they show the way in which it was reworked to produce the present rich ambivalence of tone. Originally the first sentence referred not to 'venerable' hair, but to hair that was simply, neutrally, 'white'. And only in the final text does the printed second sentence appear, with its fine patina of irony: 'The pillow-case was lightly stained by the halo of white hair.' At the same time revision saw the removal of simpler, cruder examples of irony, for instance the description of J.T.'s forehead creasing 'cautiously as if into deep thought', as he strains to break wind. Mere details though these changes may seem to be, they are in fact examples of the even-handed care Emyr Humphreys takes, from the outset, to present J.T. to us in a double focus that complicates judgement. His character is suspended somehow, somewhere, between vanity and humility, between comedy and dignity; and our judgement of him is in turn suspended between admiration and condemnation. To the very end of the novel his essential identity is as uncertain as, at the beginning, are the letters needed to fill the enigmatic blanks between his 'initials . . . stamped at a distance from each other across the front' of his collar box.

Also omitted from the printed text was the sentence, 'If he were to move his head sufficiently, and if he opened his eyes, he would see what time it was.' This makes the mistake of appearing to impute to the sleepy J.T. a lazy unwillingness to look at the clock – precisely the convenient habit of wilfully selective vision which enables him, according to hostile witnesses as different as Lydia, Isaac Dafydd and Vernon's wife Sandra, self-indulgently to avoid seeing people and situations as they really are. The novel itself, however, never fully endorses this view – hence the omission of that offending sentence. Instead, the narrative discourse in general carefully allows for the possibility of J.T.'s being selfless rather than selfish, and balances unquestionable disasters like the death of Cynwal against occasions of unalloyed altruism, such as when he gives away his grandmother's cottage. Something of a spiritual Quixote, he seems oblivious to the havoc he creates around him, whether in the comical form of a shattered butter-dish, or in the tragic shape of an embittered wife and an alienated son. The morally equivocal nature of the world J.T. inhabits is delicately suggested by the description of him waking: 'He saw the haze of light that took the colour of warmth and sunshine from the worn curtains, although it was in fact a dull day outside.' The indefatigably practical Kate has, of course, long since been downstairs, cleaning the grate, preparing breakfast and philosophically taking the gloomy August day just as it is. Is she then the very embodiment of the reality principle – a Martha to his Mary, and a Sancho Panza to his Quixote? Dumpy Kate, fishing her glass eye out of the prunes, would seem to be an altogether more robustly sensible character than the elderly J.T. who mouths benedictions, preens himself rather in front of the mirror and pores over his ancient sermons. Her strengths, however, turn out to be inseparable from her weaknesses. Her indomitable matter-of-factness makes her refuse to see the quiet despair behind Mr Hobley's attempted suicide. And although she is admirably stoical, she has never ceased to be her father's dutiful daughter, able to fulfil herself only through docile service, while irritably resenting the fact. The jealousy which was the suppressed aspect of her devotion to her rebellious sister Lydia is given full expression through her resentment of her niece Thea.

In fact, the notes suggest that *Outside the House of Baal* has been deliberately provided with a sexual subtext, the subconscious of the novel, as it were, since the text rarely acknowledges its presence. 'When I write', says Emyr Humphreys in one jotting, 'I try to be aware of Joyce and Wittgenstein, of Freud and Marx, and even of Bartok and Stravinsky and Roger Hilton' – Hilton being an artist whose abstract paintings are admired by the author. The diluted influence of Freud is, I believe, particularly evident in the key scene where the lovemaking of Lydia and J.T. is interrupted by the news that Kate's eye has been scratched out by a thorn. Kate it was, and not Lydia, who should have brought J.T. his food that afternoon, and throughout the novel the preparing and the eating of food is implicitly associated with strong emotions such as love and passion. Indeed, the later scene when Jenny Leyshon prepares a meal for J.T., in Lydia's absence, is closely modelled on this earlier scene where J.T. returns to his half-derelict cottage, tired, wet and hungry, and finds that Lydia has lit a fire and filled the house with the delightful smell of freshly baked bread. The fact that Lydia has effectively usurped her place and completed the seduction of J.T. may mean that Kate's loss of an eye is an unconscious act of self-mutilation, a gesture both of sexual revenge and of self-punishment, of the kind she perhaps repeats when she later marries the drunkard Wynne Bannister.

But Bannister first presents himself to her, of course, in the guise of a father-figure, when he comes to make arrangements for Pa's funeral. The influence of Pa on Kate's emotional life, including her sexual preference, is very deep, as can be seen from the terms of her rejection of her various suitors. Appropriately enough, she is washing Pa's drawers when she first hears J.T.'s voice – he having been brought to Argoed by Griff when Pa is away from home – and the irritable affection with which she treats J.T. in old age replicates the relationship between herself and Pa when they two alone are left at Argoed.

Lydia, on the other hand, is initially drawn to J.T. in part because Pa disapproves of his supposed levity; but her attachment to him is reinforced not only by the rivalry for his affections that develops between Kate and herself but also by the closeness between J.T. and her favourite brother and fellow rebel, Griff. In these ways J.T. is from the beginning involved, unawares, in the relatively innocent sexual politics of the Argoed family.

The intricate system of relationships that binds the family together is brilliantly suggested in the opening section of chapter 2 where scarcely a word is spoken as Ma leaves Argoed to die. As in silent films, meaning is conveyed almost entirely through an eloquent code of movements and gestures. This is a mode of signification sensitively and suggestively used throughout the entire novel – think, for example, of the way Griff, having just confessed to J.T. that he is no longer a Christian believer, puts his arm on his shoulder, as J.T. clambers up the slope to join him, so that as 'J.T. came level with him . . . Griff's arm was lifted upwards by the movement' – but in this particular scene it reaches a height of balletic perfection. The powerful impression given of a close-knit family functioning as an organic feudal unit serves partly to offset the subsequent impression formed of exploitation and dissension, and so lends some colour of credence, at least, to the later nostalgic yearnings of Lydia and Kate for the good times at Argoed. Equally important is the way Emyr Humphreys follows this scene with a picture of young Joe disconsolately sitting alone on the window-sill of the classroom, keeping watch while his father is secretly refilling his whisky flask. The contrast between the two scenes is further pointed up by the way they are made to interlock. At the end of the Argoed scene Ned looks down at his trouser-leg because 'Ma had reached out to tug his trousers'. At the beginning of the schoolroom scene, Joe rubs 'his chin against the darnings on the knees of his stockings' – in a self-comforting gesture that is thus made poignantly expressive of his motherless state. Later, it is precisely this unselfconscious air of helplessness that makes the adult J.T. so attractive to certain types of women. At the same time, the habit of self-sufficiency, which he has had to learn early, helps him develop into a spiritual loner, an inner-directed character.

This arrangement of short scenes to chime, contrast, cross-refer and interact is, of course, the primary means by which Emyr Humphreys 'makes meaning by moulding form' in *Outside the House of Baal.* He himself felt the technique was similar in some ways to the exploration of consonances and dissonances in modernist music (hence the references to Stravinsky and Bartok) and in particular to the language of form and colour in abstract art – a feature he specifically discussed, when working on the novel, with his friend the eminent painter Patrick Heron. Undoubtedly, however, the extensive experience he had gained during the fifties from working in radio and television drama greatly influenced his method of working. Most strikingly, it caused him to revise his opinion of the way in which novels were now being read – and to deduce from this a theory of how they should be composed. He formed the view that the new media were sensitizing audiences to certain signs, or signifiers – close-ups, cuts from shot to shot, attitudes, gestures, asides, undertones – and felt a novelist should be taking advantage of the current economy of meaning made available through a sophisticated general awareness of these conventions. At the same time there were older novelistic conventions – of authorial omniscience, dense dialogue, psychological analysis etc. – which, he believed, were now superannuated.

Whatever the validity of these theories when regarded as a general principle, they undoubtedly served Emyr Humphreys well as working hypotheses. His scenic structure proved flexible enough to produce a brilliant variety of interpretive effects, as well, of course, as making it easy for him to range over extensive time and space. Note, for instance, the way in which Pa is caught, in an early scene, as his tears are dropping into the clock he is mending. This endears him to us in a way that is never completely cancelled out by all the succeeding episodes in which he almost invariably appears tyrannical and mawkishly self-pitying. One of the latter is the scene where Kate mollycoddles him with hot milk and whisky – an incident resonantly juxtaposed to the one in which J. T.'s father is found dead on the mountain, an empty Lysol bottle by his side. A poignant impression of mutability is created by the way Aunt Addy makes her one and only appearance in the novel, in the scene describing Ma's departure from Argoed, which follows on from the moment when Kate, startled by the sounds of J.T. flushing the toilet upstairs, lets slip and breaks the butter-dish that 'was a present from Aunt Addy of Denbigh, given to her thirty-four years ago'. Water connects the end of one scene in which Ifan Cole, suffering from a hangover, vomits over the small anvil, with the beginning of another in which Lydia takes Ma's picture apart, in her frantic search for Pa's secret lover. And once this connection is perceived, the reader can reflect that, in their different ways, both Ifan and Lydia are natural rebels. Little Thea, playing on her uncle Ned's northern farm, where her mother has taken refuge from the horrors of the south Wales Valleys, exclaims that 'everything is hungry'. She is referring to the pigs and the hens and the cattle, but in context her childish cry serves to underline the difference between this rural region of plenty and the social deprivation in the depressed industrial areas. Examples could be multiplied endlessly of the ways in which some of the subtlest effects in the novel are the product of the fluid interrelationship of scenes.

It is, however, equally instructive to notice the gaps in the narrative structure, and precisely where they occur. What is remarkable is that silence falls at several of the most crucial points. Ma's death, Kate's reaction to losing her eye, the marriage of Lydia and J.T., the death of Pa, J.T.'s reaction to the death of Lydia – these and other seminal events are bypassed. Considered in conjunction with the scenic structure mentioned above, this practice reminds us that *Outside the House of Baal* is, in Roland Barthes's now familiar terms, a 'writerly' rather than a 'readerly' text. In other words, the reader is called upon to participate very actively in the process of producing meaning – and thus in effect 'writes' the interpretive script for himself or herself.

Barthes was led to this distinction partly through the study of the theory and practice of Bertolt Brecht, and it is worth noting that during the period leading up to the composition of *Outside the House of Baal*, Emyr Humphreys had himself become very interested in Brecht's work. The aspects of the plays that most fascinated him were those recently well described by Catherine Belsey:

> Brecht's solution [to the reader's passive, uncritical acceptance of the world as pictured in a text] was to write a new kind of text, foregrounding contradiction rather than effacing it, and distancing the audience from both text and ideology. In . . . the interrogative text there is no simple hierarchy of discourses such that the reader is offered privileged access to the work's 'truth'. Instead the reader constructs meaning out of the contradictory discourses which the text provides. Barthes speaks of the multiplicity of voices of indeterminate origin in the writable text, the polyphony which deprives the implied author of authority so that the truth of any one of the discourses is not guaranteed by a knowledge of its origin or source.[15]

Compare this with the full text of a notebook entry by Emyr Humphreys, part of which has already been quoted: 'The voice that tells the tale colours everything and invalidates each event. Therefore I am absent & I do not press myself on you.'

It is only by ignoring the polyphony of the text that, it seems to me, readers can, without hesitation or qualification, reach conclusions like the following about *Outside the House of Baal*:

> The book is a full-length portrait of J. T. Miles – a Calvinistic Methodist minister who is the very type of 'the good man' . . . The unfolded narrative shows him 'betraying' Argoed – here the symbol for the older Calvinistic Wales – by marrying the light-minded Lydia rather than her elder sister, Kate.[16]

There is surely, at the very least, much more to be said for Lydia than this, and moreover the novel, in one of its voices, says it. And if one is interested not in the least that can be said for her but in the most, then a powerful case could be made for regarding Lydia (along with other women from Kate, through Mrs Bayliss and Jenny Leyshon, to Norman's neglected Marjorie) as the tragic victim of a complacently masculine world. She escapes from servitude with Pa only to become the 'slave', as she angrily puts it, of the ineffable J.T. A Thea ahead of her time, she is allowed no scope for the exercise of her considerable energy; a feminine Griff, she is denied the opportunities he is given to develop in his own way.

Of course, this is a novel in which every thesis is accompanied by its antithesis, and so a persuasive case counter to the above could be made on behalf, let us say, of J.T. But what is important to realize is that readers are not only openly encouraged (by the way the novel is structured) to enter into the 'debate', they are also made to reflect on the terms of their own preference. This, again, is a Brechtian feature of *Outside the House of Baal*: the novel is designed to bring readers face to face with their own presuppositions and hidden value systems. Moreover, it contextualizes these, showing them to be not uniquely personal to its readers, but rather embedded in a specific period and in a social background. In other words, like Brecht's plays, the novel not only shows us 'history', it leads us to experience ourselves as historical beings. So, for instance, our sneaking preference for J.T. (or of course, for Lydia) is represented to us by the noncommittal text in a manner which makes clear the social origins and ramifications of our judgement. The novel deals as equivocally with time as it does with the main characters, refusing to let the past entirely get the better of the present, or the present of the past. The title would seem to endorse J.T.'s view of contemporary Wales as pub- and club-land, but even in the matter of drink the inhabitants of the past seem scarcely more abstemious than those of the present, and J.T.'s fierce hostility to the 'House of Baal' is understandable in view of his alcoholic father. When Pa querulously complains about the new maid, Kate reminds him of the sharp practices of Mary Parry Rice in the old days. The advances made in medicine are emphasized, and J.T. himself is impatient with the nostalgic maunderings of Henry Bowen, with his lament for the loss of law and order and his complaint about the disrespect of the young. But at the same time, J.T. cannot suppress a pang when he realizes the young photographer with the pigeon on his shoulder has no idea that the dove is the symbol of the Holy Spirit.

The younger generation in the novel is in most other respects more knowing, and also sometimes more honest, than its elders. Thea openly flirts with her father, teasingly treating him as her beau. Norman is more honest about his contribution to the breakdown of his marriage than J.T. ever managed to be. Such frankness, particularly in sexual matters, is graphically suggested by the wartime scene in which J.T., crossing a field on his way to visit Vernon, finds his attention unwillingly riveted to a woman's half-naked body: 'Her white belly and her black pubic hair that were meant to be hidden, had become the centre of the whole landscape.' But his subsequent (and consequent) argument with Ronnie in that same scene brings out the glibness, flip reductiveness and selfishness of his son's outlook on life.

Change itself is shown by the novel to involve unexpected continuities as well as differences. Vernon is very much his father's son, idealistic to a fault. Even Dan Llew's 'modern' mercenariness has its antecedent in Pa's lifelong habit of lifting the stair-carpet, and the old tyrant of Argoed is indeed proud of a son who has prospered because he followed the biblical injunction not to 'bury his talent'. The sad Christian farce performed at Oberammergau is paralleled by what has long been going on in nonconformist Wales. Yet when all is said and done, some of the most powerful scenes in *Outside the House of Baal* are those which plangently convey a scene of the passing of a world, memorably instanced by J.T.'s heart-breaking attempt to speak, on tape, to Lydia's relatives in America. Emyr Humphreys sketched in his notebooks the kind of change he there had in mind: 'Man lives longer – no other physical change but the world frame of his imagination shattered . . . [J.T.'s] children lose faith; his country decays; his family becomes estranged – like Job long ago.' Nevertheless the relationship between past and present in the novel as a whole is more complex and subtle than this. In the last scene but one in which J.T. is featured, we see him poignantly at a loss to prevent the mistakes of the past from being repeated, but this time in a harsher key.

That scene revolves around the incident in which a forlornly lost little boy dirties his pants, and so after a fashion there is a reference right back to the opening paragraph, in which J.T. breaks wind. It is, in fact, noticeable how often 'gross' bodily functions are mentioned in *Outside the House of Baal* – farting, shitting, urinating, vomiting and so on. These are strong reminders that human life, however spiritualized a view of it one takes, inescapably involves an existence in and of the body, an existence which thereby has its comic, distasteful and grotesque aspects with which any serious spiritual philosophy has got to come to terms. The novel shows traditionally puritanical nonconformity, in the shape of the main characters, endeavouring to recognize that, as one of the notes has it, 'the body [is] not an evil thing'. When, therefore, J.T. comes face to face with these physical facts of life, or is simply juxtaposed with them, the maturity of his spiritual vision is implicitly put to the test, as it is when he is seen to struggle, along with Kate, to cope with the potentially humiliating physical disabilities and general bodily decrepitude that accompany old age.

If *Outside the House of Baal* is, as I believe it to be, the best novel that has yet been written in English about Wales, then that is due in no small measure to the central division of mind and of feeling out of which it came, and which it clearly reflects. This division has already been explored, in several of its different manifestations, in the main body of this essay, but in conclusion it may be approached once more via the comments Emyr Humphreys made about the novel *Traed Mewn Cyffion* by his late friend, the great Welsh short-story writer Kate Roberts. His remarks about her talent, and her achievement, apply almost equally to himself as author of *Outside the House of Baal*.

> Kate Roberts belongs to that select category of artist whose work emerges from a given landscape and society with the numinous power of a megalith or a stone circle. This is a status not easily achieved. It requires a combination of servitude and revolt which reflects the relationship between the artist and her society. In retrospect, it is product of a life-long struggle and a life-long commitment: the unceasing urge to be both a free artist and a responsible member of a society under siege from hostile historical forces . . . On the surface the novel would appear to be in the mould of the 'three generations sagas' of popular fiction. But because of the special nature of Kate Roberts's gift and her response to the crisis in the life of her community and the wider upheavals of her time, the novel takes on several of the features of an epic in the classical sense. For example, although her style is bare and her prose is deliberately unadorned, there is throughout the work a note of intensity, a

> quality of song, that echoes the timeless celebration of tribal and social qualities characteristic of epic poets from Homer to the Hengerdd. Almost in spite of the modern critical mode there is an underlying current of praise-poetry. With all their faults and shortcomings these are her people to whom she is tied by indissoluble bonds of attachment.[17]

When the publishers first received the typescript of *Outside the House of Baal* they announced their enthusiasm for it in the form of a telegram to the author which read: 'VERY PLEASED STOP WRITING.' Since Emyr Humphreys happened to be away at work when the telegram arrived, it was opened and read by his young daughter, who then excitedly reported to her baffled father over the phone that his publishers had told him to stop writing immediately. Fortunately Emyr Humphreys did not take that advice – indeed during the third of a century since the novel appeared in 1965 he has published upwards of ten other novels, including the impressive Amy Parry sequence. But *Outside the House of Baal* remains the single best work he has ever produced; a masterpiece among Welsh novels, and a marvellous combination of 'servitude and revolt'.

Notes

1 The remark was made during a discussion with R. S. Thomas, in the programme *Mother's Tongue, not Mother Tongue*, presented by M. Wynn Thomas (BBC Radio 4, August 1986).

2 See John Harris (ed.), Caradoc Evans, *My People* (Bridgend, Seren Books, 1987).

3 For the general background see Kenneth O. Morgan, *Rebirth of a Nation* (Oxford, Oxford University Press, 1980).

4 Emyr Humphreys's own view of this period is to be found in *The Taliesin Tradition* (Bridgend, Seren Books, 1989).

5 For further information about these figures see Meic Stephens (ed.), *The Oxford Companion to the Literature of Wales* (Oxford, Oxford University Press, 1986).

6 Another notable 'rebel' Nonconformist minister of the inter-war years mentioned by Emyr Humphreys in his notes for *Outside the House of Baal* was Tom Nefyn (Williams) (1895–

1958) whose controversial life furnished models for certain events and characters in the novel. Tom Nefyn saw action both in the Dardanelles and in the Middle East during the First World War, and in the process underwent a religious conversion which influenced the remainder of his life. On his return he entered the Calvinistic Methodist ministry where his unorthodox theology, allied with his evangelical readiness to preach a radical social gospel, made him a figure revered by some but disapproved of by others.

7 George M. Ll. Davies, *Pilgrimage of Peace* (London, Fellowship of Reconciliation, 1950), 13.

8 *Pilgrimage of Peace*, 14.

9 In this section I draw heavily on the working notebooks which Emyr and Elinor Humphreys kindly allowed me to consult and that are now in the National Library of Wales. References to *Outside the House of Baal* are to the expanded text published by Seren (1996).

10 Wittgenstein, *Tractatus Logico-Philosophicus*, tr. D. F. Pears and B. F. McGuinness (London, Routledge & Kegan Paul, 1966), 151.

11 This quotation is taken from Emyr Humphreys's notebook. In the translation by Pears and McGuinness the sentence reads: 'It is not *how* things are in the world that is mystical, but *that* it exists' (p. 149).

12 Claudio Magris, *Times Literary Supplement* (7–13 December 1990), 1332.

13 *Tractatus*, 115.

14 Dietrich Bonhoeffer (1906–45) was arrested by the Nazis in April, 1943, imprisoned in Buchenwald and hanged two years later at Flossenburg.

15 Catherine Belsey, *Critical Practice* (London, Methuen, 1980), 129.

16 *Companion to the Literature of Wales*.

17 Emyr Humphreys, 'Under the Yoke', *New Welsh Review*, 3 (Winter 1988), 9–10.

8

Killing John Jones: A Writer Looks Back

TONY CURTIS

I wanted to kill John Jones.

With my bamboo sword I had squeezed through the wire between the concrete fence posts which divided our houses and was charging after him as he scrabbled to the safety of his back kitchen door. My cane rattled once in rage at that tear-blurred door before I turned, wet with anger and frustration, and returned to our garden and the floury aprons of my mother and Gran.

That was in the summer of 1950 and I was in my fourth year to heaven – hell-bent on revenge for god knows what wrong my friend John had committed. Whatever marble-snatching, face-pinching hurt it was I cannot tell, but my Gran Curtis, whose house it was, did not talk to the Joneses at Number 51 next door for over twenty years; and then only when Ernie Jones died. Ernie rode on his polished bike, ticking his way past our gate, every morning for those twenty years and more. He set type in the printing shop of the *Carmarthen Journal*.

Ernie had a bad limp, but coached athletics with the Carmarthen Harriers. In 1958 he was an official in the Commonwealth Games when they were still Empire. He wore his green blazer with pride. I admired that blazer and envied John Jones his three older brothers; muscular men they were already when John, an afterthought, and I, an only thought, played and fought and made up and made up war and the wild west and the Cup Final and the Arms Park and the cricket tests with Brylcreemed Compton, who smiled down on us as Evans the barber basined us tidy.

We were joined together, John Jones and I, in a street of council houses built in 1927 to the north of the town, with fields between us and the cattle mart. Sometime before, and I cannot be clear whether this was a true memory or a memory made up from being told, the field and pond were drained and flattened to make the biggest mart in west Wales. That was our gym, our concrete pitch, our leisure centre of stalls and metal bars and great sliding doors for goals. It was our patch, our secret, our territory. And John Jones always beat me with an instep shot or a wrist-twisting googly, all skills he had got from his brothers, who passed on secrets I had to learn second-hand, by losing to John.

The open side of us was Mr and Mrs John. He worked down the engine sheds, where my Uncle Des rose to be a driver. Mr John was always as black as an African, from the soot inside the boilers he cleaned. As sure as any miner's his lungs were putting on blackface for a grimmer carnival than one we had for the Coronation in our street. On the other, joined side of John Jones was Mr Elias who sat in the summer's sun at the back door making coracles. The wicker frame he bent over was transformed by canvas and pitch into a fishing shell. He would black turtle his way, properly licensed, to the Towy River where we must never play, because boys drowned.

That summer of 1950 my grandmother Williams came down to visit from Lancashire and died at the tea table in our front and only room.

> Remember
>
> Granma Williams dying at tea
>   best china
>   butter and scones
> the whitest of tablecloths.
>
> And I, not understanding, fetching the neighbours
> To gawp.

That bit of clumsy stuff is from *Walk Down a Welsh Wind*, my first publication, a Phoenix Pamphlet done by Harry Chambers in Manchester in 1972. It is from a poem called 'Lay Traps' and talks about another Carmarthen character:

Mr Jones the Lamp, living down Mart Lane
Cut away the hours of his age
Fashioning a peacock out of privet.
Proud, majestic, daft green bird
grew out of itself
back into a hedge
Unseen by the old man, escaping his worrying shears,
His snips and preening.

Early memories of living in Pentrefelin Street are mixed in with references to Vernon Watkins and Dr Bartley – two teachers of mine from the mid-1960s in Swansea University. The Watkins-influenced refrain

Take a branch of holly
Crush the berry
Walk down a Welsh wind
Lay traps to your mind

Shadow a high buzzard
Catch a soft breath
Race the white curling tide
Remember death

sandwiched the fragments in the piece. Give me the child until he is seven. Well, at the end of 1953 I was seven and there was too much left for me to learn to say that I was fixed in any way.

I was born on Boxing Day, 1946 – one of the baby boom, that bulge of births in celebration for the defeat of Hitler and the Japs. Emerging from the five-year tunnel of dark war people married and started children, or started children and married. In the future lay normal life; though the war lived on powerfully in the imagination of boys – I deployed Dinky armoured columns over the carpets, cartwheeled my Spitfire through clouds of bedclothes on summer's nights absurdly light long after bedtime. Donner und Blitzen, Stuka, Hitler, he only had one . . . Belsen.

A few years ago my mother sent me a cutting from the *Carmarthen Journal*: Nurse Evans had died in her eighties. Nurse Evans had been midwife to the town and she brought me to life kicking into a Christmas cold coming. In 1946 being a breach birth stacked the odds against you. In addition to my arrival, and survival, in Pentrefelin Street, 1946 was notable for the birth of Iago Prytherch in *Stones of the Field*, published by Keidrych Rhys's Druid Press a stone's throw away in Lammas Street. In London a young medical student from Cardiff had his first book of poems, *After Every Green Thing*, accepted by Hutchinson.

The year 1946 – *Stones of the Field: The Dark Philosophers: Deaths and Entrances.* A few hours after my birth, Dylan Thomas was up in London giving a talk about the 1946 he had had, 'The Crumbs of One Man's Year':

> Slung as though in a hammock, or a lull, between one Christmas for ever over and a New Year nearing, full of relentless surprises, waywardly and gladly I pry back at those wizening twelve months and see only a waltzing snippet of the tipsy-turvy times, flickers of vistas, flashes of queer fishes, patches and chequers of a bard's-eye view.
>
> Of what is coming in the New Year I know nothing, except that all that is certain will come like thunderclaps or like comets in the shape of four-leaved clovers, and that all that is unforeseen will appear with the certainty of the sun who every morning shakes a leg in the sky; and of what has gone I know only shilly-shally snatches and flecks and dabs, dazzle and froth; a simple second caught in coursing snow-light, an instant, gay or sorry, struck motionless in the curve of flight like a bird or a scythe; the spindrift leaf and stray-paper whirl, canter, quarrel, and people-chase of everybody's street: suddenly the way the grotesque wind slashes and freezes at a corner the clothes of a passer-by, so that she stays remembered, cold and still until the world like a night-light in a nursery goes out; and a waddling couple of the small occurrences, comic as ducks, that quack their way through our calamitous days; whits and dots and tittles.

For us, the days to come were to be calamitous. The year before, 1945, had seen the death of my grandfather Curtis, and my parents had moved from their flat in Ammanford to Number 50 with my Gran, supposedly so that my father could care for her. She was built like a farm woman and was more likely to care for them and her new grandson, whether asked or not. Then 1947 was surely 'the black colossal year', for within weeks of my birth on the Boxing Day of 1946 my Grandfather Williams became seriously ill with cancer. My mother took the train back to Warrington and stayed there for weeks to nurse him. Weeks and weeks as he died and the winter forgot to end, giving Britain its worst snow of the century. In that snow all those miles drifted us apart. She lost me to my grandmother Curtis whose Pembrokeshire farm daughter's hands held me firm through much of my first year. I was torn untimely from my mother's arms and it was a wrench which severed whatever semblance of unity there might have been at Number 50. You can see it in all the photographs:

The Shutters

I take a rotten photograph
I always have.

Mother, what the album shows again and again
is the three of us – two women separated
by a generation, a marriage bed
and a single, spoilt son.

We three pose at the backdoor –
you hold the pedal car I steer
but Gran perches my bear on the bonnet
and I'm looking at her.

Down our garden path at Pentrefelin
I threaten the flower border,
toddling towards the camera
buffered at chest and bottom by her strong hands.

On the green at Llanstephan
I sit smiling, on the bench next to Gran
and, Mother, you are looking knives
into the side of her head.

Was that a minute before or after
the one that has me in the crook
of her broad arm, tickled while Dad jokes
to hold his pipe to her smoking ear?

In all those snaps
Gran took a good photograph,

face set to the lens. A look
that unnerved my father's grip –

each print has strokes of wild light
that flamed through the clumsy shutter.
What shapes us is clear, developed, fixed tight.
The two of us are still there, Mother.

My father worked as an auto-electrician, never a mechanic, in Nelson's Garage and with his nous and my mother's inherited house proceeds from Lancashire he kept us in material goods that were, I suppose, flash. We always had a car, and a car and another car; so many different cars that sometimes coming home from school I would walk past my house by mistake. And we travelled the country, from Newbury where the Curtises began, to the Lancashire of my mother's Barlows, down to Pembrokeshire where the Barrahs and Thomases had farmed, up to Bangor where the Williamses had sailed their coasters the Welsh way up the western coast with slate.

My father worked on cars in those days when you actually repaired them. You removed parts, stripped them and put them right. I would visit him in a devil's kitchen of a place in a lane at the side of the Nelson's Arms, across from the garage. A bare light swung from the ceiling over the guts and organs of cars and great, thick-glass tubs of acid sizzled in their nesting wickerbaskets. His work mate was Willy Wilkins who had saved up and bought a new Austin which he kept locked up at home and would not take out if rain threatened. In order to supplement his income from Nelson's, my father did fiddles for farmers and townsfolk: we often had fresh chickens, not to mention salmon and sewin in under-the-arm sacks as part payment. Later in the 1950s my father erected a new shed, a place to do his fiddles. To pay for the trips, to pay for the cars, to pay for the cigarettes:

My Father

My father is a shadow
growing from my feet.

This shadow grows from one minute
past the noon of my life
and trails me like water.

My father is mending all fifty-three of his cars.
He works in a garden shed
by the caged light of an inspection lamp.
The red glow at his lips shows constantly
small and fierce like an airline overhead
or the startled eye of a fox.

Ash falls onto the greased parts
of the dynamo.
He hawks and spits through the door.

His hands and nails black with grease
come out from the old paint tin
he has filled with petrol.
Like rare birds they rise
their plumage glistening and sharp
spilling green and blue and silver.

Those hands that my forehead meets
briefly and shivering.
Those rough hands I run from
like the borders of a strange country.

The only member of my family who did not earn his living with his hands was my uncle Ivor, my father's Pembrokeshire cousin and headmaster of a tiny school in Angle. Driving the tortuous twists of the A40 to Pembroke, waving to other, occasional and rare cars, we would escape from Number 50 to visit the Old Rectory in Pwllcrochan, some five miles further. Schoolmaster or not, Ivor dirtied his hands in the fields he had planted with potatoes. This was my country heaven, my Fern Hill, where my tractor-driving, shotgun-toting cousins had acres of crows and trees and furrowed earth and cornucopian hedges. Also, the reed-rich, low-bridged stream at the bottom of their lane opened into a treasury of shale and shells with the deep, dangerous haven of Milford stretching out like a lake. Here were the edges of fields crumbling open to reveal roots and the secret underneath of things. Further on up the Cleddau river at Picton Ferry Graham Sutherland was seeing the same thing and turning it into art. I remember the labouring neighbours – Jack Watts, the Merlin of muck, the stockbroker of the seasons:

Jack Watts

squints across a sprouting field,
chews at a leaf, then weighs your crop
to the nearest bag.

Soft cap down to the eyes
and what had been somebody's suit
held by baling cord;
he is pigmented with dirt
as if washing would have drained
away the years' knowledge.

The whole county waits:
in April the Pembrokeshire Earlies come
a stiff, dark green out of the ground.
Jack and his tribe pour
like Winter rats from their cottage.

Jack stops at the stile,
pushes the cap back to the perch of his head,
then walks along a row to what becomes
the centre of the field.
He delivers a potato from the earth,
soil spilling from the web of tubers,
shaking from the clumps.
He scrapes through dirt and skin;
the sweet flesh goes between his leather lips,
a nugget lodging in the jags of his teeth.

He closes his eyes on the taste –
it is the soil crumbling, the crush
of frost, the rain carried in on the sea,
the sweat of planting.

He holds the ridged sweetness to his nose,
between finger and thumb it glistens,
the rarest egg, the first
potato and the last.

Just down the road was Bush Grammar where my three cousins would go on to school. There, just before my John

Jones-warring summer, Roland Mathias appointed Raymond Garlick to an English post. Around the time of my third birthday, Raymond Garlick first published a quarterly local magazine called *Dock Leaves*, a slim booklet of thirty pages. This included four poems by Roland Mathias, a story and four poems by Garlick and 'The Opportunist', a story by Morwydd Rees, whose house in Manorbier, forty years later, my mother was to clean for her sister, who gave me the copy I am reading this from. This is the last verse of Roland's 'A Winter's Day':

> The old tide rocks at the turning, mild
> In his ribmarks over the disappointed sand.
> A youngster who did not smile, or smiled,
> Could lose himself a friend.

Well, I made friends again with John Jones: he had his brothers and his father's blazer, but we had the cars to escape to England and Pembrokeshire. John and I rigged up a tin-can telephone between our cheek-to-cheek bedrooms and swapped our muffled secrets down the tinpot string. The memories I have are of all the absurdly light evenings of summer when bedtime was impossible. The sky clear as the hills up the Towy Valley, the dusk cut by the whistle of trains and the pathetic bleating of lambs in the slaughterhouse at the end of the mart.

> Outside, catching the leavings of light, old Mr. Ives wheezes his way through the apples, fuschias, roses and honeysuckle of his ordered garden. The wheezes are joined by pants and gasps as Mr. John creaks up from inspecting his cabbage, dusted lungs as perforated as any butterfly-crotcheted leaves in his garden. The evenings are radio dramas with predictable, dependable characters, except that I too am included: I can dive bed-rivers, fire bed-guns, at the encircling savages, squirm round pillar rocks, pinned down almost but never quite unto death, by the twanging arrows of pursed lips.
>
> It is a Saturday.
>
> Saturday's marts are bigger than Wednesday's: the dung-smells hold the air until night damps them down.
>
> Mart-dung wafting the town over is a trade-mark.

It has the shit-rich smell of growing things and the fearful stink of death.

It is gone-ten: the last trickles of the hosed pens are far-sluiced; the rolling, late farmers have stumbled back to the cabs of the cattle-trucks and barged their way out of the lorry-park. As they rattle over the grid at the gate their cargoes, wedged smothering sheep, a solitary calf straw-sprawled, cry blindly through the air-slits.

If it is quiet
If the wind is an East wind

In 1953 my Dad brought home a huge, sealed cardboard crate. On the first and only television in the whole of Pentrefelin Street we watched the grey, ghostly shapes of the Coronation. It was magical and murky, like events on another planet. Still, the three or four hours of evening television posed little threat to the golden age of British radio. *Dick Barton Special Agent* and Sunday roasts with *Take It from Here* – Professor Jimmy Edwards, Dick Bentley and, of course, June Whitfield – ooo, Ron! – was always absolutely fabulous.

Out in the world, that sunny seventh summer also saw 60,000 North Korean troops invade the South to provoke a war that would cost dear the Americans in UN helmets and their allies. Six days before, on 11 June, two Jews were electrocuted in Sing Sing. Julius and Ethel Rosenburg were convicted as atom spies. Tom Hopkinson, who was to play such an important part in the success of the Journalism School in Cardiff, resigned from *Picture Post* after James Cameron's story of South Korean brutality was censored. But we were allowed news from James Morris of the conquest of Everest and a new queen, and the party in Pentrefelin Street became a jelly and buns carnival of fancy dress. Britain ruled the world. Including Cyprus, Kenya and Egypt.

Dylan Thomas had spent from that February to June in the United States for the first of his four visits; he returned to Caitlin and his children in the Boat House in Laugharne. The place had been generously provided for him by Margaret Taylor, whose cuckolded husband would – look, nothing up my sleeves or auto-cue – use television to locate us all in our history. In this year Dylan began working on *Under Milk Wood*. In April Frank Sinatra signed for Capital Records and recorded *Songs for Swinging Lovers* – 'Mere alcohol doesn't thrill me at all.' Terifffffically too! In the year of my birth he had filled auditoria with bobby-soxers who screamed louder than anything until the Beatles. In Rhymney, poor Idris Davies, who had come to Wales to die with his mother, finally deserted Gwalia.

Dock Leaves, no.11 (now grown to sixty-eight pages) came out that summer and included a story by the young Swansea reporter Paul Ferris and 'Border Blues' by R. S. Thomas, whose volume *The Minister* was well received by Raymond Garlick. He noticed too the energy of 'Mr Dannie Abse, who edits the distinguished Anglo-American Review Poetry and Poverty [and who] hails from Cardiff'. In 'Poem on my Birthday' he looks back upon his childhood in Wales:

> Quick let me depart from the clock that never
> goes back unless I intrepidly turn it,
> back to that small Jewish boy applauding
> the corner-street heroes, a tree with a lamp-post in it,
> and a red pillar-box post back my tears' arrival;
> and later, my appointments with rare wonder
> kicking the flames back into the ashes of the mind,
> and later a whole catalogue of kisses
> from fast-giggling Gwen and hymn-singing Shan
> into the Welsh houses smelling
> of wet mackintoshes and camphor.

But in the month of my seventh birthday *Dock Leaves,* no.12 would report the death of Dylan Thomas on 9 November in a New York hospital. Alun Talfan Davies spoke of 'his noble humility, patient sincerity and pride of craft'.

Years later, when I became interested, my father said he had seen Dylan many a time in the Nelson's Arms across from the garage supporting the bar and supporting himself with pints and halves from farmers who would pay for verses and rhymes incorporating their names. My Gran declared that Caitlin was 'no better than she should be. Scandal after scandal, that Catling. And wicked.'

In the following issue of *Dock Leaves* the winner of the 'Elegy for Dylan Thomas' competition was printed. It was judged by no less a person than Louis MacNeice. The winner was a young student from Bangor University – Tony Conran. You will have to dig out that issue yourselves to determine the extent to which it was itself affected by Dylanisms.

Two years before, in *Dock Leaves*, no.5, there were photographs of the 'Festival of Britain exhibition of Welsh paintings and Pembrokeshire books and maps displayed in the hall of the grammar school, Pembroke Dock'. You can make out a Frederick Konecamp and Kyffin Williams's portrait of Hugh Thomas (Kyffin Williams catalogue, National Museum of Wales, 1987). There's Arthur Giardelli, I think, and certainly an ebullient *Pianist* by Ceri Richards. The night before Dylan died this most notable of Welsh painters opened a copy of the *Collected Poems* and began to doodle, and then draw, then elaborate in the most marvellous way around the words and in the margins of the poems. A heron holds the fish of the title *Collected Poems* in his long beak; then becomes heron-stork with a swung, swaddling-skull, inverted to make a pot of flowers. There began a wave of poetic metaphor made visible that focused much of Ceri Richards's work until his death in 1971. Last summer, forty-five years later, I bought in Pembrokeshire the lithograph *Origin of Species*, one of the works in which the green force most notably fuses into life. It was the last thing Richards signed, in 1971.

In Number 50, Pentrefelin Street I was still filling exercise book after book with pasted cigarette cards and cuttings from the *Eagle* – birds, beasts and bombers – to make my own books. Art for me was school and crayoning and then, in 1957, after the eleven-plus, sat in the cold wall-barred gym of Queen Elizabeth Grammar School for Boys, I met Ethy. I got to the Gram. because my parents wangled (we would say now 'opted') for me to go a little way across town to Pentreporth Junior School instead of the Model School from which both my father and my Uncle Des had emerged without particular distinction. In Pentreporth Mr Lewis top class had done his stuff, and in the September of 1957 I walked up the drive of the Gram. in my creaking-new blazer and stiff cap.

John Jones went to the Model, and so continued to turn left down the road to the secondary modern. I rode my new bike for passing, turned to the right, and was soon in a different

Carmarthen. At the Gram. I loved the sport, now on grass, in teams, instead of the tarmacked confines of the Pentreporth playground. I was short, had grown plump on my Gran's and Mum's competitive cooking, so into the raw-eared front row I went – a hooker, who occasionally emerged in time to see a monkey-faced lad from our team slicing through the centre. Gerald Davies I never knew well, for he was a Welsh-speaker and the Gram. was segregated not only from the fenced-off Girls' next door, but down the middle of the language divide. Gerald, in his autobiography, talks of going up to the Gram., in 1957 under his Tony Curtis quiff, which was all the rage. I had to live with that problem too. If I had known that I was to become a writer I would have taken the Welsh way and changed my name to something more nationally correct. I am a Carmarthen-born monoglot because our Welsh died when my Grandfather Williams went from Bangor for the work in Lancashire and married a Barlow, because my Grandmother's Barrahs were Jeffreyston farmers, because the Curtises were Berkshire farm-workers. And because in Pentreporth School Miss Jenkins, the fiery-haired Welsh teacher, was also fiery-tempered. It was legend that she had broken a boy's arm the year before us. She also spat like a fire-hose on the double Ls. Last year the whole place was brought down to extend a bloody car park. And the Methodist chapel my mother took me to is now women's lingerie in the M&S store.

Teachers up at Carmarthen Gram. were, I suppose, the usual mixture of characters – inspired, frustrated and weird. Gwyn Thomas described his time as a schoolteacher in this period:

> It was a calling that yielded me much happiness and gaiety. Apart from the gruesome chore of teaching the grammar of a foreign language to lads who lived in terms of an uneasy truce with the grammar of their own country, I would have thought myself among the blessed of the earth . . . I loved the endless supply of white, free chalk and the splendid sensation of becoming invisible beneath a falling pall of chalkdust.
>
> (*Artists in Wales*, ed. Stephens, 1975.)

Next to Griffiths Chem., who bore the scars of a tank explosion in the war, and Bonzo Davies who, when you had forgotten your maths homework, slippered your backside with a dap that had the word 'Bonzo"' written on it in chalk backwards, Ethy the Art was one of the weirdest. I do not recall what we called them in those days, but Ethy was a 'Nancy', a 'bum-boy'. You filled your water-jar and rinsed your splayed brushes at the sink in the corner of his room. This was obscured by the blackboard on wheels and it was said that he would corner you in that corner, given half a chance. I cannot say whether this was true, but it made a good story. However, it also meant that I reached the age of sixteen and a fail in O Level art believing that trees were green at the top and brown all the way down to the uniformly greened ground. In his cupboard Ethy had a statue of Michaelangelo's *David*, with fig-leaves where you had to have fig-leaves in the fifties. The knack was to beknacker the David with pencilled pubes while Ethy was distracted behind the board. This contrived to encourage a rebellious approach traditionally associated with the artistic temperament as well as the useful skill of executing the lightning sketch.

Twenty years before, in 1937, when Keidrych Rhys published the first edition of *Wales* from 21a, Lammas Street, the issue included Vernon Watkins, Dylan Thomas, Glyn Jones and Ken Etheridge:

> The boy's green song and the lyric of youth
> is a spent dream in the fingertip
> of the trees.

Ken Etheridge published his book *Poems of a Decade* in 1958 and a *Collected Drawings* in 1970. He wrote on design for the amateur theatre and on traditional Welsh costume. We knew nothing of this, of course. He exhibited in London and throughout Wales, but was always destined to be a minor figure in both arts. Taking a pencil rubber constantly to the befigged genitals of David could not have helped.

I can remember little of the academic work from those three years at Queen Elizabeth Grammar School for Boys. Chemistry was a foreign language. And so was French. I remember *King Solomon's Mines* in English and *Carnival of the Animals* from music. In my second year we were all recruited for a mammoth school choir, regardless of singing ability. We practised and practised Handel's *Messiah*, eventually recording the piece for the Welsh Home Service to be used in a radio play about an idealistic music master who recruited every boy for a version of Handel's *Messiah*, regardless of singing ability. We rehearsed for weeks and were finally marched down to a large chapel in Lammas Street to record the piece. I remember listening to the play on the radio and feeling strange and proud.

Nearly forty years later I tried to dramatize and make humorous the whole Queen Elizabeth Grammar School experience.

The Grammar

They were never dull, those half-remembered,
half-composed men, our masters.

We joined with them in some conspiracy
(the grey-trousered 'Fifties needed authority)

and the hurts they did us dull down the years,
those classroom NCO's from some distant war of tears.

Some had survived, like Jenkins Chem whose face
was one big scar from when his tank bought it at Falaise.

Others missed the show, or dodged the chance to fight:
they lived through peacetime's sterile wank.

Perhaps they took it out on us, the celebration
fruit of victory over Hitler and the Japs; a generation

not long enough on the branch, fallen,
rotten on coffee and juke-box rock'n'roll.

We made them the stuff of boyhood myth, and all
colluded in that corridored game they played.

We had the hatred of all arty things
an all-male institution brings:

Roberts Music played us Chopin, the poof,
but set us shivering with that Mussorgsky stuff.

Ethy the Art taught us nothing at all. Smutty
Michaelangeloes, we'd draw in his David's classical balls

and rather die than meet him behind the board
– hands on flies, backs to the wall.

Maths when Bonzo Davies would chalk backwards on a dap
BONZO – and print it on your bum with a public wack.

And all the time the skirmishings ran on:
their job to keep us under the thumb;

our skill in changing words of the hymns
and silent, riotous farting in the assembly gyms.

Then stinging ears, arse canings.
A system of rude awakenings.

Those well-remembered, rarely-composed men, our masters,
colour in our formative years, the clever bastards.

The thing that kept me in touch with books was outside school. Mr Ives who lived two up from us, on the corner, had become too old to make it up to the town library, so I ran this errand for him. Twenty years later, in a self-published Edge Press pamphlet, I tried to write about it:

Noose and Fifty

He should have been fierce, a bellicose voice and clenched fist at our clumsy football. An old man from my first memory of him, his gentleness hung over the large end-house garden with a heady scent of honeysuckle, hydrangea and roses.

There was a richness to his vegetable patch: tight, white cauliflowers, an intricacy of high runner beans. A hedge of blood-red fuschias:

prise apart the closed bell
pull the central stamen
draw the white root across
the tip of your tongue
suck the sickly sweetness.

That portly, quiet Falstaff of a man with a soft moon-face. A walrus-moustache on folds of leathery cheeks. A voice echoing my faraway uncles in Berkshire. A passion for flowers and murder.

Saturday mornings he'd send me to the library up Town Hill. And the titles were uniform:

'Murder most Sweet'.
'Make Mine Murder'.
'The Colonel's last Call'.

Though he would never remember them from one Saturday to the next.

He used a personal symbol: a noose in thick red crayon within, the number 48, his house number. This sign was meticulously made on the inside back cover of every murder mystery he'd read. He consumed three of these books every week and they sustained him into his 80's, for apart from the hard cheese which permanently slabbed the middle of his kitchen table, and the occasional tart which Gran had taken round to the back door for 'the old man' (Gran was barely seventy) there appeared to be nothing else to nourish him.

For four years I bore the books until (like my predecessors) it seemed to me that the crime section held no volume unmarked by the noose.

His eyes, twinkling with light from their deep-set nests of wrinkled skin would cloud only at the sight of a hastily snatched or misplaced Romance:

'Soapy daft stuff!'

or a murder that resolved itself into a homicide in, say, Chicago:

'These 'merican murders ain't proper. Lotta rubbish.'
'Think they're clever!'
'Bring me no girl's stuff or Yankee stuff!'

So I stuck to the spines with stubby, smoking guns and always skip-read the first page to determine location and Scotland Yard pedigree of the sleuth. An Education: the library
had Anthropology: sexual myths of the Polynesians.
Medicine
The Occult –
root and shell
bone and blood
hoof and hawk
'Bring me no girl's stuff or Yankee stuff!'
An education:
'That's m'boy. Got me a couple of good 'uns?'

'Plenty of blood? Here sit yourself down – Have some of this'. –

DRY FLY

I

tasted sherry for the first time.
It tasted rich and heady and old:

like the mustiness of his house, and in sipping the sherry it seemed that I was partaking of his age, the essence of the man:

the dust, the wooden fireplace, the heavy volumes of the Great War, illustrated – with the jingoistic headlines of the newspapers

'The Hun Eats His Words'
'Brace Tommy Batters the Teuton'.

photos of blunt, clumsy, great guns, the cheery crippled disembarking from the blind sides of mountainous liners.

An atmosphere that was museum and real.

Every night at half past nine he walked to the end of our street, turned the corner down to the Brynmawr Arms and drank a pint of watery mild.

At ten-thirty he would slowly return, creaking like the leather of a bellows, stick measuring the pavement into lengths, becoming shorter and shorter. Up to the squeaking of his green metal gate, the click of the front door against the dark like the tick of a clock.

Those illustrated books on the First World War, together with the marvellous twenty-six-episode BBC TV series in 1984, laid the foundations for my history poems of the 1980s which form the core of a selection of such work published by Seren as *War Voices* in 1995.

In 1957 Miles Davis was *Miles Ahead*, but he, of course, did not feature on the wind-up player at the corner shop across from the Gram.'s front gates. This was where the slicked-back boys bought their single Woodbines – always very conscious – and, before Conti's cafe in town cottoned on with a juke-box, the milky steam of frothy coffee. The echoey, biscuit-tin percussion of Buddy Holly was riveting. And Elvis with that leather voice before it got caramel-sweet and smooth. And the Everlys' sweet harmony.

> The movie's over:
> It's twelve o'clock
> And we're in trouble deep.

Ah, neat inversion, so easily forgiven. But for me the movie had just begun. In the Lyric and the Capitol we matinée'd into fumbling puberty – to the backdrop of black and white thrills, murderers on the stairs, teenage rebellion in mayhem and sleaze which was always announced by bebop from blowing hot and cooling Miles and balloon-cheeked Dizzy Gillespie. And, in the middle of *Three Coins in the Fountain* I made it to the back row and my first kiss from a girl who limped – well, I was fat and short, and that bit of hair at the back just would not stay down, so the odds had to be short too.

Couples from the Fifties

Vague shapes stiff and grey all those miles away
The Coronation in our front-room — dull monotype, limited edition.

I smelt the Alvis's leather back seat as my father's radio declared
War on Egypt – the Suez route to India, East of Anthony Eden.

Mau Mau, Eoka, National Service, Singapore, Berlin.
The war won, the Empire dimming, the curtains coming down.

Rock'n'Roll came to Carmarthen, two years late – the usherettes
Amazed as kids jived in the *Lyric*'s aisles, just like the *Pathé News*

Buddy, Elvis, Cliff, Gene, the original Comets and Bill.
The sweetest love-song ya ever heard – Don and Phil.

The outcasts, the lunch-time loners, the misunderstood
We trekked to the lost geyser springs of Fecci's espresso.

Coffee steam blends with Woodbine smoke and through it all
The Mekin juke-box doing slow-motion card tricks.

In Blackpool I held out my autograph book for David Nixon – in colour!
Who made cards machine-gun, vanish, then float back into view like gulls.

Dad's challenge – up the Lynton hill in the little black Austin, first gear:
Then back down on the brake to what the sea had left of the sea-wall, Lynmouth.

In the grey-dark matinées of the *Lyric* I plundered
The idea of oysters in a coral reef of petticoats.

The year 1957 also saw the publication, by *Dock Leaves,* of Roland Mathias's *Eleven Men of Eppynt.* Also T. Harri Jones's *The Enemy in the Heart,* while the two young lions of English poetry – Gunn and Hughes – were well received, in turn, by Roland Mathias. Jonah Jones was glad to have David Bell's *The Artist in Wales,* but concurred with the author that the painter in post-war Wales was having a hard time of it. Ethy certainly would have agreed. *Dock Leaves* no.22 signed off on that note and, in the following year, 1958, became the *Anglo-Welsh Review incorporating Dock Leaves,* Vol.9, no.23. In his first editorial under that title Raymond Garlick applauded the establishment in 1957 of the W. D. Thomas Memorial Lecture at University College, Swansea, especially as the speaker, Professor Gwyn Jones, had chosen Anglo-Welsh literature as his topic. Raymond Garlick said:

> It is thus a cause of the greatest encouragement that at last a lecture has been delivered before the University whose whole subject-matter was Anglo-Welsh literature, and that a publication of the University of Wales Press (namely the printed form of this lecture) should bear on its opening page these words, albeit as a subtitle. 'The First Forty Years: some notes on Anglo-Welsh Literature'.

So 'Anglo-Welsh' was to be the call to arms in publishing and education. It was significant, too, that 'the University whose four colleges have bred so many of the writers to whom the term is properly applicable, but to whose achievement the University has been so indifferent a mother', had conferred an honorary doctorate on Mr Richard Hughes.

The newly titled magazine provided the same mixture as before – creative writing, reviews, articles on Welsh affairs and useful (despite the grey and white printing) reproductions of art from Wales. No.23 provided examples of John Elwyn's work which, following the 'Four works, with notes' features on Brenda Chamberlain and Kyffin Williams, set a standard of concern for arts beyond the written. *Planet* has notably continued that concern, while the *Anglo-Welsh Review*'s successor, the *New Welsh Review,* whose editorial board I have recently left, seems regrettably set against the visual arts.

In 1958 that first issue also reviewed Paul Ferris's first novel, Dannie Abse's *Tenants of the House* and Emyr Humphreys's *The Italian Wife*. Another ten years on saw my first poems accepted (and paid for) by Roland Mathias, who would take over the editorship in 1961. That was the moment for me when the aspirations and pretensions earned credibility, and 7*s.* 6d. for two Berni Inn steak meals in Swansea High Street.

But that was another decade, another place. Reached via Pembrokeshire. In the last winter months of the 1950s my Aunt Annie from Kilgetty came up to my Gran, her sister, to die. My father had just left Nelson's Garage and was trying to earn a white-collar, fingernail-clean living selling insurance. With the promise of a job for him with the Pru, we prepared to move out finally from Number 50. My mother grabbed at the freedom, my father, who had always claimed that the weather always cleared as we drove past the county border sign westwards through the village of Red Roses, dreamed his dreams.

That last Carmarthen summer was the summer of the Park and girls. The Park had always been an important place – sports ground, adventure space. Swings and slide and a roundabout and a football pitch surrounded by the cambered concrete of a cycling track. We had Reg-Harrised our interminable way around and around that track and dizzied hours away on the roundabout with shoes pared to nothing by the braking. But in 1959 and 1960 me and my mates from the Gram. watched Ronnie James strut his stuff with Gram. girls and then tried it for ourselves. Ronnie was just a couple of months older than me, but he was cocksure, with hair just like Phil Everly's. We tumbled down the grass embankments and chased squeals around the bandstand. Ronnie left school early and went to work in a garage. It could have happened to me too, except that Aunt Annie died and I left the bad lot I had got in with at Queen Elizabeth and started in Greenhill, Tenby, in September 1960. At the beginning of August I went up the Park for the last time in my new Tenby blazer, with blue piping round the lapels and hems. And got it muddy.

Round and round and more of the same – I played rugby, better this time – winning a Pembrokeshire schoolboy county cap. When we played Carmarthen District it was in Carmarthen Park, the corner flags tucked tight and perilously into the cycling track. I still played hooker. The Carmarthen scrum-half, who proved a nifty number nine, was John Jones. After that season came O levels – I got four – and then I was traumatized by another big freeze – this was the worst since 1947. I was in Haverfordwest Hospital, 1962, with an appendix removed and some junk left in my stomach by the butcher who did it. I remember staggering from bed to look in the mirror in the toilet one morning and seeing a thin kid staring back at me. My parents were snowed out and apart from me by the fifteen miles that separated Kilgetty from Haverfordwest, and I got very, very miserable.

The Wilderness of Bone

Frost and snow
Form an efficient cage,
Whose crystal bars cannot be melted
By the heart's rage.

as R. S. Thomas wrote back in 1946, the year of my birth.

The abscess burst eventually and the experience was one of an intense awareness of mortality. I remember to this day the moment when I first realized that there was death. Just after my Grandmother Williams died at our tea table in Pentrefelin Street, my mother was taking me to Pentreporth infants. At the edge of the road I stopped and said, 'Gran who came is dead, isn't she?' In Withybush Hospital, with my self-portrait in that mirror, death for me ceased to be a third-person event.

I had scraped into the sixth form after resitting two of my failed O levels and did English and history in a classroom overlooking Kiln Park, the golf course and, beyond, Caldey Island, where the poet David Jones had first become the painter. Here the accents were more mixed, more English, and the school was mixed. In my third-year sixth I wrote my first poem. Forced to do something for the school magazine, I thought that a poem would be the quickest thing. It was a dull thing about getting up and catching the bus in to school, but they took it, of course, and the bug had bitten. I liked the tidy shape of words in the poems we had studied and at the end of my first term at Swansea University I asked for a typewriter for Christmas. That was serious stuff.

The Tenby Arts Club always remind you when you visit them that in 1952 Dylan Thomas gave them a world-première reading from the script that was to become *Under Milk Wood.*

Dylan Thomas at Tenby

Into the pause, while peppermints were passed
after the strong piano's breathless Brahms,
he walked and took his place, sat down and cast

(expressionless of face) an eye abroad,
moving the carafe with a marked distaste.
His fame proclaimed, he looked politely bored

and crossed his legs and lit a cigarette,
screwing his eyes up at the smart of smoke.
So all was done and said. The scene was set

for speech, and nervously he stirred and spoke –
shuffling the pack of papers on his knee,
at random drew one, stared at it and woke

into awareness. Now the sleeping town
under the wood of Wales sat up and sang,
rose from its river bed and eiderdown

of ducks, strode heron-stilted through the dark
and rode white horses, nightmares from the sea,
across a cantref to this bay's bright arc

and the Noah of a poet calling there
to his creatures to come. Two by two, word
by word they marched from his mouth, pair by pair

to the beat of the drum of his tongue
and the trumpet of his lips. In the ships
of his speech the sage sailed and was sung.

And Tenby, their harbour, attended.
It was October, the month of birthdays.
The saga was nearly ended.

That was how Raymond Garlick remembered it anyway. Some of my teachers at Greenhill School were Arts Club members, but no one thought fit to tell us about that notable evening. At UC Swansea a few years later I remember being told that, as we were probably fed up with Swansea's poet, we would not be studying him on the modern British and American course which I had opted for. I had to dig out the poems for myself later, and largely owing to the influence of Vernon Watkins. 'Swansea's other poet' had retired from the bank and was made Guggenheim Fellow at the university. He gave classes to my modern option group in the 1966/7 year. These were unstructured and confusing affairs. He knew everything, and every poet, while we knew next to nothing. He was, though, no teacher of wet-behind-the-ears undergraduates, and attendance fell away until most weeks there were just two of us left, and sometimes just myself.

We would watch out for him making his way down the mall past the library, at about the right time in about the right direction, and collar him, guiding him into a room, or on to a bench at Singleton Abbey. I remember from those sessions only fragments – some Wilfred Owen and Dylan Thomas. What stuck was the enthusiasm for the work and his anecdotes – Watkins cycling down to Yeats's tower for tea; Watkins, at Eliot's behest, signing the petition from poets to the American authorities to spare crazy Pound from the firing squad; Watkins firmly declaring his friend Dylan to be a Christian poet. I found both Dylan's and Vernon Watkins's own poetry beyond me at that point. The same was true of Kathleen Raine, who had been invited to the English Society that year at his request. The society was lively with visits from W. R. Rogers, again via Watkins, Dannie Abse, that funny, gloomy man B. S. Johnson, and Jon Silkin, whose four visits coincided with the appearance of *Stand Quarterly*, which he would press on to you in the lunch-time refectory, but were also not unconnected with a female postgraduate student who had a room in the Mumbles.

Vernon Watkins died in the fall of that year, 1967, in Seattle, playing tennis with the net up, as always. Frost's dictum regarding rhyme, taking no account of a weak heart.

In my postgraduate certificate year, 1968/9, I won the university's Clyne Poetry Prize of £5; then my poetry-proselytizing zeal cut its teeth, and almost broke its back, on the pupils at Dyffryn School, Port Talbot. Richard Burton's old school stank with the steel works' filth and was clogged with the frustration of the teachers' tasks. The university 'poets' had been invited, by Sally Roberts Jones, I think, to offer our uncut gems at an evening of folk-music at the Afan Leisure Centre. I remember turning up absurdly early and having our enthusiasm worn down by hour after hour of folk-music. I can still remember the length, if not the gist, of their final offering – a ballad commemorating the Munich air disaster player by player, rivet by rivet. It made *The Ancient Mariner* seem like a sonnet. But he fixed us with his glittering eye and we suffered in hope. The Manchester United dirge was completed, the whole folk-club fraternity packed up, leaving us to read our poems to each other and a very patient Sally Jones.

Later that year the young bards of Swansea eventually found a more receptive audience in Cardiff, where our contemporary but already famous fellow poet Peter Finch had started the No Walls readings.

In that winter's edition of the *Anglo-Welsh Review* I made my first contribution to Anglo-Welsh letters. In an issue which noticed Emyr Humphreys's *Natives*, Ralph Maud's *Poet in the Making* and Dannie Abse's *A Small Desperation*, as well as the first publication of Peter Finch's much-anthologized 'A Welsh Wordscape', Roland had taken the two poems – 'In my Tower' and 'The Garden':

> Coming back to this garden
> After a growth of years
> I am aware of its sameness:
> All is in place, but smaller
> Now that I am man-tall over
> The jungle of beans, curly kale
> And the clustered bright mass

Of dahlias bursting in the sun.
The wood of the fences,
The leaning trestles around the lawn,
These still stand, their brown greening
And flaked by the worrying seasons:
I had not thought them such a colour
Nor the lawn and its apple-tree to be so small.
The clear lake of sailing boats puff-blown
Is a clouded rain-barrel
Rusting now in its uselessness
Leaving me to stare back at myself in its water.

That publication and the Berni steaks, overdone, and rare for students, were a celebration which made up for other disappointments in that last year of the 1960s. Back in the summer I had spent my last student vacation with my parents in Begelly. My father had run out of jobs and luck and money, and was trying to make a go of a tin-shack village store in Begelly. We lived hand-in-till to mouth in a caravan at the back of the plot. I felt that there could well be a Pembrokeshire-based literary magazine, edited, of course by me, and wrote to the fledgeling Welsh Arts Council for support and advice. The literature director called in on me when he was next in Pembrokeshire. A big man came to the village who was big in Sion. And he did come from the book of *Poetry Wales* and confused the young man with words – of Waldo Williams and *Dock Leaves*. And he did slap the boy down.

The rest of the decade I spent in England, in Cheshire where I had my first teaching post – the headmaster was impressed by my Welsh accent and rugby experience. Then followed a post in the West Riding, the Phoenix Pamphlet, a Gregory Award, an LP record, *Five Yorkshire Poets*, with me and Philip Larkin, a trip to America, where I broadcast poems and a talk at SUNY Binghamton's campus radio station in upstate New York State. There I spoke about the roots of my writing, including my having classes with Vernon Watkins. August 1972. The student working as duty engineer came out of the box at the end, shook my hand and said, 'I'm Vernon's son.'

Poems written from that trip to America led to my winning, with Duncan Bush and Nigel Jenkins, the Welsh Arts Council's Young Poets prize. The literature director, mindful of the fact that they had mistakenly awarded the previous prize to Glyn Hughes, that well-known Yorkshireman, phoned me up in the West Riding. 'Where were you born? Are you Welsh?' he said.

Well, what do you think, Meic?

9

'Weaving a Cymric Web'? A Perspective on Contemporary Anglo-Welsh Poetry

SAM ADAMS

A survey which would do full justice to the number and quality of the poets currently writing in English in Wales, or from Wales, would need far more space than can be allowed in this essay. Although mainly concerned with the contemporary scene, it provides some necessary background of the history of Anglo-Welsh poetry since the 1930s during which several major figures, some still writing, are mentioned but without commentary. The work of poets like Dylan Thomas, Vernon Watkins and David Jones among the dead, and of R. S. Thomas and Dannie Abse who continue to flourish, is sufficiently well known to be passed over in this way with little fear of loss. It is, I am afraid, less satisfactory that distinguished poets like Idris Davies, Glyn Jones, Alun Lewis, John Ormond, John Tripp and Harri Webb are given scant attention, along with a number still happily practising their craft and art, Leslie Norris, Roland Mathias, Emyr Humphreys, Sally Roberts Jones, Raymond Garlick and Anthony Conran, all of whom came to the fore in the 1960s or somewhat earlier. Apart from the still-active older poets mentioned above, the outstanding writers of the 1990s were, with a very few exceptions, born in the 1940s and came to prominence in the 1970s. It is to these – Gillian Clarke, Duncan Bush, Tony Curtis, John Davies, Sheenagh Pugh, Robert Minhinnick, Mike Jenkins and Nigel Jenkins – that the greater part of the essay is devoted.

The first anthology of Anglo-Welsh poetry appeared in 1917. It was edited by A. G. Prys-Jones, himself a poet, whose roots lay deep in the Welsh-language culture and heritage of Wales. His aim in publishing the book was 'to give collective utterance to the English-speaking poets of modern Wales *and to show that they too have their message*' (my italics). He clearly had in mind three constituencies: the Welsh-speaking community to which he belonged; the monoglot English-speakers of Wales who appeared to lack a distinctive culture and voice; and readers in England, for the book had a London publisher. 'Prys', as he became widely and affectionately known, chose as the title of his anthology *Welsh Poets*. That should have been self-explanatory, but was not. It might have signified writing translated from the Welsh; indeed, in part it did. The first poems in the book are such translations by H. Idris Bell (later Sir Idris), who was born in Lincolnshire, of a Welsh mother, in due course held the posts of keeper of manuscripts and Egerton librarian at the British Museum, and, having learned his mother's tongue, became one of the outstanding scholars and translators of Welsh literature into the second half of the century. It was he who in 1922 coined the term 'Anglo-Welsh' to denote the work in English of writers Welsh by birth or, like himself, by parentage and allegiance. During the 1930s it acquired currency as a convenient label and has been applied generously also to those who are Welsh by domicile and choice, or willy-nilly by adoption – as from time to time, depending on the anthology you select, Wilfred Owen, Edward Thomas and Gerard Manley Hopkins.

That a similar hyphenation is not applied to writing in English from the other Celtic countries of these islands is probably due to the differences in linguistic balance between their Gaelic and English, and Welsh and English in Wales. In any case, 'Anglo-Irish' has a different connotation and one not entirely irrelevant to this discussion. 'Anglo-Welsh' makes sense because there is still a substantial Welsh-speaking population which has its own splendid literary heritage, its own important contemporary writers, its own media. Those of us who write in English, whether we like it or not, belong to that mainstream of English literature that goes back to Beowulf and a form of the language of which few now have any understanding. The Welsh writers, while by no means insulated from the influences of Anglo-American culture at the end of the twentieth century, have an unbroken lineage extending to the sixth-century poets Aneirin and Taliesin. It is not widely appreciated that publishers in Wales bring out about 500 Welsh-language books each year, more than double the number of books they produce in English, or that financial support for Welsh-language magazines (from the Welsh Office or the Arts Council for Wales) substantially exceeds that for their English-language counterparts. Rather less than a fifth of the population of Wales are able to benefit fully from this provision; by an unexpected irony they are also probably the biggest buyers of Anglo-Welsh material. For Gwyn Jones, novelist, short-story writer, editor, great survivor of the burgeoning of Welsh literary talent in the 1930s, they represented an 'inherited fund of Welshness' that guaranteed the continued existence of Anglo-Welsh writing, as distinguished, he might have added, from writing anywhere in England. As he gathered his thoughts for a public lecture he gave in 1957, he had in mind a corpus of work that, while written in English, was recognizably Welsh by virtue of its content and/or its distinctive modes of expression, as his illustrations from Glyn Jones, Idris Davies and Vernon Watkins, and references to Caradoc Evans and Dylan Thomas among others, amply demonstrated.

Nevertheless, 'Anglo-Welsh' has always been obnoxious to some, because it carries an insupportable taint of colonialism. The views of a few writers, Emyr Humphreys, who for many years has declined to be associated with any publication bearing the label, most prominent among them, have won increasing support in the past decade. It is certainly as common now to hear the alternative, 'Welsh writing in English'. This is an old debate that it might be thought hardly worthwhile to rehearse here. Yet it is shot through with contemporary concerns, particularly in view of the radical political stance of a number of influential younger writers. And, though Gwyn Jones's 'fund of Welshness' is (Praise be!) still there to be drawn upon, would he, if he were giving his lecture today, find as much evidence of it in the work of contemporary English-language writers?

From his vantage point in 1957, Gwyn Jones surveyed the literary scene not focusing on what was around him but on what lay behind - the sudden emergence in the decade 1935–45 of a recognizable group of writers in English who were Welsh by birth or connection. He proposed that it had come about because of a combination of social circumstances: the decline of the Welsh language coinciding with the growth of a large English-speaking population in south Wales; the 'great flowering of Welsh secondary education between the wars'; and the 'intermittent existence of two literary journals, *Wales* and the *Welsh Review*'. This is a sound analysis, though something like chance is also involved in the appearance together of what Gwyn Jones, transferring his metaphor, was later, in his introduction to the *Oxford Book of Welsh Verse in English* (1977) to refer to as 'a sudden flowering' of writing 'associated with the names . . . of David Jones, Idris Davies, Glyn Jones, Vernon Watkins, Brenda Chamberlain, Margiad Evans, R. S. Thomas, Dylan Thomas, Alun Lewis, and maybe a score of others'. The two magazines did not make writers of them, but they were certainly a stimulus and served to identify them, to themselves as well as to the world, as a group. Editorial policy emphasized (in Gwyn Jones's words again) that the writers 'belonged with and to each other . . . [and] . . . despite the barrier of language, that they belonged with and to Wales'.

When Gwyn Jones was penning his lecture, both *Wales* and his own *Welsh Review* had ceased publication, and the only showcase for Welsh writing in English was *Dock Leaves*, the journal of a local arts group in Pembroke Dock, which was growing in ambition and significance under the inspired editorship of Raymond Garlick and steadfast encouragement of Roland Mathias. No wonder Gwyn Jones was disposed to look back. A handful of important poets, notably R. S. Thomas, Glyn Jones and, for a while longer, Vernon Watkins, continued to attract serious and favourable critical attention, but apart from these monuments on the skyline, the literary landscape was for the most part peculiarly bare. Two of the conditions for the development of Anglo-Welsh writing mentioned by Gwyn Jones, a still-growing English-speaking population and a strongly English-orientated secondary education, were still in place, but on their own could not reproduce the burst of talent that had so distinguished the late 1930s and early 1940s. A fresh stimulus was needed. This came with the transformation of *Dock Leaves* into the *Anglo-Welsh Review* in 1957, still initially with Raymond Garlick as editor and, from 1961, Roland Mathias, and the first appearance in 1965 of *Poetry Wales*. The latter was founded by Meic Stephens who, with a brief intermission, remained its editor until 1973. He was also for the first seven numbers publisher and salesman. But *Poetry Wales* was never a small magazine in the usual sense: it always possessed the editor's sense of style and highly developed awareness of literary standards. Within two years, Bryn Griffiths, editor of *Welsh Voices* (1967), the first anthology of 'new Welsh poetry' (though it contained only writing in English) since 1944, was giving much of the credit for the discovery of 'a new generation of poets' and 'renewed vigour in Anglo-Welsh verse' to the magazine. This view met substantial agreement, including from the poets themselves, among whom John Ormond and Leslie Norris stand out, not only for their major contributions to Welsh writing in English, but also for the peculiarity they share that, having first made their marks as poets during the 1940s, they fell silent for some fifteen years, as though waiting to be stirred again to creativity. John Ormond has since told how his 'block' (that Vernon Watkins had, perhaps inadvertently, manœuvred into place) suddenly ended in 1965 with the composition of 'Cathedral Builders', which appeared in the fourth number; one of the first poems in Leslie Norris's mature manner, 'Elegy for Lyn James', was published in the second.

Not long after, in an article in the Winter 1967–8 *Poetry Wales* (no.7), Meic Stephens traced its short but striking history, gave a typically frank, and deserved, critique of the editorial shortcomings manifest in *Welsh Voices*, and painted a fresh scene in which 'Anglo-Welsh poets at last seem to be as numerous as blackberries in the woods'. The title he gave his article, 'The Second Flowering', derived from Gwyn Jones, has acquired a place in the literary nomenclature of Wales. In its first half-dozen numbers the magazine published poems by, among others, R. S. Thomas, Vernon Watkins, Dannie Abse, Roland Mathias, Raymond Garlick, Emyr Humphreys,

Anthony Conran, Leslie Norris and John Ormond (as we have seen), John Tripp, Harri Webb, A. G. Prys-Jones, Alison Bielski, Douglas Phillips, Sally Roberts (Jones), Peter Gruffydd, John Stuart Williams, Herbert Williams and Tom Earley – a remarkable roll-call of poetic talent. Although he could identify a few 'lone wolves' among them, Meic Stephens considered that the new poets in his magazine recognized that they had a great deal in common in their social background and were 'willing to associate as Welshmen and have their work discussed with reference to the culture of Wales'. In this respect he felt they differed from the poets of the 1930s, but he was probably wrong. The evidence indicates that differences in social background were barely, if at all, perceptible and there was just as much sense of association among those who contributed regularly to *Wales* and the *Welsh Review*. What was new, as Meic Stephens goes on to suggest, was 'the growth of national consciousness that [had] taken place in Wales since the war'. With due allowance for the influence that his own active involvement in politics with Plaid Cymru at this time might have had on his judgement, it remains true that a large majority of the poets of the 1960s wore on their sleeves their allegiance to Wales. Glyn Jones's affirmation in *The Dragon Has Two Tongues* (1968), 'while using cheerfully enough the English language, I have never written in it a word about any country other than Wales, or any people other than Welsh people', might not strictly apply to all his fellow writers, but most, at the time, would have heartily endorsed the principle. The great majority would also have fitted that characteristic Anglo-Welsh template of nonconformism in religion and radicalism in politics, because, like the writers of the 1930s, they had been born and brought up in a peculiarly homogeneous working-class society. A good many had origins no more than a hefty stone's throw from a coal mine. They were at least culturally nationalist; if they were not naturally Welsh-speaking, they were learning the language and taking pains to repair the vast holes left in their knowledge of the history of Wales and of Welsh and Anglo-Welsh literature by an education that, for the most part, avoided all reference to them. They applauded the stance of the *Anglo-Welsh Review*, by this time a bulky journal that gave careful critical attention to the whole spectrum of the arts in Wales, which in its editorial columns constantly railed against the neglect of Welsh culture and heritage by schools and the University of Wales, and the blind eye metropolitan reviewers turned on contemporary Anglo-Welsh literature. Several were politically involved, including one or two who were declared Welsh socialist republicans. Harri Webb, John Tripp and R. S. Thomas expressed in their writing views that were variously critical of the abject apathy of the Welsh, the Labour Party, the 'bourgeois establishment', the destruction of landscape by forests and reservoirs, and of a unique and irreplaceable society by tourists and incomers. A poster was made of Harri Webb's inelegant but memorable squib 'Advice to a Young Poet': 'Sing for Wales or shut your trap – / All the rest's a load of crap.'

The Lilting House (1969), a landmark anthology of Anglo-Welsh poetry edited by Meic Stephens and John Stuart Williams, demonstrated that, notwithstanding the gap of years, there was continuity from 1939–45 into the 1960s. A number of poets in its contents list, notably Glyn Jones and R. S. Thomas, of course belong to both periods – and to the 1990s for that matter. There was also the perception, highlighted by Raymond Garlick in his introduction to the anthology, that (as suggested above) some of the poems from both periods were written 'for Wales: in other words, they do not differ in intention from poems written in the Welsh language'. Indeed, by that time Meic Stephens's strong plea (in his 'Second Flowering' article) for a *rapprochement* between the Welsh-language writers and the Anglo-Welsh had been granted, and Yr Academi Gymreig, a long-established elective academy of Welsh-language writers, had opened its doors to an English-language section. *The Lilting House* shows that there are common characteristics also in the poetry of the two periods, beyond the level of specifically Welsh themes and references. Many of the poets are seen to be preoccupied with form and verbal texturing to a degree unfashionable elsewhere. In the 1960s, it was suggested that they were echoing, consciously or otherwise, the metrical intricacy of Welsh poetry. (A similar argument was extended – with Anglo-Welsh adoption papers – to the Metaphysical poets Vaughan, who was certainly Welsh,

Herbert and Donne.) There was an element of truth in this; it had become fairly common for Anglo-Welsh poets to familiarize themselves with *cynghanedd*, a system in Welsh prosody involving specific patterning in the repetition of consonants and internal rhyme, and for some to adapt it to serve their creative purpose – as Gerard Manley Hopkins had done. The subtle chiming of unaccented and accented end-rhymes, from the Welsh *cywydd* metre, was similarly exploited by a few. Over and above this influence, which was not antiquarian because the traditional metres of Welsh poetry are a vital part of the equipment of contemporary practitioners, there were the powerful examples of Vernon Watkins and, especially, Dylan Thomas. These two, however different they may have been in other respects, were alike in their interest in metrical discipline and the sonority of poetry. In their early writing, a number of important poets of the second flowering, notably Leslie Norris and John Ormond, were too obviously influenced by Dylan Thomas. The poems they wrote in the 1960s, however, reveal a technical accomplishment which is their own. As displayed at the climax of Leslie Norris's much anthologized 'Ballad of Billy Rose' and offered here out of context, it may seem overdone, but it is certainly distinctive:

> Ripped across both his eyes was Rose, but we were tough
>
> And clapped him as they wrapped his blindness up
> In busy towels, applauded the wave
> He gave his executioners, cheered the brave
> Blind man as he cleared with a jaunty hop
>
> The top rope.

A great deal of Roland Mathias's poetry is also densely textured in its own uncompromising, muscular way. We have the poet's word that the influence in this case was Edith Sitwell's *Aspects of Modern Poetry* (1934), which dwells on the use of alliteration, assonance and internal rhyme, allied to variation in the pattern of stresses and the placement of the caesura. (In drafting poems, Roland Mathias still takes endless pains with the count of feet.) Many of his earlier poems have extraordinarily complex verbal patterning, but by the 1960s his technical virtuosity had become assimilated into a characteristically taut utterance, as a few lines from 'Brynafan: First Light' must serve to illustrate –

> Within the cruck the night
> Is thick, an animal residue
> Of bones and food, the soupy wash
> Of a working stomach an hour short of its time
> When the light went out for good. To pick
> Heaven out beyond the cotton hill,
> Have knees for drumsticks and the dead hock
> Of day for gnawing . . .

With due allowance for the depredations of time and editorial whim, there are significant differences between *The Lilting House* and Meic Stephens's latest anthology of poetry in English from Wales, *The Bright Field* (1991). Still greater differences are observable between *The Lilting House* and *Burning the Bracken* (1995), an anthology compiled from the work of poets published in the last fifteen years by Seren, the most constructively ambitious of Welsh publishers, which claims to be a definitive sampler of contemporary Anglo-Welsh poetry. Most obviously, there has been a progressive increase in the number of 'Anglo-Welsh' writers born in England or elsewhere. Whereas only seven of the thirty-nine poets in *The Lilting House* were not Welsh by birth, this is the case with more than a quarter of the twenty-six in *The Bright Field* and almost half the forty-six in *Burning the Bracken.* The greater mobility of the population is the likeliest reason. Most of the English-born poets in Seren's list had their university education in Wales and have been employed and resident here for several years. Some have Welsh parents who found *their* jobs and settled in England. A few, like Brian Aspden, with no such familial link, are so rooted that they have become Welsh-speakers, as, at an earlier time, did the Londoner Raymond Garlick. There are also significant differences in the number of women represented in these anthologies: three in *The Lilting House*, six in *The Bright Field*, and seventeen in *Burning the Bracken.* This change is of a piece with developments in the arts and society generally, but it is perhaps more marked in

Wales where, historically, few women have made their mark as writers, though recent research has unearthed a handful from the meagre ranks of the Welsh gentry. Gwyn Jones's *Oxford Book of Welsh Verse in English* (1977), which provides an overview of poetry in Wales from the sixth century, has only three.

The poets of the 1990s, already posited collectively as a 'third flowering', display a different array of characteristics from those that, superficially at least, distinguished the 1960s group. This is, of course, a broad generalization, not least because a number of 1960s poets, and a few of earlier vintage, have continued publishing throughout. None the less, a fault line is perceptible between the poets who first came to prominence in the 1970s and those who had acquired a reputation earlier. With a few notable exceptions, the former are less overtly nationalist in outlook than the latter, less moralistic, less interested in God and spirituality, more concerned about the environment and social issues, more worldly-wise, better travelled and likelier to draw upon their experience of other countries, especially the United States, readier to exploit scholarly interests in their writing. Most have consciously discarded the common markers of Anglo-Welsh poetry, such as use of Welsh place names and reference to Welsh myth and legend. The change is neatly summed up in John Davies's ironic instructions on 'How to Write Anglo-Welsh Poetry':

> First apologise for not being able
> to speak Welsh. Go on: apologise.
> Being Anglo-anything is really tough;
> any gaps you can fill in with sighs.
>
> And get some roots, juggle names like
> Taliesin and ap Gwilym, weave
> a Cymric web. It doesn't matter what
> they wrote, let's not be naive.
>
> Now you can go on about the past
> being more real than the present –
> you've read your early R. S. Thomas,
> you know where Welsh Wales went.

In its rejection of old values this might be seen as a keynote poem, but by a further irony, in important respects the poet is a good deal closer to the 1960s than most of his contemporaries. John Davies has continued to write about home, family and Welsh origins and places, and (as the quotation suggests) is a traditionalist in his frequent use of regular stanza forms and rhyme. He shares with Duncan Bush and Tony Curtis familiarity with the United States and contemporary writers there from having spent a good deal of time in that country, but unlike them, he is constantly aware of linguistic and cultural tensions. The reasons may lie partly in his upbringing in industrial south Wales, and partly in the linguistic divisions within his own family. He does not speak Welsh while those about him do, as 'Sonnet 9' from *Visitor's Book* (1985) describes:

> My wife and daughter speak it, strumming
> on the green places, a running water-beat
> beyond me. But though I've picked up some
> of the words, they do not sound like mine.

In this, his second major book (a pamphlet, *Strangers*, was published in 1971) and in *Flight Patterns* (1991) which followed it, groups of poems are devoted to Wales, his origins in Port Talbot and his family in his present home in Prestatyn on the coast in the north, while others deal with his experience of the USA, where at different times and in different places he has spent three years teaching. The American poems also often refer back to Wales; a reflection couched in American demotic can draw a contrast between attitudes to life and love there, transmitted over the airwaves in popular songs, and those at home:

> To be on their wavelength
> I'd need me a Ford pickup and more.
> Folk I was raised with kept their griefs
> well under wraps . . .
>
> ('Country')

The tension is creative. In poems about his first American journeys, recorded in *At the Edge of Town* (1981), he recognized that rootedness can become 'a cell, / unlocked door tight shut, the window clouded' ('Small Towns'); and yet '. . . there's a tug. You keep looking back' ('Starting Point'). He carries in America the exile's heightened sense of his own country, not that it necessarily weighs heavily upon him. At a post office in the small township named Wales in Utah he writes to a friend –

> Mary Davis scanning
> my postcard asked if that's Welsh. 'No, that's
> my writing,' I said.

Sensitivity about loss of the language is stirred more at home – by a Welsh funeral, or attending the performance of a Welsh play at his daughter's school, where, while wishing he could 'grasp its drift', he falls into a daydream ('The Learning Tree'). There is a good deal of self-deprecating, wry humour in John Davies, and of broad humour too, as in 'Things to Do When the Town's Closed', which celebrates the ridiculous in ordinary life. Indeed, he is a highly complex poet whose work frequently demands careful reading, and a very competent artist into the bargain. He is a gifted poet of landscape and covering sky, of geology and water-seep; water imagery proliferates. His technical virtuosity is displayed in a historical, topographical sonnet sequence, 'Burying the Waste' and, very effectively, in 'Decoys', which contrasts the products of his woodcarving skill with the single-minded purpose of the game-bird hunter. His American experiences have stimulated the adoption of personae, men and women, and the use of free-verse to convey their idiom. Although all the poems exploit colloquial language and imitate the rhythms of speech, in the main, free verse is the medium of those on American themes, while more regular stanzaic forms and rhyme are employed for the Welsh.

'Picture Time', the first poem in *At the Edge of Town,* is about looking at family photographs. A wedding snapshot prompts a reflection about the clan:

> . . . all of us
> made almost each of us quite sure, for once,
> just what we were . . .

A doubt persists with 'almost', and in the end, for John Davies, the question of identity will not go away. The mind can be distracted from it:

> Sometimes staring at Where again
> eases the strain
> of Who . . .

– but not for long.

Gillian Clarke was almost a 1960s poet. Her work appeared for the first time in the Summer 1970 number of *Poetry Wales*. Further poems were published in the autumn and winter numbers and by the end of the year she was well launched as a writer. It is not an exaggeration to say that those initial poems, short lyrics about love, birth, nurturing, partings, loss and death, were a revelation. No previous Anglo-Welsh poet had drawn so consistently upon women's domestic and familial experience, or written about the countryside from so clearly a feminine viewpoint. The poems were not feminist, nor were they sentimental in the way that so much of women's magazine fiction was at the time, although the subject matter was not dissimilar. There was a distinctive shaping power in the diction and imagery, and an artistic objectivity, that lifted these acute observations of ordinary life far above the commmonplace. In 'Birth', the finest of the 1970 poems, she conveyed the physical reality and wonder of the experience through seeing and remembering:

> Hot and slippery, the scalding
> Baby came . . .
> We waited while the calf struggled
> To stand, moved as though this
> Were the first time. I could feel the soft sucking
> Of the new-born, the tugging pleasure
> Of bruised reordering, the signal
> Of milk's incoming tide, and satisfaction
> Fall like a clean sheet around us.

The poem comes to a conclusion as neat as a laundered sheet. This was not always the case with the early work; several of the domestic poems narrowly avoid descent into bathos, especially in their final lines, but there were always also fresh perceptions and images of startling originality. Death recurs frequently as a theme in her early books, the pamphlet *Snow on the Mountain,* and *The Sundial.* Poems record the deaths of creatures, of friends, of strangers, by the slow attrition of sickness, suicide and accident, and through bravado. Gillian Clarke uses a sheep's skull as a stimulus in her creative writing courses and a *memento mori* seems always within reach, from the very early 'little, silver skulls [of lambs that] eyed us darkly' in 'The Fox', to the 'white, fine skull, full up with darkness / As a shell with sea' of a young woman who is the subject of a 'Lunchtime Lecture' at the museum, and later to the horned skull whose 'mortality gapes in the craters of his face' ('Ram'). Death presents the writer with a fact that cannot be explained and an artefact that gives no answers but is peculiarly beautiful. The imagination can dress the young woman's skull with flesh, 'hair and colours and the rustling / Blood' but to what purpose? 'We stare at each other, dark into sightless / Dark, seeing only ourslves in the black pools.' The consolation of religion is absent. At best, there is only the memory of loved ones, which, once it has become objectified, can become the stuff of poetry. It has taken a long time for the poet to come to terms in this way with the death of her father, memorialized in her latest book, *The King of Britain's Daughter* (1993). What hope there is for the future lies in continuation of the species and the cycle of the seasons: down the curving horns of the ram's skull 'a cornucopia of lambs is bleating'.

As might be expected, Gillian Clarke's poetry has become more politically aware, more environmentally concerned. It is hardly possible to live, as she does, in a cottage in rural west Wales, without being conscious of the threats posed by disasters like Chernobyl, or of the low-flying manœuvres of military aircraft. There has been a greater change in the self-critical development of her craft, although her mature voice was there from the outset. She has written herself, in *The Bright Field,* that many of the early poems were 'artlessly, instinctively written', and distinguishes these from her 'deliberate' poems, one of the first of which was 'Letter from a Far Country', collected in the book of the same name in 1982.

This gives expression to feminist anger at the casual discounting and demeaning of the traditional roles of motherhood and home-making, depicted in the lives of her own 'dead grandmothers'. The graceful, intuitive lines that distinguished her earlier writing do not occur so readily in this long poem (nor, indeed, in poems to male ancestors in the same volume), but 'The Hare', an elegy for Frances Horovitz, memorably combines assured technical skill with a profound emotional charge:

> . . . Different
>
> as earth and air, yet in one trace that week
> we towed the calends like boats reining
> the oceans of the world at the full moon.
>
> Suddenly from the fields we heard again
> a baby cry, and standing at the door
> listened for minutes, eyes and ears soon used
>
> to the night. It was cold. In the east
> the river made a breath of shining sound.
> The cattle in the field were shadow black.
>
> A cow coughed. Some slept, and some pulled grass.
> I could smell blossom from the blackthorn
> and see their thorny crowns against the sky.

In 'The King of Britain's Daughter', commissioned for an oratorio, acute memories of childhood holidays on the coast of west Wales and of a father's love and wonderful, strange knowledge are mingled with the myths of Branwen and Bendigeidfran. This long poem sequence has clear links with the poet's early lyrical impulse and frequently surprises with the power and precision of its imagery. At this stage in her career, Gillian Clarke continues to be more closely aligned to the poets of the 1960s than to those who began publishing at about the same time and continue to flourish. Her subject matter is still to be found in the Welsh countryside and coast, in her roots in the rural west and north, and in Welsh myth. She has learned the language.

Apart from John Davies, who, as has been already indicated, is much preoccupied with identity and roots and his own ambivalence towards Welsh, the other poets who emerged about the same time as Gillian Clarke, notably Duncan Bush, Tony Curtis, Sheenagh Pugh and Robert Minhinnick, have different attitudes to Wales and the language. In the case of Duncan Bush this was not apparent at the outset. 'Pneumoconiosis', one of his earliest published poems and probably still the best known, emerged whole in one brief creative surge. Its subject, the dreadful coal-dust disease that afflicts miners, elicits a prompt and angry response in south Wales, and would no doubt in any coalfield region. If, however, it is seen as a 'Welsh' poem, then it is unusual. Duncan Bush considers himself cosmopolitan and, though he has roots in Cardiff, he does not spend time exploring them. In a long and illuminating interview with Richard Poole (in *Poetry Wales*, July 1992), he dismisses the personal perspective, the 'I' and 'we' which dominated much of the poetry of the 1960s – 'To promulgate the personality or personal circumstances of the poet . . . seems to me excessive', and the overt display of Welshness – 'The only recent, new, or future writing in Wales that has been, is, or will be of any use at all is that which has found its way out of a forest [of leeks, the national emblem], or never set foot in it.' In an earlier response to the magazine (20, no.1, 1984) he said,

> You ask to what extent my own work has been influenced by writing in Welsh (or from the Welsh as it would have to be in my case). The answer is not at all . . . As an English speaker I don't incidentally feel less Welsh because of this.

Whether it expresses an allegiance to Wales or not, 'Pneumoconiosis' has important pointers to the poet's subsequent development in its relaxed free verse form, the use of the colloquial language of an adopted persona, the former miner with his 'lung full of budgerigars', and its political thrust. The poem is a reaction to the denial of compensation to the disabled. The plight of mining communities again stirred him to a poetic response at the time of the miners' strike – 'Summer 1984'. Though it is natural to locate his concern close to home, that is not necessarily the case, for the most powerful images of the strike came from Yorkshire, through the medium of television. That television can have a profound impact on a writer whose antennae are well adapted to detect the violent interplay between the oppressed and their oppressors, victim and assailant, wherever and whenever the drama is enacted, is demonstrated by a poem of extraordinary power, 'Living in Real Times – Summer, 1995'. Pictures from the war in Bosnia and from a test match, shown simultaneously on the banks of TV sets in a shop window, are the starting-point for a meditation on man's propensity for inflicting suffering upon his fellow, while others are preoccupied with trivialities. The cricketers on their channel throw up their arms to celebrate a wicket, echoing the gesture of a dying man, shot in a street in some Bosnian town:

> Sarajevo? Mostar? Vukovar? . . . TV's intimate and
> generalising eye makes everywhere somewhere else:
> a province of that small, remote country
> of which we, famously, know little
> still . . .

The viewer recognizes the inevitability of it all: 'Over and over. And forever / and for ever. No Amen.' This is one of those rare exceptions – a poem that employs the first person singular, but to personalize the shared guilt. It is a political poem; consistent with a great deal of his work, it expresses his commitment, not to partisan interests, but to democratic, humane, liberal ideals which, closer to home, lead him to focus upon the inequities in society and the plight of the underprivileged. He is also widely travelled, and exploits in his recent work experiences gained particularly in the United States and in the former Soviet Union as well as extensive reading.

Increasingly Duncan Bush has assumed the personalities and voices of characters in the midst of their dramas. *The Genre of Silence* (1988) is an extraordinary *tour de force*. It purports to be the literary remains, prose fragments and poems, of one Victor Bal, who disappeared in 1938 under the Stalin regime. In addition to Bal himself, whose voice is heard in his poems and in sections from an autobiography, there are the words of an editor, the transcript of an interview, much incidental history, for example about the Union of Soviet

Writers, to which Bal belonged and so on. The accumulated weight of circumstantial evidence is such that at least one reviewer was convinced of Bal's existence. The book was generously praised in some quarters but has not yet received the wider recognition it deserves. In the poet's latest book, *Masks* (1994), the characters are men and women not far from the end of their tether. The mode of expression is soliloquy and the complexities of character and circumstance are such as to require sequences for their expression rather than individual poems. In Brussels a South African mercenary takes a black whore:

> After what these good Belgians did
> to her country and its people,
> can it matter what you or I do with her?'
>
> ('European Capital')

and, his shoe gradually filling with blood from a wound in his thigh, observes people in bars and cafés and meditates on other times. A Welsh farmer's widow contemplates the changing landscape, the pointless destruction of a birch tree, and the equally pointless persistence of the spring sap rising in the stump. Most memorably, in 'Are There Still Wolves in Pennsylvania', a Vietnam veteran, scarred by more than the shrapnel wound he suffered, and his wife move through their personal dreams inexorably towards a violent denouement, though in the characteristic obliqueness of these sequences conclusions can only be guessed at. Free verse, the predominant form in all the books, is used successfully in these poems to convey colloquial speech and distinguish character. It might be thought that with such chameleon qualities Duncan Bush lacks a 'voice' of his own, but that is not so. The quality of intellect that informs all his work is distinctive. Combining as he does intellectual strength, versatility and facility in verbal and dramatic invention, he is a writer of substantial achievement and still greater promise.

After R. S. Thomas and Dannie Abse, Tony Curtis is probably the best-known contemporary Anglo-Welsh poet. This position has been gained, he makes no bones about it, by working at it. He is energetic and prolific, a notable competitor in sport and in his writing. He won the National Poetry Competiton in 1984 and was a runner-up in the Observer/ Arvon competition in 1985. Having studied creative writing at Goddard College, Vermont, he currently heads a similar course at the University of Glamorgan, where he is Professor of Poetry. He is as frank in his poetry as he is at interview (with Robert Minhinnick, *New Welsh Review*, 8, 1990). On the issue of Welshness for example, he believes that a non-Welsh-speaker's 'grip on a Welsh identity is at times precarious'. He sees Welshness as 'a territorial thing' in his poetry, 'but whether . . . racial or cultural I don't know . . . I should learn Welsh, yes, but I'm not taking anything new on board at the moment.' Much of his writing is territorial in the simple sense that the many poems about home, roots and family are set in Wales but, given his south Pembrokeshire background, there were different expectations with regard to Welsh allegiance. In the fifth poem of the 'Pembrokeshire Seams' sequence, from *Letting Go* (1983), he writes:

> To the north, in the next county,
> cottages are put to the torch for the language,
> for the idea of community . . .
>
> Not here; below the Landsker
> we've been eased out of such extremes.

In the long elegy to John Tripp, 'Thoughts from the Holiday Inn', first published in *A Cardiff Anthology* (1987) edited by Meic Stephens, he identifies the time when the momentum of nationalist sympathies sagged, in the wake of the defeat of the plan for a Welsh Assembly in the devolution referendum, 1 March 1979, and the assuaging concessions that followed: '. . . The din / Of justified protest settled after '79 – Welsh cheque books, Channel Four.'

If Welshness and identity receive at best an uncommitted response, he has a wide range of other interests and concerns that have become the carefully cultivated sources of poems. In addition to family and origins, his own children and their well-being, he is deeply interested in art, artists and photography, in the history of both world wars and the Russian Revolution, and in the casual cruelty of oppressors and the fate of the oppressed in any land or time. In the interview with Robert Minhinnick he describes how he was led from an initial interest in the war artist William Orpen to research about the painter's chauffeur, one Grover Williams, who became a motor-racing driver and, in the Second World War led a French resistance cell against the Nazis, was captured and sent to a concentration camp. This in turn led him to read Ellie Wiesel's account of his experiences in Auschwitz. From these sources and others have come poems about the Holocaust and the prize-winning 'The Death of Richard Beattie-Seaman in the Belgian Grand Prix, 1939'. The method he has come to adopt, which he sees as rather like that of Robert Browning, is essentially narrative. In his view, poetry is 'an excellent way of telling a story'.

It is not necessary to seek or guess the major influences on the poetic development of Tony Curtis; with his customary openness, he declares them in 'First Class in the Hold', which describes how, during a rough ferry crossing to Cherbourg, he reads and reflects upon Robert Lowell's *Life Studies* – the major influence:

> I never met or even saw you read
> but it's clear your ghost rides
> in the poets that survive:
> Heaney, Walcott, Dunn,
> write your continuing elegy.
> Unsettled spirit, I'd gladly have
> you shoulder me.

Apart from his postgraduate studies there, he has visited the USA many times and is very familiar with contemporary American poetry, especially of the confessional kind of which he considers Lowell the master. It confirmed a tendency in his own early work, particularly on the theme of mutability. Change and decay and death are continuing concerns. *Letting Go* has as its epigraph Billie Whitelaw's words in a television broadcast about Beckett, 'Death doesn't make any sense if you can't use it'. In Tony Curtis's writing the 'making sense' includes poems like 'On Skrinkle Beach', in which a foul reminder of death, the carcass of a rabbit, and news of other human deaths become an awful warning about the vulnerability of children, and 'That Last Evening', which describes the death of his father. More recently 'Reg Webb', in *War Voices* (1995), an elegiac piece about a seaman who spent the war dodging Atlantic U-boats, reveals the poet's affection and human sympathy as much as his honest gaze at the decay and decrepitude that accompany ageing. It concludes: 'He's lost now, with fire in the hold, and a hard stoke / for one last evasive action, making smoke.'

The confessional poetry and the poems about Pembrokeshire roots usually share these same qualities and are rich in allusion generated from strong narrative structures. The less successful read like superior journalism – which is perhaps not far from the poet's intention. These are as far from 1960s 'texturing', as exemplified by Roland Mathias's work, as it is possible to get. Occasionally, prosiness and more conventionally poetic utterance occur within the same poem, as in 'At Sligo, 1976' where the lines 'I and George and Marjorie from California / join the folk-night crowd' are followed soon after by

> There is a facile purging
> in the fists of drunks,
> a hammering at the gates of life.

Perhaps taking his cue from Walcott in particular, although work of this kind has long been part of his poetic repertoire, he has increasingly adopted personae to tell his stories. There are many examples in his latest book *War Voices*. A few earlier poems, republished here in an appropriate context are less complex and demanding than those composed recently, but all are readily accessible. The stories they tell and the significant detail they contain, given and imagined, are striking. Several are embellished by a kind of historical counterpointing, when the 'now' of the poem recalls past events, or, more tellingly, those that will occur. The poem about the death of Richard Beattie-Seaman is one such, another is 'Portrait of the Painter Hans Theo Richter and his Wife Gisela in Dresden, 1933' which looks out from the peace and beauty of the artist's relationship with his wife to the gathering horror of Hitler's Germany and forward to the fire-storm. It concludes:

From Otto's window the sounds of day –
The baker's boy calling, a neighbour's wireless
Playing marches and then a speech.

There may be a formulaic tendency in re-creations of history, but it is largely avoided in these poems which, at one level, appear as moving human documents. Tony Curtis has found in his selected narratives the means of expressing his instinctive emotional response to life and humanity. Poems like 'Soup', 'Incident on a Hospital Train from Calcutta', 'Trials' and the very remarkable 'The Last Candles', a fragment of history from the Russian Revolution, seem destined to be regular anthology pieces.

Sheenagh Pugh, now also lecturing at the University of Glamorgan, is of mixed Welsh-Irish stock. She was born and brought up in England, but she holidayed in Wales as a child and, in 1971, after studying Russian and German at Bristol University, found employment as a civil servant in Cardiff. Soon after, her poems began to appear in Anglo-Welsh magazines. From information she gave in an interview with Richard Poole (in *Poetry Wales*, January 1995) she appears to have been precocious as both reader and writer. Her choice of reading when young was discriminating and idiosyncratic. Not for her Blake, the Romantics, Hopkins and selected modern Americans, the usual fare of budding poets in the 1960s, but rather those neglected fifteenth to sixteenth-century figures Robert Henryson and Sir Thomas Wyatt. This is characteristic of the poet; she is strenuously individualistic. In her response to an invitation to contribute to a symposium on women's poetry (*Poetry Wales*, 23, no.1), she wrote, 'I object violently to being shunted into some sub-group of humanity and judged as anything but an individual.' She will not accept the label 'woman poet' because she believes poetry should be 'universal and unifying'. In the same piece she stated bluntly, ' . . . if there is such a thing as a poetry which is limited to part of humanity, I think there is a simpler name for it than women's poetry, black poetry or whatever. I think the word is mediocre.' As a student of languages, she has an uncommon depth of knowledge about language *per se* and is a gifted translator. Her fourth book, *Prisoners of Transience* (1985), consists of translations from French and German poets, and in the final section of the latest, *Sing for the Taxman* (1993), verses translated mostly from the German. As translator, she has a regular client in the German poet Hans-Ulrich Treichel and won the Babel prize for translation in 1984.

She is also keenly interested in history and has travelled widely. Experiences gained from books and directly from places overseas, especially in Iceland and more recently, still in pursuit of the Norse theme, the Shetlands, are the most important sources of inspiration in her writing to date. Sorley Maclean, the Gaelic poet from Raasay in the Hebrides, and George Mackay Brown, a man of Orkney, whose work also draws a great deal from Norse saga, are newer enthusiasms. Another, Robert Browning, provided a precious insight into the planning of a sequence of poems about a historical character.

Confessional poetry is not her normal mode. The rare exceptions stand out the more strongly – like 'M.S.A.', the poem with which she won the Welsh Arts Council's Poem for Today competition in 1988. This long, free verse piece takes as its starting-point a television news item about the Iran–Iraq war and tells of the poet's encounter with a party of young Iranians in Berlin sixteen years before. It discusses the differing roles and attitudes of the young men and the one woman in the group, and imagines how the former must have lost that serious, soft innocence they once possessed to become persecutors or victims, 'when one/ murdering old con-man replaced another' in their country. The complicity of our society and ourselves as individuals in barbarism is clear;

> it's the likes of me who counsel
> compromise; who settle for less
> than truth, because it isn't that simple,
> who grow fat at the centre of a web
> of coke pushers, or peddle nerve gas
> to good customers and no questions asked.
> I am the enemy now.

More usually, even an elegy is almost depersonalized. She has written of 'A Matter of Scale' (in introducing her selection of poems in *The Bright Field*), '[it] is about a friend who died in a motorbike accident, and is sincerely meant, but it's true that I loved the sound of the word "Aldebaran" and enjoyed balancing the poem around it.' The necessity of artistic detachment is a problem familiar to poets who write out of sympathy for the suffering of others. In her own case, Sheenagh Pugh explains, 'I hope "detached" doesn't equal "callous", but I don't think poets can work effectively without being somewhat detached from their emotions.' She is a cerebral poet, but not a cold analyst; her wit, her enthusiasms, both recherché and, like snooker, widely shared, contradict that charge. Gwyn Jones, world authority on the Icelandic sagas, would applaud her affection for Egil Skallagrimson. The way in which this, the greatest of the skaldic poets, saved himself from beheading in York by cynically composing a panegyric on his captor, Eirik Bloodaxe, becomes an apt analogy for an ageing popular singer, in the title poem of *Sing for the Taxman*, painfully on the road again, ostensibly to pay his tax debt. But, the poem asks

> who, hearing,
> could ever suppose you had a choice,
> or could do anything but sing,
> as long as the words were there, and your voice?

This celebration of all who have the skill to sing, who can say with Egil:

> I didn't mean
> a single glittering phrase, but Christ,
> can't I craft them, just.

is a delight, and more revelatory of the poet than many 'confessional' poems. 'Sing', it concludes

> for whatever makes pain speak,
> whatever makes grief delight in music.
> Sing because you're the best; because you can,
> and sing – why not? – for the taxman.

'Mozart Playing Billiards' is in a similar vein of wit and has the same purpose of celebrating skills of all kinds performed with panache. It is a rather rare example of writing in persona which makes its serious point with a light touch and with unobtrusive but impressive technical accomplishment.

That artistic detachment from issues which are painful, referred to above, is displayed in several poems in *Sing for the Taxman*. It is achieved through the use of personae, as in 'The Last Wolf in Scotland' and 'The Turkish Policeman's Testimony', which reflect the poet's concerns for the environment and for human rights, and through the use of elaborate verse forms, as in 'Jenny', about a lost child. If 'Sing for the Taxman' might be said to be at the apex of the book, then its supporting pillars are the two sequences, 'Climbing Hermaness' and 'Five Voices'. The former, a free-verse record of and meditation upon the climb on Unst, the most northerly of the Shetland Isles, incorporates some exquisite descriptive writing with the idea of a quest, which is finally an allegory for life itself and its inevitable conclusion:

> that place
> of ultimates with no end
> but light itself.

Robert Browning's plan in *The Ring and the Book* was to present 'the same transaction from a number of different points of view'. This is the approach adopted in 'Five Voices', to provide, in persona, five different views of the life and violent death of Lieutenant Hans Hermann von Katte, whose wit, elegance and devil-may-care attitude to the most serious of projects, the spiriting away of the Crown Prince of Prussia from his bullying father, have been of consuming interest to the poet. Further poems in the book show how she has pursued the lieutenant beyond the history text where she first found him to his home and the family mausoleum where his remains are displayed, minus sundry bones and teeth filched by souvenir-hunters.

Sheenagh Pugh shares a number of concerns with her contemporaries: as mentioned above, she is a defender of the planet and the environment, and she speaks for the rights of individuals, not least those of children, and freedom from persecution. She stands apart from them in her refusal to be aligned with 'The Movement' or any other fashion in poetry, and in not finding inspiration in the USA. Her sheet anchor is a kind of academic rigour which dictates that her passions – von Katte, the Norse sagas and snooker alike – have to be pursued long and seriously; the wit and lightness of touch which distinguish many of her poems may be deceptive. She brings the same intensity to the making of her verses; technically, she is the equal of anyone writing in English today, and a good deal better than most.

Robert Minhinnick's first published poems appeared in a special 'New Poets' number of *Poetry Wales* I edited in Autumn 1972. He was just twenty. Only a few years earlier, as a sixth-former, he had been given a copy of *Welsh Voices* and realized for the first time that there were Welsh poets who wrote in English. He had already at that time decided that what he wanted to do was write. The poets with whom he was most familiar were those normally encountered in school at that time, and soon after them, R. S. Thomas, Edward Thomas and Dylan Thomas, John Tripp, Roland Mathias and Meic Stephens. His literary heritage thus differed little from that of earlier generations of Anglo-Welsh poets, and his outlook and literary aims are similar. Although he has travelled widely, and the range of his writing in prose (he is a gifted essayist and polemicist, especially in the cause of conservation) and in verse reflects this, he is still essentially a poet of and for Wales. 'It's where I am,' he said in a *Poetry Wales* interview (September 1989), 'it's where I've lived and worked, it's also where I've published. It's inevitable. I wish I could write in Welsh, but what Welsh I know I've had to learn and it's inadequate.' Again his poetic technique has affinities with the writers of the 1960s. He can say with Roland Mathias and others, 'I try to create a texture in my poems' and the evidence of this is in his adherence to stanzaic forms and to language which is peculiarly enriched. Although he makes use of colloquialisms and speech rhythms, he cannot write a prosaic line. From the outset his poetry has been distinguished by striking visual imagery in particular, for which he draws on an interesting range of experience, including working in a scrapyard and on the docks in Cardiff, as well as his observations of the countryside and domestic interiors.

The punning title of his third book, *Life Sentences* (1983), identifies an essentially personal collection; many of the poems are portraits of people and places, and responses to events in the home and the locality. Death, especially violent death, a recurring theme, makes its entry with 'The Death of Johnny Owen', the Welsh boxer killed in the ring in Los Angeles. Other poems contain narratives about suicide, murder and public execution. Two of the sequence of seven poems that compose 'Inventing a Childhood' involve butchering animals; 'The Party', about killing a pig, tells how the youngest child was 'placed inside the split carcase / And lifted out laughing from the wound's long slit'. This charade or ritual is echoed later in 'Catching my Breath', which describes the birth of the poet's daughter (and makes an interesting comparison with Gillian Clarke's feminine perspective on the subject). The visual images are precise – '. . . her skin like grapeskin, / A blue colour . . . the long birth cable trussing her like flex' – and the emotional response is painfully honest: the birth was observed 'With strange dispassion' and afterwards, 'There's no feeling yet; only a place where it will be'.

Robert Minhinnick's recollections of childhood are predominantly rural and he finds weathers and seascapes to reflect his moods:

> On this bleached day even gulls are mute;
> The waves rush to the feet like lathered dogs.
> And yet I court bad weather, the avoidable
> Blast . . .
>
> Then I kick over a mussel-shell
> Luminous with the tide's use. I would be
> Like that, allowing a little light,
> Reflecting one thin ray.

In this book he is nothing so much as a modern Romantic. 'Gale Warning' reveals him 'grown ugly, unable to think', so that 'even the storm is puny, I can laugh / It off.' Those few poems where irony and sudden access of the wider world outside home and the locality intervene are still driven by the perceiving and reflective 'I', as when he climbs the roof to fix a television aerial, suppressing vertigo:

> Until at last I'm taller than the house,
> The aerial turning like a weathervane
> In my hands . . .
>
> In a room below a screen has cleared;
> The world hurls images we can't escape:
> I'm overwhelmed by sudden freezing vision,
> A man who climbs, a searching fragile shape.

The Looters (1989), his fifth book, introduces a number of fresh developments, notably an overt political stance in poems like 'Ants', a disturbing piece about the oppression of Australian aborigines, which some have seen as an allegory of colonialized Wales; 'YOPS', about unemployed youth; 'Development Area' where 'sulphur falls with the dew' and:

> On the glacier of the city's
> Rubbish the children pick
> For futures already discarded

and 'Sunglasses', which casts a jaundiced eye upon politicians, their protectors and outmanœuvred protest. A revolution in style occurs too, in symbolist poems many of which carry important messages. In 'The Hothouse', a nine-poem sequence, this approach is used to make analogies between breakdown in human relationships, madness and environmental destruction. While the imagery often scintillates, the meaning is sometimes obscure; a few are riddles by design. This book also contains further poems about family and childhood recollections and reflections on recent events – such as the looting of lorries abandoned 'like dislocated vertebrae' on a snow-bound motorway, the theme of the title poem.

With *Hey Fatman* (1994), there is a return to earlier concerns and more immediately accessible writing. The sequence 'A History of Dunraven' fills some gaps in the family history which began to unfold in *Life Sentences*. It concerns the mansion, since demolished, where his mother was once employed. Recollections of childhood, schooldays and friends underline the strong personal element in the collection. Many of the poems have more than a touch of the macabre and imagery that conveys heightened anxiety; he is particularly adept at communicating a *frisson* of unease. Others are melancholic, looking back with regret as though from a great age. The elegiac tone of a great deal of Robert Minhinnick's poetry might be considered characteristically Anglo-Welsh. This is not the character of the brilliant title poem. Its setting is a squalid, beachside bar in a hot, exotic city. The characters, apart from the poet-observer, are the barman, four whores and their clients, and local insect life – 'a moth . . . with wings like two South Americas' that immolates itself on a neon sign and, at the end of the poem, floats down 'like charred paper' while 'Over the walls the baby roaches ran / Warning of fire, waving their brown arms'. 'Hey fatman' is the whores' taunting invitation to dalliance:

> *Hey fatman*, that's what they said;
> Almost without saying it, if you know what I mean,
> Because that's all it takes in a place like that.
>
> And they'd suck their drinks and circulate,
> Trailing a perfume through the room
> Of their own sweat, like a herb crushed underfoot.
> *Hey fatman*, it said to the night,
> To the brass propellors of the fan
> That uttered ceaselessly its quiet scream.

This writing, highly coloured yet relaxed, colloquial and still elegant, marks a further stage in the development of Robert Minhinnick's craft. In this poem at least a process of Americanization has occurred that sits well enough with his established skills and might be the means of introducing him to the wider audience he deserves on the other side of Offa's Dyke.

Mike Jenkins is the most overtly political of contemporary Anglo-Welsh poets, inheritor of the mantle of John Tripp and Harri Webb. Like them, he is a socialist, if not from the cradle, then from the experience he has had as a teacher in schools serving working-class communities in Wales and in Northern Ireland. As a member of Cymru Coch, the Welsh Socialist

Party, he does not toe the Labour line: he is as committed to cultural and political nationalism as he is to socialism. In the statement he submitted to Meic Stephens with the poems he selected for *The Bright Field*, he writes of the Welsh language as 'a significant underlying presence in my poetry. I hear it in work. I learn it and my children go to a Welsh-medium school; it's a measure of our striving for identity.' His commitment is clear from his work as writer and editor (he was in charge of *Poetry Wales* for several years from 1980). He pledged the royalties from one of his books to the anti-poll tax campaign.

As a notable performance poet as well as for his political stance and accessibility as a writer, he has considerable popular appeal. His sense of mission inclines him to satire and the exploitation of sardonic humour. He has employed sophisticated narrative techniques in pursuing his anti-establishment goals: 'A Dissident Voice', from the 1990 volume of the same name, about the murder of the peace campaigner Hilda Murrell, is planned (like Sheenagh Pugh's 'Five Voices') as a sequence of persona poems, each throwing light on the subject. He is also capable of great sensitivity and, on occasion, sentimentality, as were John Tripp and Harri Webb. In poems about his family in particular he achieves warmth and delicacy, but again and again his human sympathy, and his anger, are stirred by the daily round of deprivation and mundane cruelties that afflict hopeless families in blighted post-industrial communities. Often the poem gives a child's-eye view or, as in 'An Escape', it is the voice of a child that speaks:

> My Mam's at work again, on the tills
> handling all that money which flows
> through her like the facts
> they funnel into me at school . . .
>
> It's the rain I despise . . . nagging me inside
> with memories of screaming, fighting . . .
>
> But here comes Lisa with our dog
> and her friends all wild in the wind;
> and we're off to the little river,
> to the tree-trunk bridge where our heads
> will be leaf-light and reeling.

He gained notable success in *Graffiti Narratives* (1994), his fifth book, with poems written in the local dialect of Merthyr Tydfil. This choice of register presents a challenge to the writer, who must avoid seeming to patronize his subjects. The poems are humorous, some indeed wildly funny, and the satirical edge strikes not at the people but at the politicians and planners who created the estates they inhabit –

> I come from-a ewgest 'state in town,
> second ewgest maze in Ewrop, they say,
> coz planners potched it up, the clowns;
> I'd give em a proper lampin
> on'y they've all gone away . . .

The range of themes in Mike Jenkins's poetry is narrower than in that of his contemporaries, but he makes up for this lack by the depth of sympathy and understanding he constantly shows for his human subjects.

His namesake, Nigel Jenkins (they are not related) shared the Welsh Arts Council's 1974 Young Poets prize with Duncan Bush and Tony Curtis, and in 1996 won the Council's Book of the Year prize, pushing R. S. Thomas's *No Truce with the Furies* and Gwyneth Lewis's *Parables and Faxes* into second and third place respectively, with *Gwalia in Khasia*. This is a lively and perceptive prose account of his journey to the Khasi Jaintia Hills in north-east India, in the footsteps of Welsh Calvinistic Methodist missionaries who, in the nineteenth century, brought Christianity, literacy and peaceful coexistence to the region, at the cost to their converts of many centuries-old rites and customs. The religious and cultural colonization of another land by the Welsh, who, in the view of the author, have been colonially exploited to the verge of extinction, adds a twist of irony to the book.

Like Mike Jenkins, he is an overtly political writer with strong Welsh nationalist views. His aim as a poet (again set out in *The Bright Field*) is to 'culture the pearl of independence (i.e. liberation from the British State into a more active relationship with the wider world)'. He shares Gwyn Jones's perception that the fate of a distinctive Anglo-Welsh poetry, and of Wales as a separate country with its own cultural identity, is bound up with the fate of the Welsh language – 'The poem loses its strength as the language dies back, removing from the anglicized majority all but a trace of how once, here poetry played a central role in the national polity and everyday life.' He is keen to post warning of this threat to the wider public and has lost confidence in magazines as a means of doing so. He fears that they reach only other poets and their 'academic pilot-fish'. Instead, he puts his energies into giving public readings and 'writing messages on walls'.

His third book of poems, a substantial volume, *Acts of Union: Selected Poems 1974–1989*, appeared in 1990. It reveals him to be, as might be expected, vigorous and forthright in the expression of his political beliefs, but there are also poems which treat other acts of union, notably that of man and wife, with warmth and gentleness, as in 'Shirts':

> I am the place
> he returns to, his
> hunger's home.
> I build every day
> a house full of rooms,
> of walls to enfold
> the things that he loves.

The title of the book is a neat play on words that represents the range of themes. As well as marital union, these also embrace relationships between the poet and his origins on a Gower farm, between his people and their roots, albeit occasionally in poems about deracination and loss, and between Wales and England since political annexation by the Acts of Union of 1536 and 1543. 'Yr Iaith' ('The Language') offers a sad commentary on his grandmother, who exchanges the 'dung-filled yards' of the family home, and the violin and harp of social music-making, for rooms where 'the brass gleamed, the crystal rang' and 'an evening ends with colour tv', while the Welsh language she possessed has been almost forgotten for lack of use. 'Land of Song' contrasts with the gentle, elegiac tone of 'Yr Iaith'. It is a vitriolic attack on the 'shame dressed as pride' the poet sees personified in rugby supporters in their 'oggy oggy toyland'. The savage bitterness of the poem was stirred by the negative majority at the devolution referendum, as 'I.m. 1 iii 79' appended to the title reminds. Like Mike Jenkins, he finds much in the present condition of Wales exasperating, and he is equally concerned about infringement of human rights throughout the world and the threat of nuclear disaster. It is sometimes difficult for him to contain the energy and commitment he brings to writing within the confines of a poem. While the anger and compassion are obvious, there is not always enough detachment and application of the technical skill he certainly possesses to satisfy artistic criteria. The great strength of much of Nigel Jenkins's work is, as he intends, in its ready communication of ideas to an audience at a live reading.

I am unable even to guess how many of the poets with whom I have dealt at some length above would take offence at the use of the term 'Anglo-Welsh' in connection with them. In one sense at least it is useful: it is readily inclusive of gradations of 'Welshness' from those born and bred in Wales and Welsh-speaking, to those who have no greater connection than a vague sense of allegiance. It allows the list of poets who merit at least mention in this survey (many deserve a great deal more) to be extended to include, for example, Blackburn's Brian Aspden; Nigel Wells, born in Northampton; Penny Windsor from the West Country; Chris Torrance of Edinburgh; John Powell Ward, a Suffolk man; and Hilary Llewellyn-Williams who hails from Kent. All are writers of some distinction, have spent a considerable time in Wales and contributed a great deal to its culture – John Powell Ward as, among other things, a former editor of *Poetry Wales*. If the label 'Welsh writing in English' is preferred, with its implication of exclusivity, would any qualify? What of Hilary Llewellyn-Williams's part-Welsh parentage? Is Brian Aspden 'naturalized' by virtue of being a Welsh-speaker? (Was George Borrow Welsh by the same criterion?) Does Nigel Wells's success in winning a Welsh Arts Council prize with *Wilderness / Just Bounce* in 1987 make him Welsh? What of a poet like Steve Griffiths, born in Anglesey, who has lived and worked in London since 1970? At the very least it is probably true to say of all of them that their work is better known in Wales than it is in England. All, along with John Barnie, Peter Finch, Christine Evans, Catherine Fisher, Douglas Houston, Huw

Jones, Stephen Knight, Oliver Reynolds and Graham Thomas, are represented in *The Bright Field* – the most useful anthology of contemporary poetry from Wales currently available.

The names of Stephen Knight and Oliver Reynolds who, alone in the list above, have London-based publishers may be recognized elsewhere. The latter in particular attracted widespread note by winning the Arvon Foundation international poetry competition in 1985. His subjects are common enough in Anglo-Welsh poetry – the fine and permeable division between town and country, the decline of heavy industry, the heedless destruction of the environment – but he brings to bear on them a fresh eye and a melancholy wit, and imagery which is always precise and often has a cutting edge. Peter Finch has some twenty volumes of verse to his credit, and his *Selected Poems* appeared in 1987. He is the outstanding experimental poet in Wales, and has been since the launch, in 1966, of a little magazine he named *Second Aeon.* Under his inspired editorship the magazine broke fresh ground in the welcome it extended to 'concrete' poetry and to avant-garde writers from overseas, especially the USA. It is a great pity that he wound it up in 1974 on taking the post of manager of the Welsh Arts Council's Oriel bookshop. There is much sheer enjoyment in his poetry which exploits the techniques of modernism in continuous experiments with form. Though his poems are intended to entertain, they contain serious messages about the human condition, the state of Wales and the fate of the Welsh language. Describing the position at which he has gradually arrived, rather than one adopted at the outset, he says Wales is 'a permanent undercurrent to almost everything I do'. Christine Evans, originally from west Yorkshire, has lived in Wales since 1967. She teaches in Pwllheli, where her father was born. Her home is a smallholding and her husband a fisherman, so that she is constantly in touch with the Welsh-speaking local community and its rural and seafaring traditions. She began writing in 1979 and won a Welsh Arts Council prize with her third book, *Cometary Phases* (1989). Her meditative voice, with quiet persistence, unfolds her experiences of a pastoral existence in a harsh land, of growing children, her own and the pupils she teaches, and the human and animal cycle from birth to death. Christopher Meredith, a Welsh-speaker, was born in Tredegar, a former industrial town in the Gwent Valleys. For a time he worked in a steel plant but now lectures at the University of Glamorgan. Much of his poetry is personal, of family, domestic tasks, common experiences, and riddled with the many ironies of life. His first novel, *Shifts* (1988), won a Welsh Arts Council prize, and his second, *Griffri* (1991), was favourably reviewed in the metropolitan press. Catherine Fisher, who is also a successful writer of children's fiction, was born in Newport, Gwent. Her first volume of poetry, *Immrama* (1988), gained a Welsh Arts Council prize, and in 1989 she won the Cardiff Literature Festival poetry competition. Her poetry is technically accomplished – she frequently uses modified traditional stanza forms – and employs a diversity of adopted personae. In common with many of her contemporaries, she is a concerned environmentalist, but she is unusual in finding inspiration in the mysterious and magical and drawing on Celtic mythology and the Celtic saints for her themes and allusions.

Gwyneth Lewis emerged as a poet too late to be included in *The Bright Field.* She is that rare phenomenon, a bilingual writer who is creatively at home in both English and Welsh. She first attracted attention as a teenager in the 1970s when she won prizes for poems in Welsh at the Urdd National Eisteddfod, and her first volume was *Sonedau Redsa* (i.e. 'Redsa's Sonnets', Redsa being the name of her godchild in the Philippines), published in 1990. Her second, *Parables and Faxes* (1995), has been enthusiastically received by readers and reviewers in England and Wales. In her Welsh-medium secondary education she imbibed that complex system of prosody, *cynghanedd,* still practised by many Welsh poets. In her own Welsh poetry she employs it flexibly, rather than according to the classical rules of the 'strict metres'. In a conversation with Richard Poole (*PNReview*, 113) she speaks of the delight she found in 'these subtle shifts of vowel and consonant patterns' and describes them as 'one of the most important metrical scaffoldings in my work in both languages'. This is the source of the music in her writing in English, heard at its richest (because 'musicality needs to be in proportion to the subject in hand') in a poem like 'Going Primitive':

Who can resist a didgeridoo
in the middle of Queen St – not one, but three
from the Northern Territory,
each one more deeply, eucalyptically rude?

This is closely akin to that texturing that was a preoccupation of many of the Anglo-Welsh poets of the 1960s and of a few since. It comes to Gwyneth Lewis as naturally as breathing and directly from her Welsh literary roots.

She does not have a problem of Welsh identity, still (as we have seen) a common source of anxiety among Welsh writers in English. She does not need to employ the usual marks of identity caricatured in John Davies's 'How to Write an Anglo-Welsh Poem'. When, occasionally, she uses Welsh words in a poem explanations are not needed, and the purpose is not to make a statement about Welshness:

Welsh was the mother tongue, English was his.
He taught her the body by fetishist quiz,
father and daughter on the bottom stairs:
Dy benelin yw *elbow*, dy wallt di yw *hair.*

Parables and Faxes is unlike any other collection by an Anglo-Welsh poet of the 1990s; only the symbolist poems of Robert Minhinnick's *The Looters* come close to it in their inventiveness and imagery and their stanzaic forms – though in Gwyneth Lewis's hands the traditional sestina and villanelle also flourish. She is a gifted technician, perhaps as a result of her early training in Welsh versification. Her subjects are relationships, places at home and abroad, people, mutability, incidents recorded and reflected upon. All are touched by a transforming wit that renders the familiar strange. Fantastic as many appear, all her poems 'are rooted in specific, actual expeiences'. Transformation itself is a theme – 'We are all transformers: we change what we see' – and there is a superabundance of word-play. The ludic element is perhaps what most of all distinguishes her work from that of her contemporaries, men and women. Her writing is consistently as stimulating and entertaining as it is thought-provoking. Her view of the world is feminist, but not stridently so; she is supremely confident in her art and herself. She has so far felt no need of adopted personae to add diversity to her output; her own voice has variety enough. In her freshness of vision, wit and musicality – and her unselfconscious Welshness – Gwyneth Lewis is a bright hope for the continuation of distinctive Welsh writing in English into the next century.

Note

(An abridged version of this essay appears in *Comparative Criticism*, Volume 19, *Literary Devolution: Writing in Scotland, Ireland, Wales and England*, edited by E. S. Shaffer (Cambridge, Cambridge University Press, 1997).

Meic Stephens: A Bibliography

A Periodicals edited

The Dragon/Y Ddraig, the Magazine of the University College of Wales, Aberystwyth, lxxxiii (Spring 1961).

The Nationalist, 1 (June 1963).

Poetry Wales. Cylchgrawn cenedlaethol o farddoniaeth newydd. This magazine was founded by Meic Stephens and first published by his Triskel Press in Merthyr Tydfil in Spring 1965. He edited the first seven numbers until the issue for Summer 1967 (vol.3, no. 3), when he handed over the editorship to Gerald Morgan and Gwilym Rees Hughes, but resumed the editorship after three numbers in Spring 1968 (vol.4, no. 3), remaining as editor of the next sixteen numbers until Spring 1973 (vol.8, no. 4), when the editorship passed to Sam Adams.

B Anthologies edited

Caneuon Rhyddid Cymru/Songs of Welsh Freedom (Merthyr Tydfil, Triskel Press, 1963).

Burning the Hands of the Clock: Poems by Eight Young Cardiff Poets. (Cardiff, Triskel Press, 1967).

The Lilting House: An Anthology of Anglo-Welsh Poetry 1917–67 (with John Stuart Williams; London/Llandybïe, J. M Dent & Sons in association with Christopher Davies, 1969); with an introduction by Raymond Garlick.

Green Horse: An Anthology by Young Poets of Wales (with Peter Finch; Swansea, Christopher Davies, 1978); with an introduction by Roland Mathias.

A Book of Wales: An Anthology of Verse and Prose (London, J. M.Dent & Sons, 1987).
A Cardiff Anthology (Bridgend, Seren Books, 1987; reprinted 1996).
The Bright Field: An Anthology of Contemporary Poetry from Wales (Manchester, Carcanet, 1991).
A Rhondda Anthology (Bridgend, Seren Books, 1994), with an introduction by Dai Smith.

C Verse

Triad, with Peter Griffith and Harri Webb (Merthyr Tydfil, Triskel Press, 1963), with an introduction by Anthony Conran; edn. limited to 500 copies.
Exiles All (Swansea, Christopher Davies, 1973), with an introduction by Sam Adams.
Ponies, Twynyrodyn and Other Poems (Cardiff, Combrógos, 1997); edn. limited to 150 copies.

D Sociolinguistics

Linguistic Minorities in Western Europe (Llandysul, Gomer Press, 1976); translated into German by Susanne Kalweit as *Minderheiten in Westeuropa* (Husum, Matthiesen Verlag, 1979).
La llengua i els mitjans de comunicació social al País de Gal.les avui (CIEMEN,1981; Catalan translation of lecture, *La langue galloise à l'heure actuelle*, given at St Michel de Cuixha, 1980).

E Bibliographies edited

A Reader's Guide to Wales: A Selected Bibliography (London, National Book League, 1973), compiled by members of the staff of the National Library of Wales.
A Bibliography of Literature in Twentieth-Century Wales (London, British Council, 1995).

F Serial publications edited

'Writers of Wales' with R. Brinley Jones (Cardiff, University of Wales Press, 1970–); the series, which comprises eighty-eight titles to 1998, continues.

'Artists in Wales' (Llandysul, Gomer Press, 3 vols., 1971, 1973, 1977).
'The Gregynog Poets/Beirdd Gregynog' (Newtown, Gwasg Gregynog, 12 vols., 1989–90).
'Changing Wales' (Llandysul, Gomer Press, 14 vols., 1992–7).

G *Miscellaneous books compiled and edited*

The Welsh Language Today (Llandysul, Gomer Press, 1973).
The Arts in Wales 1950–75 (Cardiff, Welsh Arts Council, 1979), with an introduction by Raymond Williams; Welsh version, *Y Celfyddydau yng Nghymru 1950–75* (Cardiff, Welsh Arts Council, 1979).
The Oxford Companion to the Literature of Wales (Oxford, Oxford University Press, 1986); Welsh version, *Cydymaith i Lenyddiaeth Cymru* (Cardiff, University of Wales Press, 1986); second impressions, 1990 and 1992.
A Dictionary of Literary Quotations (London, Routledge, 1989); reprinted as *Collins Dictionary of Literary Quotations* (London, HarperCollins, 1991).
The Oxford Illustrated Literary Guide to Great Britain and Ireland (with Dorothy Eagle; Oxford, Oxford University Press, 2nd edn., 1992); reprinted as a paperback, *The Oxford Literary Guide to Great Britain and Ireland* (1993).
A Most Peculiar People: Quotations about Wales and the Welsh (Cardiff, University of Wales Press, 1992).
Take Wales: Cinema in Wales (Cardiff, Wales Film Council/Screen Wales, 1993).
A Little Book of Welsh Quotations (Belfast, Appletree Press, 1997).
Cydymaith i Lenyddiaeth Cymru (Cardiff, University of Wales Press, 1997); an English version, *The New Companion to the Literature of Wales* (Cardiff, University of Wales Press, 1998), a completely revised edition of *The Oxford Companion to the Literature of Wales* (1986).
A Little Book of Welsh Sayings (Belfast, Appletree Press, 1998).
Entries on Welsh and Anglo-Welsh writers in Colin Matthew (ed.), *New Dictionary of National Biography* (Oxford, Oxford University Press, 2004).

H *Translations*

The White Stone: Six Essays by T. H. Parry-Williams (Llandysul, Gomer Press, 1987).

For the Sake of Wales (trans. of Gwynfor Evans's memoirs, *Bywyd Cymro*; Cardiff, Welsh Academic Press, 1996), with an introduction by Dafydd Elis Thomas.

The Basques: Their Struggle for Independence (trans. of Luis Núñez Astrain, *La Rázon Vasca*; Welsh Academic Press, 1997), with an introduction by Ned Thomas.

Monica (trans. of Saunders Lewis's novel, *Monica*; Bridgend, Seren, 1997), with an introduction by Bruce Griffiths.

An Anthology of Welsh Short Prose (trans. of fifty-two essays by Welsh writers; Cardiff, Welsh Academic Press, 1998).

Shadow of the Sickle (trans. of Islwyn Ffowc Elis's novel, *Cysgod y Cryman*; Llandysul, Gomer Press, 1998).

I Editions

The Curate of Clyro: Extracts from the Diary of Francis Kilvert (Newtown, Gwasg Gregynog, 1983).

The Collected Poems of Harri Webb (Llandysul, Gomer Press, 1995).

The Collected Poems of Glyn Jones (Cardiff, University of Wales Press, 1996).

The Collected Stories of Rhys Davies (Llandysul, Gomer Press, vols. 1 and 2, 1996; vol. 3, 1998).

No Half-Way House: Selected Political Journalism of Harri Webb (Talybont, Y Lolfa, 1997).

Richard Llewellyn, *How Green Was My Valley* (London, Reader's Digest, 1997).

A Militant Muse: Selected Literary Writings of Harri Webb (Bridgend, Seren, 1998).

J Miscellaneous writings and literary journalism

It would be impractical to attempt a complete bibliography of the journalism of Meic Stephens because such a list would run to several thousand items. What follows is only a selection from among his more substantial and significant writings.

'The hooters', a short story, *South Wales Echo* (3 May 1958).

'Gran's boy', a short story, *The Dragon/Y Ddraig*, lxxxiii (Spring 1961).

'Crumbs from the black swans', an article about Anglo-Welsh literature, *Lookout* (5 December 1961).

'The status of the Anglo-Welsh', *Y Wawr* (Spring 1962).

'The voice of Scotland', a review of Hugh MacDiarmid, *Collected Poems* and Duncan Glen, *Hugh MacDiarmid, Welsh Nation* (September 1962).

'Things as they are', a review of R. S.Thomas, *The Bread of Truth, Welsh Nation* (December 1963).

'The matter with Wales', a lecture delivered at Plaid Cymru's summer school 1962, *The Nationalist* (June 1963).

'The seamless web', an article about the new regional policy in France, *Welsh Nation* (May 1964).

'Where have all the Angloes gone?', a round-up of Welsh books published in 1964, *The London Welshman* (September 1965).

'How long before Welsh poets go concrete?', *Western Mail* (3 September 1966).

'A rare courage', a review of Alun Lewis, *Selected Poetry and Prose, Western Mail* (10 October 1966).

'Truth like the diamond', a review of Vernon Watkins, *Selected Poems, Western Mail* (17 October 1967).

'Today's mead and horses', an article about the Welsh Arts Council's new policies for literature, *The London Welshman* (November 1967).

'The second flowering', an article about the early years of *Poetry Wales, Poetry Wales*, 3, 3 (Winter 1967–8).

'Dechrau da', a conversation with the registrar of births about registering the birth of a child in Welsh, *Baner ac Amserau Cymru* (11 April 1968).

'Yr Academi Gymreig and Cymdeithas Cymru Newydd', *Poetry Wales*, 4, 2 (Winter 1968).

Review of Nigel Heseltine, *Twenty-five Poems of Dafydd ap Gwilym*, Herbert Williams, *A Lethal Kind of Love*, Roy Burnett, *Rhondda and the Collected Works of Dai Cottomy*, Robert Morgan, *Poems and Extracts*, and David Callard and Geraint Jarman, *Zutique*, *Poetry Wales*, 4, 3 (Spring 1969).

'Barddoniaeth Arbrofol', an article about experimental poetry, *Taliesin*, 21 (December 1970).

'Under two hats', an interview given to John Tripp, *Planet*, 9 (December 1971/January 1972).

'Moderniaeth', an article about Modernism, *Taliesin*, 24 (July 1972).

'March of the moderns', a review of Edward Lucie-Smith (ed.), *Experimental Poetry*, John Sharkey (ed.), *Mindplay*, and Duncan Glen (ed.), *Akros*, 6, no. 18, *Planet*, 13 (August/September 1972).

'Serving the books of Wales', an article about the Welsh Arts Council's policy for literature, *The Bookseller* (2 September 1972).

'Hugh MacDiarmid', an article in *Taliesin*, 25 (December 1972).

'Nid eithriad yw Voivodina', an article about the ethnic character of Yugoslavia, *Barn* (July 1973).

'Dim ond syniad bach', an article about support for the Welsh language in Cardiff, *Y Dinesydd*, 4 (July/August 1973).

'Cyril Hodges (1915–1974)', an obituary in the form of a letter to Sam Adams, *Poetry Wales*, 9, 3 (Winter 1973–4).

'Irish poetry', a review-article on John Montague (ed.), *The Faber Book of Irish Verse*, *Poetry Wales*, 9, 4 (Spring 1974).

Review of Eugène Guillevic, *Selected Poems*, *Poetry Wales*, 10, 1 (Summer 1974).

'Jack wold be a gentilman', an article about Ranulph Higden and John of Trevisa, *Barn*, 144 (October 1974).

Review of Val Warner, *The Centenary Corbière*, *Poetry Wales*, 11, 3 (Winter 1976).

'The writer as cultural worker in Sweden', two articles in *Book News from Wales* (Winter 1976–Spring 1977).

'Croeso adref, Dolores!', an article about the return to Spain of Dolores Ibarruri ('La Pasionaria') from exile in Moscow, *Y Faner* (13 May 1977).

Interview about the first ten years of the Welsh Arts Council's policies for the support of literature, *Poetry Wales*, 14, 2 (Autumn 1978).

'Cyhoeddi yng Nghymru', an interview about the Welsh Arts Council's support for publishing in Wales, *Barn*, 201 (October 1979).

'The good companion', an article about progress in the compilation of *The Oxford Companion to the Literature of Wales*, *Book News from Wales* (Summer 1981).

'Trefn y wyddor i lenyddiaeth Cymru', an article about progress in the compilation of *The Oxford Companion to the Literature of Wales/ Cydymaith i Lenyddiaeth Cymru*, *Y Faner* (24 April 1981).

Review of Kathleen Hughes and Dafydd Ifans (eds.), *The Diary of Francis Kilvert, April–June 1870*, *The Anglo-Welsh Review*, 73 (1983).

'The Vaughans and The Yat, Glascwm', an account of a family featured in the diary of Francis Kilvert, in the newsletter of the Kilvert Society (September 1987).

'Guardians of the stones', a review of David Robinson, *Heritage in Wales*, *Wales on Sunday* (30 July 1989).

'Poets who caught the bus', a review of Robin Bell (ed.), *The Best of Scottish Poetry*, *Scotland on Sunday* (13 August 1989).

Review of Marion Wynne-Davies (ed.), *Bloomsbury Guide to English Literature*, *Bulletin* of the Welsh Academy (Winter 1989); a review of the updated version appears in the *Bulletin* for February 1996.

'Gorbachev on a knife-edge', an article about the imminent break-up of the Soviet Union, *Wales on Sunday* (24 December 1989).

'From Picture Post to poetry', an obituary of John Ormond, *Guardian* (9 June 1990).

'In John Jones's country: growing up in Treforest', an autobiographical essay, *Planet*, 82 (August/September 1990).

'Poet with dragon fire in his verse', a profile of Harri Webb, *Western Mail* (7 September 1990).

'Churchman who loved and lost four women', an article about Francis Kilvert, *Western Mail* (20 September 1990).

'The Garth Newydd years', a memoir of Harri Webb in Merthyr Tydfil, *Planet*, 83 (September/October 1990).

'A bumper book of Welsh poetry', a review of Cary Archard (ed.), *Poetry Wales: 25 Years*, *Western Mail* (29 October 1990).

'Rhondda remembers a lost genius', an article about the poet Ben Bowen, *Western Mail* (6 November 1990).

'Churchill's day of reckoning', an article about the Tonypandy riots of 1910, *Western Mail* (8 November 1990).

'When the quarries echoed with anger', an article about the Penrhyn lock-outs of 1896 and 1900, *Western Mail* (26 November 1990).

'Warm welcome for Manhattan man of letters', a profile of Joseph P. Clancy, *Western Mail* (1 December 1990).

'The unlucky tragedy of Thomas's plays', an article about Gwyn Thomas, *Western Mail* (8 December 1990).

'The man who wrote Bread of Heaven', an article about William Williams (Pantycelyn), *Western Mail* (21 December 1990).

'Woeful writer's heroic failure', an article about T. J. Ll. Prichard, author of *Twm Shon Catti*, *Western Mail* (28 December 1990).

'Welsh words for the world', an obituary of Gwyn Williams (1904–90), *Guardian* (29 December 1990) and *Y Faner* (18 January 1991).

'Wales's grand old man of literature', a profile of Glyn Jones, *Western Mail* (16 February 1991).

'Folk stories from the modern Welsh', an article about urban myths, *Western Mail* (23 February 1991).

'What do we mean by Celtic?', an article about the ancient Celts, *Western Mail* (1 March 1991).

'Cyflafan y Beirdd', an article about the 'Massacre of the Bards', *Taliesin*, 73 (Spring 1991).

'One man and his Wales', a personal column, *Planet* (six nos., April/May 1991–February/March 1992).

'Cofio'n gain', a review of Derec Llwyd Morgan (ed.), *Emynau Pantycelyn*, *Y Faner* (11 March 1991).

'Mab y crydd', a review of John Ormond, *Cathedral Builders*, in *Y Faner* (19 April 1991).

'The night I held Liv Ullmann in my arms', a feature in the *Western Mail* (6 April 1991).

'Ymlaen gyda Georgia!', an article about the civil war in Georgia, *Wales on Sunday* (21 April 1991).

'A new literary broom for Wales', a profile of Michael Parnell, the editor of *The New Welsh Review, Western Mail* (30 April 1991).

'Spade money in Glyntâf cemetery', a feature in *Western Mail* (4 May 1991).

'Llyfrau o bob lliw a llun yn y Gelli', an article about the Hay books festival, *Western Mail* (19 May 1991).

'Prize homecoming for Merthyr's celebrated writer', a profile of Leslie Norris, *Western Mail* (27 May 1991).

'Ambition to explore a thousand parishes', an article about the topography of Wales, *Western Mail* (1 June 1991).

'Killed for the buttons on his coat', an article about the bone-setter John Lloyd ('Silver John'), *Western Mail* (29 June 1991).

'The Russians versus the rest', an article about ethnic tension in the Soviet Union, *Radical Wales*, 30 (Summer 1991).

'Unforgettable days at Barry Island', *Western Mail* (29 June 1991).

'Ponty's past captured in people's play', an article about the production of Laurence Allan's play, *Valley of the Kings*, *Western Mail* (1 July 1991).

'Sakartvela Mudam!', an article about the fate of Georgia during the break-up of the Soviet Union, *Y Faner* (30 July 1991).

'Caerdydd, prifddinas ein llên', an article about the literary associations of Cardiff, *Western Mail* (8 August 1991).

'Sut y bydd Cymru yn dathlu 2000?', an article about how Wales will celebrate the millennium, *Western Mail* (17 August 1991).

'Burning memories of school', a memoir of teachers good and bad, *Western Mail* (5 October 1991).

'Trying to turn down the volumes', an article about the love of books, *Western Mail* (12 October 1991).

'His name will continue reverberating', a tribute to Michael Parnell, *The New Welsh Review*, 14 (Autumn 1991).

Review of Tony Augarde (ed.), *Oxford Dictionary of Modern Quotations*, *The New Welsh Review*, 14 (Autumn 1991).

'Turkeys are the answer for this Wales', an article about the town of Wales, Utah, *Western Mail* (23 November 1991).

'An ambassador of top literary talent', a profile of Gillian Clarke, *Western Mail* (6 January 1992).

'Journey into a fictional mind', an article about Duncan Bush, *Western Mail* (8 January 1992).

'The mighty Mam behind Novello', an article about Clara Novello Davies, *Western Mail* (10 January 1992).

'Welsh bookshelf'. Meic Stephens wrote this regular column in the *Western Mail* from 6 March 1992 to 2 September 1995; it has continued to the present as 'Welsh Books'.

'Ymhob pen'. Meic Stephens contributed to this regular column in the *Western Mail* from 14 March 1992 to 21 September 1996; many articles are on literary subjects.

'Nationalism is not a bourgeois ideology', a review of David L. Adamson, *Class, Ideology and the Nation, The New Welsh Review* 14, IV, 2 (Autumn 1991).

Review of Gwyn Jones, *Background to Dylan Thomas and Other Explorations, The New Welsh Review,* 16 (Spring 1992).

'Putting on paper our overlooked culture', an article about the compilation of *The Oxford Illustrated Literary Guide to Britain and Ireland, Western Mail* (11 May 1992).

'Barcelona on guard against terror', an article about the threat of violence at the Olympic Games, *Scotland on Sunday* (26 July 1992).

'A love of language', a feature in the official programme of the Ebbw Vale Garden Festival (1992).

'Welsh literary trust makes its first awards', an article about the creation of the Rhys Davies Trust, *Book News* (10 October 1992).

'Wales: a culturgram', published as a leaflet by the David M. Kennedy Center for International Studies at Brigham Young University, Provo, Utah (1992).

'Printed on stone', a review of J. E. Caerwyn Williams (ed.), *Cerddi Waldo Williams, The New Welsh Review,* 19 (Winter 1992–3).

'Fifty years at Upper Boat', an article about the Upper Boat power station, *Trydan* (May 1993).

'The Kilvert Gallery, Clyro', *The Art Unit* (March 1993).

'Making love to a duchess', an article about working for the Oxford University Press, *Bulletin* of the Welsh Academy (June 1993).

'Y Meddyg Esgyrn', an article about the bone-setter John Lloyd ('Silver John'), in Dai Hawkins (ed.), *Llyfr Gwyrdd Fferegs* (The Radnorshire Society, 1993).

'Dylan's refuge in his house shaken by sea', a review of Kate Marsh (ed.), *Writers and their Houses, Western Mail* (26 August 1993).

'This is Planet Wales calling the world', a review of Janet Davies (ed.), *Compass Points, Western Mail* (25 September 1993).

'Y bardd a'i wraig', a review of Paul Ferris, *Caitlin*, and Jonathan Fryer, *Dylan: The Nine Lives of Dylan Thomas,* in *Golwg* (21 October 1993).

'Sad case of a "perfect" Welsh skull in a Scottish cupboard', an article about Hugh MacDiarmid's plagiarism of a story by Glyn Jones, *The New Welsh Review,* 23, VI, 3 (Winter 1993–4).

Review of Tom McArthur (ed.), *The Oxford Companion to the English Language*, *Bulletin* of the Welsh Academy (January 1994).
'Valley of inspiration', an article about the literary associations of the Rhondda Valley, *Western Mail* (5 February 1994).
'At the edge of things', an interview with Leslie Norris, *Books in Wales* (Spring 1994), reprinted from Eugene England and Peter Makuck (eds.), *An Open World*.
A review of Ian Hamilton (ed.), *The Oxford Companion to Twentieth-century Poetry,* Bulletin of the Welsh Academy (March 1994).
'A small house in Meadow Street', an essay on change in a working-class community, *Planet*, 105 (June/July 1994).
'Y gwr ifanc o Gaerdydd', a review of Dannie Abse, *Intermittent Journals, Golwg* (18 August 1994).
Interview in David Lloyd (ed.), *The Urgency of Identity* (Evanston, Ill., Northwestern University Press, 1994).
'Twm, Jan a Mach', a review of Jan Morris and Twm Morys, *A Machynlleth Triad/Triawd Machynlleth, Golwg* (27 October 1994).
'Miner poet of the pits', an obituary of Robert Morgan (1921–94), *Western Mail* (28 October 1994).
'Llyfr y Sefydliad', a review of Jonathan Parker (ed.), *People of Today, Golwg* (1 November 1994).
Review of A. M. Allchin, *The World is a Wedding*, and M. Wynn Thomas, *Morgan Llwyd, ei Gyfeillion a'i Gyfnod,* in *Zeitschrift für Celtische Philologie*, 46 (1994).
'Mwy nag Ysbiwr', a review of Jenny Rees, *Looking for Mr Nobody, Golwg* (3 November 1994).
'The wailing princess', a review of Glyn Jones and T. J. Morgan (eds.), *The Story of Heledd, Planet* 108 (December 1994/January 1995).
'Oratory attracted many to Plaid', a tribute to Harri Webb (1920–94), *Western Mail* (2 January 1995).
Obituary of Harri Webb (1920–94), *The Independent* (3 January 1995).
'Bardd coch', a tribute to Harri Webb (1920–94), *Golwg* (12 January 1995).
'Angry summer of an unhappy miner', a review of Dafydd Johnston (ed.), *The Complete Poems of Idris Davies, The Independent* (17 January 1995).
Obituary of Harri Webb (1920–94), *Planet*, 109 (February/March 1995).
'Completing the poetic record', an introduction to a number of unpublished poems by Harri Webb, *The New Welsh Review*, 28 (Spring 1995).
Obituary of Glyn Jones (1905–95), *The Independent* (11 April 1995).
'A case of over-production', a review of Dafydd Johnston (ed.), *The Complete Poems of Idris Davies, Planet*, 111 (June/July 1995).

'Extracts from the notebooks of Glyn Jones', an introduction, *The New Welsh Review*, 29 (Summer 1995).

Review of Tony Curtis and Christine Pagnolle (eds.), *Poèmes du Pays de Galles*, *Book News* (Summer 1995).

'Pethau cyffredin', an essay about the death of his mother, *Taliesin*, 90 (Summer 1995).

Obituary of Lynette Roberts (1909–95), *The Independent* (28 September 1995).

'Writer's Dublin', an article in *Planet*, 113 (October/November 1995).

'The making of a poet', a translation of Glyn Jones's contribution to Alun Oldfield Davies (ed.), *Llwybrau Gynt*, *Planet*, 112 (August/September 1995) and 113 (October/November 1995).

Obituary of Gwyn A. Williams (1925–95), *The Independent* (18 November 1995).

'On mother's knee', a review of O. M. Edwards, *Hwiangerddi* (ed. Hazel Walford Davies), *Planet*, 115 (February/March 1996).

'Writing verse and worse', an article about the writing of poetry, *Western Mail* (3 and 10 August 1996).

'Penblwydd hapus, Rhydwen', a profile of Rhydwen Williams, *Western Mail* (24 August 1996).

'Up the Republic!', a review of Cliff Bere, *The Young Republicans*, in *Planet*, 118 (August/September 1996).

'Cymro o Sais', a profile of Raymond Garlick, *Western Mail* (21 September 1996).

'Here comes everybody', a review of Robert Welch (ed.), *The Oxford Companion to Irish Literature*, *Planet*, 119 (October/November 1996).

'Election fever', a short story, *The New Welsh Review*, 34 (Autumn 1996).

Tribute to Sorley MacLean (1911–96), *The New Welsh Review*, 35 (Winter 1996–7).

Obituary of Pennar Davies (1911–97), *The Independent* (2 January 1997).

'Book sales and subsidies', *Planet*, 121 (February/March 1997).

'Belonging', a review of three essays by Robin Llywelyn, Nigel Jenkins and Wiliam Owen Roberts in the *Places / Y Man a'r Lle* series, *Planet*, 122 (April/May 1997).

'The Third Man: Robert Herring and *Life and Letters To-day*', in Tony Brown (ed.), *Welsh Writing in English*, 3 (1997).

'Something of the Viking', a profile of Gwyn Jones, *Western Mail* (24 May 1997).

'The Welshman with an accent on the international', a profile of Ned Thomas, *Western Mail* (14 June 1997).

A memoir of Eugène Guillevic (1907–97), *Planet*, 123 (June/July 1997).

Obituary of Alexander Cordell (1914–97), *The Independent* (11 July 1997).

Obituary of Ron Berry (1920–97), *The Independent* (24 July 1997).

Obituary of Rhydwen Williams (1916–97), *The Independent* (7 August 1997); reprinted in *Planet*, 126 (December 1997–January 1998).

'Landscape with figures', a review of three essays by Christopher Meredith, Ruth Bidgood and John Barnie in the *Places / Y Man a'r Lle* series, *Planet*, 124 (August/September 1997).

'Mystery still swirls around origins of Valley author,' an interview with Susan H. Llewellyn, widow of Richard Llewellyn, *Western Mail* (20 September 1997).

Obituary of Cliff Bere (1915–97), *The Independent* (22 September 1997).

Obituary of John Elwyn (1916–97), *The Independent* (25 November 1997).

'The Apotheosis of George Thomas', *Planet*, 125 (November/December 1997).

'A Writer's Diary', *Book News / Llais Llyfrau* (Christmas, 1997).

List of Subscribers

The following have kindly associated themselves with publication of this volume in honour of Meic Stephens by subscription:

Jane Aaron, Aberystwyth
Dannie Abse, London
Jonathan Adams, Newport
Nicholas Adams, London
A. M. Allchin, Bangor
Denis Balsom, Gregynog
John Barnie, Aberystwyth
Tony Bianchi, Cardiff
J. Roy Birch, Bromsgrove
Tony Brown, Bangor
Marie-Thérèse Castay, Condom
Joseph and Gertrude Clancy, Aberystwyth
Gladys Mary Coles, Ruthin
Anthony Conran, Bangor
Fay Cornes, Dalkeith
Cynog Dafis, Llandysul
Don Dale-Jones, Carmarthen
Tudor David, London
Alun Creunant Davies, Aberystwyth
Gareth Alban Davies, Aberystwyth
Geraint Talfan Davies, Cardiff
Gwilym Prys Davies, Tonteg
J. N. M. Davies, Bath
John Davies, Cardiff

Leslie Davies, Aberdâr
Lewis Davies, Lewes
Philippa Davies, Brecon
Tom Davies, Penarth
Walford Davies, Aberystwyth
Moira Dearnley, Llandogo
Per Denez, Douarnenez
Ashley Drake, Caerdydd
Jon Dressel, Llansteffan
Owen Dudley Edwards, Edinburgh
Tom Earley, London
Hywel Teifi Edwards, Llangennech
Robert M. Edwards, Maesteg
Islwyn Ffowc Elis, Llanbedr Pont Steffan
Tom Ellis, Rhiwabon
John Elwyn, Winchester
John Emyr, Bangor
Brengain Evans, Caerdydd
Gwynfor Evans, Llanybydder
Lowri Angharad Evans, Llanllechid
Paul Ferris, Boughrood
Angela Fish, Tonteg
Raymond Garlick, Carmarthen
Chris Grace, Cardiff
B. Griffiths, Bangor
J. Gwyn Griffiths a Kate Bosse-Griffiths, Abertawe
T. Elwyn Griffiths, Caernarfon
Richard Griffiths, Reading
R. Geraint Gruffydd, Aberystwyth
Eleri a Robin Gwyndaf, Caerdydd
Sandra and Robert Harding, Llantrisant
Derek and Sue Harries, Abergavenny
John Hefin, Llandaf
Joyce Herbert, Cowbridge
Jeremy Hooker, Frome
Glyn Tegai Hughes, Y Drenewydd
Gwilym Rees Hughes, Cardiff
Emyr Humphreys, Llanfair Pwllgwyngyll
Allan James, Llantrisant
Cliff James, Blackwood

Branwen Jarvis, Bangor
Nigel Jenkins, Swansea
Bobi Jones, Aberystwyth
Doreen Jones, Cardiff
Gwerfyl Pierce Jones, Aberystwyth
Gwyn Jones, Aberystwyth
Huw Jones, Bangor
Huw Jones, Caerdydd
Ieuan Gwynedd Jones, Aberystwyth
Jonah Jones, Cardiff
R. Brinley Jones, Llanwrda
Sally Roberts Jones, Port Talbot
Nesta Wyn Jones, Dolgellau
Edgar H. King, Newport
D. E. Leitch, Glasbury-on-Wye
John Lewis, Llandysul
David T. Lloyd, Syracuse, NY
Proinsias Mac Cana, Dublin
Roland Mathias, Brecon
Ralph Maud, Bellingham, Washington State
John May, Tongwynlais
Gareth Miles, Pontypridd
Elaine Morgan, Mountain Ash
Gerald Morgan, Aberystwyth
Kenneth O. Morgan, Long Hanborough
Prys Morgan, Abertawe
Jan Morris, Llanystumdwy
Lord Morris of Castlemorris, Foolow
Leslie Norris, Orem, Utah
Glenys Ormond Thomas, Cardiff
Teifion Phillips, Barry
J. R. Powell, Pontypridd
Judith Pritchard, Hengoed
Sheenagh Pugh, Cardiff
Alun Rees, Cardiff
D. Ben Rees, Liverpool
Ioan a Margaret Bowen Rees, Bangor
John Rowlands, Aberystwyth
Ann Saer, Caerdydd
John Samuel, Sidcup

List of Subscribers

Vlad'ka and Leos Sátava, Praha
Mercer Simpson, Cardiff
Elan Closs Stephens, Aberystwyth
Heledd Stephens, Ynysybwl
Huw Stephens, Caerdydd
Lloyd Stephens, Stratford-upon-Avon
E. K. Thomas, London
Graham Thomas, Abertyleri
Gwyn Thomas, Bangor
M. Wynn Thomas, Abertawe
Ned Thomas, Cardiff
Patrick Thomas, Brechfa
R. George Thomas, Cardiff
John Powell Ward, Horton Kirby
Dafydd Wigley, Caernarfon
Cynwil Williams, Cardiff
E. O. Williams, Y Barri
Glanmor Williams, Swansea
Herbert Williams, Aberystwyth
J. Arfon Williams, Caeathro
Mansel Williams, Bangor
Marion Griffith Williams, Dolgellau

Hugh Owen Library, University of Wales, Aberystwyth
Koninklijke Bibliotheek, Den Haag
The Learning Resources Centre, University of Glamorgan
The Library, Arts Council of England
Llyfrgell Genedlaethol Cymru, Aberystwyth
Llyfrgell Rhanbarthol Caerfyrddin
Llyfrgell Salisbury, Prifysgol Cymru Caerdydd
The Welsh Academy